Radical Vision

Radical Vision

A Biography of Lorraine Hansberry

Soyica Diggs Colbert

Yale UNIVERSITY PRESS/NEW HAVEN & LONDON

Published with assistance from the foundation established in memory
of Philip Hamilton McMillan of the Class of 1894, Yale College.

Yale University Press books may be purchased in quantity for educational, business, or
promotional use. For information, please e-mail sales.press@yale.edu (U.S. office) or
sales@yaleup.co.uk (U.K. office).

Set in Adobe Garamond type by IDS Infotech Ltd. Chandigarh, India.
Printed in the United States of America.

ISBN 978-0-300-24570 7 (alk. paper)
Library of Congress Control Number: 2020943772
A catalogue record for this book is available from the British Library.

This paper meets the requirements of ANSI/NISO Z39.48-1992 (Permanence of
Paper).

10 9 8 7 6 5 4 3 2

To Rodger

Contents

Acknowledgments

I would like to thank the National Endowment for the Humanities and the Schomburg Center Scholars in Residence Program for their support. I would also like to thank Farah Jasmine Griffin, director of the Scholars-in-Residence Program, and the 2015–2016 participants, Sylvia Chan-Malik, Kaiama Glover, Tsitsi Jaji, C. Riley Snorton, Sonia Sanchez, Caree Banton, Nicole Wright, Jeff Diamant, and Adrianna Campbell, for their feedback on early drafts of this work. I also thank then Schomburg Center associate curator Steven G. Fullwood for his support of and insight on this project. The book would not have been possible without the Lorraine Hansberry Literary Trust, the Jewell Handy Gresham-Nemiroff Trust, and their co-trustee Joi Gresham. Thank you for giving me access to and permission to use the archive, for preserving and stewarding the dissemination of Hansberry's work, and for supporting and championing this project. The trusts serve an essential purpose in upholding Hansberry's legacy and impact and making her work accessible for generations to come. Thank you also to Georgetown University, Christopher Celenza, dean of the College of Arts and Sciences at Georgetown University, the support of the Georgetown University Idol Family Professorship endowment fund, and the Georgetown University Healey Family Endowed Fund for Academic Excellence for their financial support, which enabled research assistance and to obtain image permissions. Sarah Miller at Yale University Press supported this project from its inception and provided exacting feedback throughout its development. I am grateful for her careful stewardship of the volume. Thanks to Phillip King at Yale University Press for the care you showed the manuscript through helpful suggestions and for your oversight during the production process. The generosity of colleagues extends well beyond institutional affiliations, and I am grateful to many friends that have read, discussed, and offered feedback on this project.

I presented portions of this book at Boston College, Northwestern University, Cornell University, Mary Washington University, Brown University, Rutgers University, Yale University, University of Maryland College Park, the Black Thought Collective, and the Futures of American Studies Institute at Dartmouth College; I am grateful for the thought-provoking feedback I received at these events. I also appreciate the feedback I received from generous colleagues on drafts of the manuscript: Margo Crawford, LaMonda Horton-Stallings, Douglas Jones, Paige McGinley, Robert J. Patterson, Samantha Pinto, Kevin Quashie, Shane Vogel, and Isaiah Wooden. Thank you to Derek Goldman for sending me an interview with Hansberry that proved quite useful and to Maurice Jackson for sharing materials from his personal archive. I also want to thank the community of scholars and friends that have cheered on, offered advice, and made suggestions for this work: Jennifer DeVere Brody, Joshua Chambers-Letson, Erica Edwards, Régine Jean-Charles, Michelle Wallace, Delicia Lewis-Webb, Heather Graham, Candice McFarlane, Kelly Baker Josephs, Drew Lichtenberg, Imani Perry, Evie Shockley, Salamishah Tillet, and Dagmawi Woubshet. The generosity of community extends well beyond this list, and I am grateful to many friends that have discussed and offered feedback on this project.

I have learned so much from my brilliant students and especially from those in my spring 2019 James Baldwin, Lorraine Hansberry, and Nina Simone Seminar. This book would not exist if Maurice Wallace had not encouraged me to write it. It would also not be complete without the indefatigable research assistance of Fatima Dyfan, Skylar Luke, MacKenzie River Foy and Taurjahi Purdie. I am also grateful to Brent Hayes Edwards, Jarvis McInnis, Tracy Heather Strain, and Randall MacLowry for their aid in helping to locate permissions and documents. Finally, I must thank my family. I've learned over the years that writing a book has a deep impact on all of those closest to you. For your enduring support, thank you to the Brown Family, R. Harrington Diggs, Joanne Diggs, Diallyo Diggs, Rakiya Moore, and Diallyo Diggs II. And to Rodger Colbert, you gather me and make me better. Thank you!

Radical Vision

Introduction: Notes of a Native Daughter

Daddy died,
"Raisin" opened
and yesterday I got a divorce
all on March 10. 1945; 1959; 1964.

Lorraine Hansberry learned by telegram that her father died.[1] On the same day thirteen years later, her career-defining play, *A Raisin in the Sun,* opened on Broadway. The play catapulted her from obscurity to household name. Just five years later, on another March 10th, she divorced the greatest friend of her mind—Robert Nemiroff, or as she affectionately called him, Bobby.

The shadows that loomed throughout Hansberry's life cast large impressions. She lived in the shadow of her father's death; death crystallized his impact on her life. She lived with illness, wondering when she would die. She lived with the social pressure of being the face of Black theater and a Black radical. She lived with the weight of her marriage ending and the social stigma of divorce in the 1960s. Each March 10th established a loss (her father, her anonymity, her marriage) that would serve as an essential moment to her becoming free. Although not all equal in their impact on her development, they each mark key turning points in her life and work.

Lorraine's father, Carl Augustus Hansberry, represented an American type of social and political striving. Born on April 30, 1895, from Gloster, Mississippi, as a young man he migrated to the north after graduating from Alcorn Agricultural and Mechanical College. In Chicago, he began his business and political career. He met and married Nannie Louis Perry, who was from Columbia, Tennessee. She was also a college graduate, having earned her degree from Tennessee State University. Together they had four children: Carl Augustus, Perry Holloway, Mamie Louise, and Lorraine Vivian.

A well-educated middle-class couple, they lived on the South Side of Chicago. Known in the Windy City as the kitchenette king, Carl built his real estate empire, drawing from the Black adage to make a dollar out of fifteen cents. He bought single-unit properties on the South Side and chopped them up into residences for two or three families. He produced single-family dwellings that had their own kitchen but shared a bathroom, and were known as kitchenettes. These tiny units provided housing to the masses of Black migrants relocating from the south to segregated Chicago and helped establish Carl's financial empire. According to Mamie, "He made quite a fortune during the depression because the white landlord simply couldn't collect the rent, and he could. Things just grew from there. Most people were going broke. He was making quite a lot of money and set up our business. We had a maintenance crew and housekeepers, and his half-sister came as a secretary and my mother's niece was a secretary and his half-brother were collector. He'd have to go collect from all the buildings from the housekeepers, and the housekeepers would collect the rest . . . [from the tenants]. That grew and grew and things got better and better." The real estate business supported Carl's political aspirations and helped provide a comfortable life for his family. While he acquired properties, Nannie taught school and served as a ward leader for the Republican Party. Together they formed a power couple that equally invested in reserved respectability and racial uplift. Mamie described them as "stately."[2]

Although the Hansberrys found financial security during the Great Depression and its aftermath, the mass impact of the extended financial crisis caused many families to wonder about American possibility. The Hansberrys' ability to thrive in a financial climate that rendered millions of Americans destitute not only distinguishes Lorraine's family as Black Americans but also as Americans in general. Thanks to her parents' investments, she had a stable childhood, for the most part.

Lorraine enjoyed the comforts of her parents' financial stability, but racism disrupted their domestic tranquility. In 1937, Carl's economic achievements allowed him to purchase a house at 6140 South Rhodes Avenue, in Woodlawn, an all-white neighborhood near the University of Chicago. There was a racial covenant attached to the property, which set in motion a series of confrontations that shaped Lorraine's understanding of racial justice work. When Carl and his family attempted to move into the building, neighbors responded by spitting on them and jeering at them, and finally throwing concrete through their window.[3] Eventually, the family moved. Carl ultimately filed a lawsuit that ended up confirming his right to buy a home in that neighborhood, although the courts did not find, as he had sought, that the racially restrictive housing covenants were illegal. He won a battle but lost the war that segregated Black people and kept them from purchasing property in general.

Racism worked to keep the Hansberrys in their place by offering a violent rebuke to Carl's attempt to integrate the Woodlawn neighborhood of Chicago. Lorraine's childhood exposure to civil rights advocacy taught her that freedom required a multi-pronged approach, with financial, legal, social, and cultural change-makers working together. From experience, she learned that when any one aspect of freedom work functioned independently of the others, individuals could experience uplift but not freedom. Freedom, Lorraine deduced, required cultivating a set of practices over time that were coordinated with other members of a movement that addressed intersecting forms of oppression.

Lorraine's parents were the best Americans they knew how to be. They worked hard, amassed wealth, and fought for political change. Carl founded one of the first Black banks in Chicago, Lake Street Bank, but by 1946, he knew that he needed more space. Not physical space, not more land per se, but more breathing room to be at peace as a Black man living in a segregated world. The type of space he sought did not exist in the United States in 1946. With Nannie, he purchased a home for their retirement in Polanco, Mexico, a suburb of Mexico City. Before he made his retirement plans, Carl's high blood pressure showed that he had signs of cardiovascular disease. The Hansberry family hoped relocating to Mexico would help his health. In March 1946, they visited their future home where the two planned to retire as expatriates.

They did not anticipate that he would never return to Chicago. When the telegram arrived to tell Mamie that their father had died, the children must have been stunned; later they learned he had suffered a cerebral hemorrhage.[4] In a matter of days, Lorraine's world turned upside down. She lost the man who gave structure and stability to her life; the parent she could admire without having to wrangle with a gender comparison. He showed her what political striving could entail. Of course, so did her mother. And in time, Lorraine would come to understand the political lessons both her parents imparted. But her father's life and work offered her an example disentangled from respectable womanhood. Moreover, the sharp pain of her father's loss left an indelible and immediate impact. The peculiar American landscape that allowed Carl to amass a small fortune and made him a stranger in his own land prompted Lorraine to later reflect, "American racism helped kill him."[5] Later, as her ideas matured, she might have noted, American racism made him singular and, therefore, helped kill him. Hansberry eventually came to understand how isolation facilitated racism's deadly effects.

Carl's death came quickly. The devastation and loss that shrouded the civil rights movement surfaced for Lorraine much earlier than the violence that came later, from the *Brown v. Board of Education* decision in 1954 to the passage of the Voting Rights Act in 1965. Lorraine was a movement baby. She saw her parents fight for civic redress through the courts and the pursuit of public office. In 1940, her father ran for Congress, as a Republican, and lost. Both of Hansberry's parents were Republicans, and capitalists, during a period when Black people's political allegiances began to shift. Since 1936, no Republican candidate for president has won more than 40 percent of the Black vote.[6] Carl lived through Franklin Delano Roosevelt's New Deal—a deal that grew the American middle class and maintained racial hierarchies—although he died before Harry Truman ran for election in 1948 with a pro–civil rights platform.[7] An early exposure to the workings of liberalism set the foundation for Lorraine to advocate for a radical shift from the political status quo. As an adult, she not only distanced herself from her parents' politics of uplift, she also challenged white allies to call for transformation rather than reform.

The violence associated with Black striving emerged for Hansberry as a child and crystallized for her as a teenager with the loss of her father. Years later she understood that the slow death racism produces would require a revolution cooked over a slow-burning fire. Or as Walter Benjamin wrote, in 1940, "The tradition of the oppressed teaches us that the 'state of emergency' in which we live is not the exception but the rule." Benjamin's well-known statement appears in "Theses on the Philosophy of History," an essay he wrote just before fleeing Vichy France to evade capture by the Nazi Gestapo. Benjamin, a German Jew, was unable to continue his escape from France to Spain, and, as a result, committed suicide, still fearing Nazi capture.[8] Like Benjamin, Hansberry's theory emerged in close proximity to death. And just as her father's death did not come overnight, neither would the justice that she sought. Her father's life and death taught her that each individual life constituted an interval in the pursuit of freedom. The movement, as Hansberry conceptualized it, brought these discrete intervals together to form a structured and durable whole.

HANSBERRY'S RADICALISM

In 1946, when "daddy died," Hansberry suffered her first great loss. Grappling with loss informed her theories about the world, justice, and freedom. Although she idolized her father, she reflected: "Daddy felt that this country was hopeless in its treatment of Negroes. So he became a refugee from America. I'm afraid I have to agree with Daddy's assessment of this country. But I don't agree with the leaving part. I don't feel defensive. Daddy really belonged to a different age, a different period. He didn't feel free. One of the reasons I feel so free is that I feel I belong to a world majority, and a very assertive one."[9] The end of World War II marked a turning point of great global and personal significance, bringing to a close the Nazis' mass human destruction in Europe, yet also inaugurating the use of atomic weapons by the United States in Japan, and leading to intertwined post-colonial, decolonial, and civil rights pursuits. It also certified that Black Americans' willingness to fight abroad would not necessarily mean equal access to rights at home.

Hansberry's early life coincides with the civil rights movement, from the end of World War II until the mid-1960s. Many historians designate the period from the Supreme Court's *Brown v. Board of Education* decision in 1954 to the passage of the Voting Rights Act in 1965 as the classical phase of the movement; but they also agree that organizing activities in the 1940s and early 1950s laid the foundation for this decade of civil rights achievements.[10] Hansberry grew up in the midst of this civil rights activism, and it served as the foundation for her political formation. The years from 1946 to 1965 bookended the maturation of Lorraine's political consciousness, as she cultivated a theory to guide and find expression in her practice.[11]

Hansberry's writing, and writing about her, establishes her as an artist and an intellectual fundamentally committed to Black radicalism, feminism, and ultimately human beings' ability to bend history toward justice. This book proceeds from a single question: How does Hansberry's art offer a radical political vision for matters and the mattering of Black life in the mid-twentieth century? In the introduction to *Want to Start a Revolution?* Dayo F. Gore, Jeanne Theoharis, and Komozi Woodard argue, "In most historical studies, postwar Black radicalism has been defined by a limited set of principles: self-defense tenets and tactics, separatist organizations, Afrocentric cultural practices, and anticapitalist philosophies, as well as a rejection of the practice of lobbying the state." While Hansberry's work adheres to some of these tenets (self-defense and anti-capitalism), like other Black women radicals, she collaborated with organizations that sought to redress inequality based on sexuality or gender.[12] She worked with white-led gay and lesbian organizations as well as communist-led groups. Her intersectionalist Black radicalism focused on the distinctive qualities of Black women's liberation and the material conditions necessary in their becoming free.

While Hansberry's political commitments and personal relationships with Paul Robeson, W.E.B. Du Bois, Louis Burnham, Alice Childress, and others situated her squarely within the Black radical tradition, existentialism, particularly Simone de Beauvoir's *The Second Sex,* deeply influenced her. Existentialists, including de Beauvoir, Jean-Paul Sartre, Frantz Fanon, and Albert Camus, were concerned with the relationship between human thought and action. They considered how experience shaped the individual's ability to give meaning to life and pursue freedom. Hansberry's writing affirms existentialist ideas of the individual's transformational capabilities *and* it challenges one of its central presumptions, that becoming emerges through individual antagonism.

Hansberry's Black radicalism accounts for Black women's labor and sexual exploitation and the incommensurability of interracial experiences; together these positions informed her artistic and political practice. She used her art to showcase encounters (political, sexual, personal, and historical) with witnesses, and she purposefully concentrated most of her energies on a form with witness built in—theater. In so doing, she called attention to how one establishes intimacy that leads to collaboration across differences. Political encounters provide the opportunity to work through differences and deepen consciousness. As Lori Jo Marso describes de Beauvoir's use of encounters, "Without struggle, *sans encounter,* freedom cannot emerge."[13] Encounter serves as a moment of friction that may result in greater clarity for all, those involved in the encounter and those that bear witness to it. Her art expressed her political vision, a vision that responded to the immense suffering of Black people not only through the act of encounter but also through witness. Her contribution to social movements included acts of imagination that would usher forth new forms of collectivity based in mutual exchange and historical specificity.

Hansberry understood freedom as a process rather than a destination, and existence as a mode of being through action. Her writing (creative and nonfiction) produces an understanding of personal and political becoming and social transformation as a collective endeavor not solely a matter of individual transcendence.[14] A central concept of this book, "becoming free," names the processual nature of Hansberry's work, the ideas that underpin it, and its place in a long history of emancipation. The Black radical tradition emerges through a deep understanding of material history, particularly trans-Atlantic slavery. For Hansberry, the process of becoming free required understanding how daily practices contributed to and sustained the long history of abolition, or what she called "the movement." At the same time, existentialism taught her about the difficulty of connecting across differences. Hansberry's experiences (from her middle-class childhood filled with masculine models of leadership to her adult experiences as a woman and a lesbian artist and activist) called into question the unity of blackness and that isolation could be overcome through shared but not necessarily commensurate visions. I mean vision here both in the conceptual and physical senses.

Radical Vision explores the contexts, schools, movements, and histories that shaped and distinguish Hansberry's thought. Necessarily, it takes up her personal life and how the personal impacted her work and politics. Given the distinction between Hansberry's public self and the one that emerges in her private writing, I refer to the public figure as Hansberry and the private person as Lorraine. Of course the two blended into each other, but part of what this book establishes is how the public image enabled and limited the visibility of her radical vision.

The violence Hansberry saw, coming of age in Chicago, informed her political theory and political and aesthetic practices until her death. This book tells the story of Hansberry's ideas. Following the great tradition of African American life writing, from *The Narrative of the Life of Frederick Douglass* to *Zami: A New Spelling of My Name,* the book foregrounds Hansberry's writing to highlight Black self-invention.[15] Black life writing has a long history that intertwines with Black liberation struggles. Lisa Lowe writes of formerly enslaved abolitionist Olaudah Equiano, "The autobiographical genre illustrates how liberal emancipation required a literary narrative of the self-authoring autonomous individual to be distilled out of the heteronomous collective subjectivity of colonial slavery. This is as much a literary critical question of how the autobiography is interpreted . . . as it is a historiographical matter of which archives, events, temporalities, and geographies will be privileged."[16] Understanding that the archive, the primary source used here, only gives partial access to Lorraine, the book sifts through Hansberry's rich and vast papers to depict how her writing shaped her public image and reflected her private thoughts, as it acknowledges that the archive does not have the capacity to represent the individual.[17] Additionally, this book differs from the aforementioned autobiographies in that it does not tell the individual's life story but rather the story that emerges from a life of writing.

Delving deeply into Hansberry's archive offers a fuller picture of her contribution to midcentury thought through her principled investment to resist the angel of death that seemed to shadow her and all Black people. Thanks to the diligent stewards of her papers, Robert Nemiroff, Jewel Handy Gresham-Nemiroff, and Joi Gresham, many of Hansberry's published works, drafts, and unpublished works remain available for consideration. In addition, her personal writing in journals and on scraps of paper, as well as her correspondence, helps to shed light on the intimate details of her life and thought. As a story of her ideas, this book focuses on Hansberry's written work and the work written about her. There are inconsistencies in what she wrote about herself; her journal states that her father died in 1945, although it was actually in 1946.[18] These slippages may reflect a lapse in memory, but they also could be evidence of the active way Hansberry wrote herself into being. She created a timeline, from 1945 to 1964, marked by two historical turning points—the end of World War II and the passing of the Civil Rights Act. Hansberry did not live to see the Voting Rights Act passed in 1965, but her work suggests that she knew the movement was shifting direction, from civil rights to Black power. Hansberry's slippage shows the archive as a space of both evidence and invention. A photograph taken in 1959 captures different sides of Hansberry, changing and attending to them through the composition, just as her writing produces multiple versions of herself (through her use of pseudonyms and the demands of different publishing venues) that together do not capture the complexity or compelling interiority of Lorraine but do tell a story about a radical thinker and artist. The writing offers a nuanced understanding of her thoughts, commitments, and desires. As in all life writing, I contend with the types of evidence that remain in the archive. At the same time, I focus on Hansberry's writing specifically because she chose to express herself artistically and politically as a writer. In her work, we find her vision for becoming free.

Her papers, housed at the New York Public Library's Schomburg Center for Research in Black Culture, reposition her in mid-twentieth century cultural production and thought, demonstrating her deep political investments in Black internationalism and civil rights as they pertained to gays and lesbians, women as well as people of color. In addition to the political stakes of her writing, she also intervenes in formal debates, exploring different modes of realism. In so doing, she seeks to reorient the viewer. Distinguishing her work from that of Richard Wright, Hansberry asserts, "Naturalism tends to take the world as it is and say: this is what it is, this is how it happens, it is 'true' because we see it every day in life that way—you know, you simply photograph the garbage can. But in realism—I think the artist who is creating the

Lorraine Hansberry at 337 Bleecker Street, April 1959, photographed by David
Attie for *Vogue Magazine*

realistic work imposes on it not only what is but what is possible . . . because
that is part of reality too."[19] The imposition of the possible speaks not only to
Hansberry's aesthetic vision but to her philosophical and political ones as well.
Her use of realism, and her assertion that "every human being is dramatically
interesting," reflected her commitment to the everyday as a source for

transformation in art and politics.[20] Only attending to the published writing constricts her aesthetic and political vision.

Hansberry's vision accounted for how daily and repeated action could build the infrastructure for Black freedom movements *and* the institutionalization of anti-Black racism. Through institutionalization, anti-blackness materializes in laws, policies, and culture. The archive offers an introduction to Hansberry's writing as a practice that she worked to refine over time. But for Hansberry, the act itself served as a form of protest. Therefore, in engaging with the finished and unfinished work, one finds the process at the heart of becoming free requires repeated, incremental, and perpetual action that resisted racism's material impact. Hansberry's understanding of the material costs of racism motivated her to consider how Black people pursue freedom in relationship to and in spite of the state. Although she became a part of what she would call the Black intelligentsia, she often called for a focus on the Black working class. She animated her understanding of incommensurability in collaborations, political and artistic, and her aesthetic choices not to take over but to make room. While Hansberry's fame and class privilege may have limited the potential for state violence, she nevertheless understood the ever present threat it posed for most Black people. And even those shielded from the gross violence of the state suffered uniformly from the slow death racism caused.

Telling the story of Hansberry's intellectual life presents challenges because it requires speculating about her choices, motivations, and investments. Although she amassed a substantial amount of published work while alive, her unpublished work dwarfs the volume of the work in print. Additionally, much of the unpublished work remains unfinished. To wade into the waters of the Hansberry archive and return with a cohesive narrative requires stitching together details, ideas, lines of thought, and historical contexts that were, for the most part, left undone. This work of putting the pieces together must attend to the times, rhythms, and social conventions of the mid-twentieth century. At the same time, writing the story of Hansberry's ideas requires understanding that by every indication she was ahead of her time. The interplay between careful reading, contextualizing, and speculating serves as the basis for this volume, which draws from Hansberry's finished and unfinished work and her personal and public writing. Together these works evidence her ideas, investments, desires, imagination, and thoughts (both well established and percolating).

Although in many ways Hansberry lived her life out loud, never hiding her commitment to radical politics, the success of *A Raisin the Sun,* a family drama, constrained her public image, and facilitated its profitability. The play's success produced a public image of a liberal darling rather than a radical. The

Hansberry you meet in her vast archive, therefore, challenges popular perceptions of her as a one-hit wonder or an accommodationist. The scholarly and
biographical work of Margaret Wilkerson and Imani Perry has clarified the
breadth of Hansberry's radical political vision and, for Perry, the significant
personal impact of engaging Lorraine's life and legacy. In addition, Cheryl
Higashida and Mary Helen Washington have chronicled Hansberry's important contributions to the left. Steven R. Carter and Tracy Heather Strain have
examined the profound importance of Hansberry's drama. Kevin Mumford
has explored Hansberry's sexuality, and Monica Miller's forthcoming work
examines Hansberry's internationalism.[21]

I build on and depart from this exciting body of work by offering a vision
of Hansberry that attends meticulously to the figure buried in the archive,
foregrounding how her writing, published and unpublished, offers a road map
to negotiate Black suffering in the past and present, which remains an important part of understanding Hansberry's legacy and freedom dreams and practices. Revealing the breadth and depth of her writing through an exploration
of unpublished work that has yet to garner attention situates this book in the
history of ideas by accounting for the magnitude of archival evidence and
committing more deeply to the intellectual context in which Hansberry was
enmeshed. For Hansberry, loss and despair characterized most of her life. She
suffered from depression and contemplated suicide. She understood intimately
the feeling of being ravaged, physically, politically, socially, and personally, by
impossibility. And, nevertheless, she believed in the possibility of transformation. Her intimacy with death and belief in the collective human capacity to
transform the world distinguishes her voice and her legacy.

DADDY DIED: A CRISIS BOTH SUDDEN AND ROUTINE

The loss of Carl came quick, but, upon reflection, Lorraine knew it had been on
the horizon for a while. She stated firmly that American racism contributed to
her father's death. Carl's passing showed Lorraine how racism eats away at Black
people, slowly destroying them through the daily onslaught of seeming minor
and innocuous attacks. The devastating impact of her father's death transformed the nature of crisis for Lorraine. She saw crisis as a material outcome of
systems and structures that required constant cultivation and concealment. The
loss of her father prepared her to offer a different context for the Holocaust and
the use of atomic weapons by the United States, and therefore a feeling other
than despair about these historical events. To quote de Beauvoir, she could not
think in terms of despair or "happiness but in terms of freedom."[22]

The cultural impact of the Cold War and the willingness of the United States to use atomic warfare to end World War II recaptured national and international attention on October 22, 1962. That day, President John F. Kennedy told the American people that the Soviet Union was building a missile base in Cuba. The potential of a Soviet-controlled base just ninety miles from Florida that could enact a nuclear attack on U.S. soil turned the simmering international threat of nuclear war into a rolling boil. Over the thirteen days of October 16–28, an international standoff unfolded between the United States, the Soviet Union, and Cuba that would create one of the most frightening political events in modern history. The Cuban missile crisis threatened the complete annihilation of Cuba, parts of the Soviet Union, and an area that housed at least a third of the U.S. population. In addition, military action would result in long-lasting environmental damage. At the time, the United States had a missile base in Turkey that had the potential to strike the Soviet Union with nuclear weapons. The Soviets sought to even the international playing field by capitalizing on the preexisting antagonism between the United States and Cuba over American interference in Cuba's governance as a sovereign nation.

In 1959, Cuba ended a revolution led by Fidel Castro, which ousted President Fulgencio Batista and resulted in Cuba becoming a socialist country. In 1961, the U.S. Central Intelligence Agency undertook a military operation, the Bay of Pigs invasion, in Cuba to support Cuba's Democratic Revolutionary Front. In three days, Castro's Cuban Revolutionary Armed Forces defeated the invading forces, leaving a bitter relationship between Castro and Kennedy. Given an opportunity to limit U.S. international aggression, Castro welcomed the Soviet military base. He differed with Nikita S. Khrushchev, the Soviet premier, on tactics, however. Khrushchev thought the base should be set up in secret, while Castro believed the sovereignty of Cuba gave it the right to set up the base openly. Ultimately, Khrushchev's plan won the day.

On October 16, 1962, Kennedy's national security assistant, McGeorge Bundy, brought the president photographs of nuclear-armed missiles in Cuba. Over the next week, Kennedy contemplated how to respond. His address to the nation on October 22 demarcated the historical period of mass destruction in the twentieth century and articulated a familiar brand of American freedom. Looking to recent history as a point of reference, he claimed: "The 1930's taught us a clear lesson: aggressive conduct, if allowed to go unchecked and unchallenged, ultimately leads to war. This nation is opposed to war. We are also true to our word. Our unswerving objective, therefore, must be to prevent the use of these missiles against this or any other country, and to secure their withdrawal or elimination from the Western Hemisphere."[23] Kennedy's presentation of America's opposition to war did not account for the CIA's subversion of the Cuban government, effectively masking American imperialism by trumpeting national values. His speech established the strength of the United States without conceding his role in stoking the crisis.[24] He assured Americans, "We will not prematurely or unnecessarily risk the costs of worldwide nuclear war in which even the fruits of victory would be ashes in our mouth; but neither will we shrink from that risk at any time it must be faced."

His address, in its final moments, affirmed how American exceptionalism feeds U.S. imperialism and, most important, the ability of the former to cover for the latter. American rhetoric of ever expanding freedom provides the basis for the U.S. government to interfere in the sovereign operation of other states that it deems less free. Demonstrating the ease to export and, therefore, produce the governing logic of the hemisphere, Kennedy speaks directly to Cuban citizens, saying: "Many times in the past, the Cuban people have risen to throw out tyrants who destroyed their liberty. And I have no doubt that most Cubans today look forward to the time when they will be truly free—free from foreign domination, free to choose their own leaders, free to select their own system, free to own their own land, free to speak and write and worship without fear or degradation. And then shall Cuba be welcomed back to the society of free nations and to the associations of this hemisphere." Ironically, Kennedy offered an ideal of freedom predicated on the limit of governmental interference. His statement established a version of freedom emerging through a curtailed relationship with government. Hansberry had a similar understanding of freedom predicated on limiting governmental interference and understood that the shell game of American political practices required extra-governmental means of becoming free as well.

In the midst of the ongoing crisis, Hansberry gave a speech at a mass meeting at the Manhattan Center on October 24.[25] According to the FBI, the New York Council to Abolish the House Un-American Activities Committee (NYCAUAC) sponsored the event. Although Hansberry later had a meeting with Attorney General Robert F. Kennedy on May 24, 1963, that is more well known, her invocation of the federal government and the president in 1962 offers an early example of her publicly intervening in a crisis. She said: "I think that it is imperative to say 'No' to all of it—'No' to war of any kind, anywhere. And I think, therefore, and it is my reason for being here tonight, that it is imperative to remove from the American fabric any and all such institutions or agencies as the House Committee on Un-American Activities which are designated expressly to keep us from saying 'No!' "[26]

Hansberry used her public visibility for political ends. Her invocation of John F. Kennedy through the call for "we the people . . . to oblige all, the heads of all governments responsible to us, the world's people" produces an encounter that cultivates the relationship between the speaker and her audience.[27] In so doing, the speech addresses invisible power structures. Hansberry draws into view the ghostly presence of the state in order to make it answerable to the citizens gathered in protest and the global community of radicals that inspired her vision. In her comments, she sought to make the U.S. government and the heads of all governments accountable to the artists that she maintains the House Un-American Activities Committee sought to quiet.

The speech ends with refusal. Hansberry drew force from a counterhistory that she mapped in the preceding moments of the address, asserting, "that maybe without waiting for another two men to die, that we send those troops to finish the Reconstruction in Alabama, Georgia, Mississippi, and every place else where the fact of our federal flag flying creates the false notion that what happened at the end of the Civil War was the defeat of the slavocracy at the political as well as the military level."[28] Intimately aware of how loss could inform one's sense of power, she responded to despair by tapping into a long history of Black political thought based on her practice and depiction of *the encounter*. Given the devastating impacts of World War II, human and environmental, feelings of powerlessness and, therefore, despair characterized Hansberry's political and intellectual age. Instead of conceding to the history of American liberalism that Kennedy used to establish the ethics of American force, Hansberry's words disrupt.

A moment of encounter also serves as the basis for establishing the other in Frantz Fanon's *Black Skin, White Masks* and de Beauvoir's *Second Sex*. In *Black Skin, White Masks,* Fanon depicts an encounter with a boy on a train. The child's perception, which he summarizes with the phrase "Look a Negro!" comes to represent for Fanon the implementation of an ontological condition established through the trans-Atlantic slave trade.[29] The exchange of looks followed by the child's summary evaluation locks Fanon in a history that he cannot yet escape. In *Second Sex,* de Beauvoir writes, "traveling, a local is shocked to realize that in neighboring countries locals view him as a foreigner; between villages, clans, nations, and classes there are wars, potlatches, agreements, treaties, and struggles that remove the absolute meaning from the idea of the *Other* and bring out its relativity; whether one likes it or not, individuals and groups have no choice but not to recognize the reciprocity of their relation." In the case of the foreigner, de Beauvoir does allow a reprieve. She writes, "But in order for the Other not to turn into the One, the Other has to submit to this foreign point of view." And asks, "Where does this submission in woman come from?"[30]

The problem, for Fanon and de Beauvoir, resides in a historical condition that situates Black men and white women respectively in a position to submit to the "foreign point of view." De Beauvoir concludes that material structures and conditions foreclose individual women from achieving "autonomous freedom."[31] She also criticizes women's willingness to collude with these structures. De Beauvoir makes a clear case for how materiality—material conditions and the physical body—shapes women's appearance as the other, and depicts the collective transformation of those conditions as the route to freedom. Nevertheless, in a book review of *The Second Sex* filled with praise, Hansberry criticized de Beauvoir's failure to "embrace a more far-reaching historical materialist view of life."[32] Hansberry's criticism of de Beauvoir calls attention to the difference in their understandings of history, particular histories of political struggle. De Beauvoir depicts collective freedom as a yet to be attained political horizon. Hansberry sees it as ongoing unfolding intervals. Hansberry's historical materialism accounts for the underground networks that sustain Black freedom struggles in periods of extreme political repression. From the nadir of race relations that ended Reconstruction to the public decimation of the Popular Front following World War II, Hansberry understood how Black activists sustained movements during dark times.

As a result, Hansberry sees the point of encounter as having the ability to disrupt history. In the moment of disruption, she concurs with de Beauvoir that one may feel ambiguity, or what Hansberry would call twoness following the Black cultural tradition of W.E.B. Du Bois. Encounter produces an awareness of one's self and attention to the other. It has the potential to steward collaboration and, perhaps, mutuality. For Hansberry, the experience of being Black in American already produced twoness; encounter heightened internal and external attention to Black people's bodies and their collective economic conditions.

Drawing from the Black radical tradition of the commons forged through difference of ethnicity, age, gender, sexuality, to name a few, Hansberry's understanding of being has resonance with "what Jean-Luc Nancy calls being-singular-plural: 'Being cannot *be* anything but being-with-one-another, circulating in the *with* as the *width* of this singularly plural coexistence.'" Hansberry's experience in the 1950s working simultaneously with the feminists of the Sojourners for Truth and Justice, the Black radicals on the journal *Freedom,* and leftists as a part of Camp Unity materialized her understanding of being together in difference. In *After the Party,* Joshua Chambers-Letson describes a form of communism "founded in difference, rather than a relation of equivalence." He explains:

> In place of racial capitalism's market-based commons of race, sex, gender, and class stratified, yet formally colorblind equivalence, a communism of incommensurability is a sphere of social relation structured less by social fictions of possession, equality, and exchange, than by collective entangled, and historically informed practices of sharing out, just redistribution, sustainability, and being together in difference. This kind of communism might take its cue not so much from the failed political parties of historical communism, as from the parties the SNCC activists threw while listening to Simone's records or the performance-rich parties of queer of color nightlife. Not because these spaces were perfect— they were and are replete with their own violences—but because they were trying to produce *something* else, *something* we don't even have a vision of. Yet.[33]

Hansberry understood that historical and ideological conditions (from slavery to Jim and Jane Crow) shaped Black people physically (in terms of how they labored and lived) and positioned them economically. Her historical materialist point of view steeped in Black radical thought allowed her to serve as a conduit across political groups with disparate focuses (gender, sexual, racial, or economic liberation) yet entangled histories. Her work to create space in common, public and underground, served the process of becoming free. Hansberry understood "freedom less as a point of arrival, or as a right that one possesses, than as an ephemeral sense and a practice of becoming that is performed into being by the body within tight and constrained spaces." In a study of improvisatory dance, Danielle Goldman describes performance as a "practice of freedom."[34]

Riffing on the well-known encounter in *Black Skin, White Masks* that produces alienation both immediate and historical, Hansberry participates in and describes in her work several encounters that challenge the conclusions of Fanon and de Beauvoir. She stages encounters in her plays, fiction, letters, and activism. Although most well known for her writing, "she also marched on picket lines, spoke on street corners in Harlem, and helped to move the furniture of evicted black tenants back into their apartments in defiance of police."[35] Hansberry's intervention into existentialist thought produces resistance to racism's slow structuring death through moments of political emergence that reveal underground forms of grassroots organizing and forecasts of things yet to come. The call in her speech to "empty the southern jails of the genuine heroes, practically the last vestige of dignity that we have to boast about at this moment in our history; those students whose imprisonment for trying to insure what is already on the book is our national disgrace at this moment" draws the activism of the Student Nonviolent Coordinating Committee's "jail no bail" protest into the history of the Cold War, once again staging a politic commons that does not evacuate each coalition of its specificity.[36]

Hansberry's speech in 1962 not only drew on the history of the civil rights activist close to the national crisis of the Cold War, it also called attention to her in order to redirect it to the students on the ground in South Carolina. This tactic of redirection recurred in her meeting with Robert Kennedy in 1963 and set the frame for understanding how her writing offers a Black radical reframing to writing the self. Hansberry's primary mode of becoming was her writing; Hansberry's writing, however, resists the subordination of the collective to the individual by repeatedly drawing attention to and calling forth the voices and experiences of grassroots organizations, including the Student Nonviolent Coordinating Committee. A true theatrical artist, Hansberry paints the historical backdrop to her story and casts it as an ensemble. Hansberry's writing, when understood as writing her life, challenges the conventions of autobiography, which "encourages readers to understand the emancipation of the individual *as if it were* a collective emancipation."[37] Drawing from a Black radical tradition of mass transformation, Hansberry calls for collective emancipation as a constitutive part of her becoming free.

Throughout her work, Hansberry surfaces histories of Black radicalism to support contemporary justice work and stave off the feeling of isolation, a precursor to despair. For Hansberry HUAC's attacks on her mentor Robeson and the subtler silencing of friend Childress stood in the forefront of her thinking about how the state curtailed artistic expression. When Hansberry moved to New York, she quickly became a part of Black radical and leftist organizations. In chapter 1, I examine her participation in various groups advocating for racial, gender, and sexual rights, including the editorial team of Robeson's periodical *Freedom*. Hansberry's work with *Freedom* served as a training ground for her thinking about Black struggle intergenerationally and internationally. Due to the operation of HUAC, much of the work that Robeson and his generation of leftists undertook necessarily occurred underground. Childhood experiences, intergenerational friendships, and studies specified Hansberry's conception of time. She understood the movement as emerging through the resistance of the enslaved and not beginning with responses to the Cold War.

Given the immediate concern of a potential nuclear missile attack, it seems odd to hold a protest about HUAC. Characteristic of Hansberry's writing, her work often appears to be on the wrong historical register, either belated or too soon. Hansberry's participation in the protest ties the Cuban missile crisis to a longer history punctuated by World War II of U.S. aggression that sought to reinstate the deteriorating empires of the West by convincing independent nations to side with the United States and Europe in the Cold War. The international game of chicken that could have resulted in nuclear catastrophe posed an undeniable threat to life. The fate of entire nations lay in the hands of three men, leaving everyday people feeling completely devoid of agency and power. Hansberry's speech enters into an atmosphere of doom with a historical lesson that places the current condition in relation to a longer history of state action. Her speech works on history not only as an act of historiography but a political one that draws from her investments in historical materialism as a necessary foundation for daily acts of insurgency. Her work and legacy explore the role of the artist in the ever-present context of American crisis.

Understanding the current crisis as an incident within a longer time frame enabled Hansberry to situate, historicize, and frame the anxiety it produced. Instead of conceding to the powerlessness of the individual in moments of national crisis, particularly in the nuclear age, in the published version of the address, she asserted: "It is perhaps the task, I should think certainly the joy, of the artist to chisel out some expression of what life can conceivably be."[38] Chisel provides a metaphor for revolutionary process: to chisel, to reform rock with blade, to shape the unmalleable. Hansberry sought to recast fixed ideas about society and about race and gender, which many midcentury Americans thought were biologically determined and therefore unchangeable. Hansberry's pen served as her chisel.

Her writing and activism activate the body as a site of meaning. The exchange between speaker and audience, real and imagined, animated and intervened in relationships. In Hansberry's speech, she explained that the contemporary climate of fear "is the direct and indirect result of many years of things like the House Committee and concurrent years of McCarthyism in all its forms . . . the climate of fear, which we were once told, as I was coming along . . . would bear a bitter harvest in the culture of our civilization, has in fact come to pass."[39] Kennedy used his address to the American people to establish the necessity of international governmental action to curb a purported threat to American freedom. Hansberry offered another example of U.S. governmental action that threatened American freedom, but her example is national.

More personally, she began the speech with self-reflection on the mechanisms that have encouraged her silence. She wondered about her recent lack of visibility, which the editors of *A Documentary History of the Negro People of the United States,* volume 7, where the speech is anthologized, attribute to her failing health. Her archive, however, suggests that the struggle to craft a public self, attentive to her political investments and the maintenance of her social power, greatly informed her limited visibility. Hansberry's popularity and influence traded in her public recognition as a young, beautiful, middle-class Black wife. Her public statements, however, unequivocally express her radical vision for social organization.

In the speech, she explained that political calculations have informed her public absence and that she had been working on a play, likely an early version of *The Sign in Sidney Brustein's Window*. In the play a German novelist describes to an American how "the better portion of the German intelligentsia" came to "acquiesce to Nazism."[40] The novelist goes on to say that in exchange for silence the Nazis made the German citizens feel separate from and unable to intervene in the conflict. Their sense of futility created comfort. The antagonism between apathetic comfort and politically engaged struggle animated Hansberry's thinking from her childhood until she died, because she understood that in order for U.S. democracy to tout freedom from interference while engaging in imperialism at home and abroad required despondent citizens.

Hansberry questioned the perception that people cannot effect change or challenge the violence being committed by their governments. In the published version of the speech, she writes, "It is [writers], in whom we must depend so heavily for the refinement and articulation the aspiration of man, who do not yet agree that if the world is a brothel, then someone has built the edifice; and that if it was the hand of man, then the hand of man can reconstruct it—that whatever man renders, creates, imagines, he can render afresh, re-create and even more gloriously re-imagine."[41] Referencing Jean Genet's play *The Balcony*, Hansberry categorized the cynical view of society as permanently structured by sexual exploitation in an alluring house of mirrors. In her writing, sex serves as a form of labor, enables human reproduction and situates women in social hierarchies. Here she depicts a type of exploitive labor that perpetuates the artist's alienation from society. She calls for artists to awaken to this dynamic and affirm commitment to politically engaged art.

Hansberry completed her speech by asserting, "if we are to survive, we, the people still an excellent phrase—we the people of the world must oblige the heads of all governments to become responsible to us." The ability to challenge government action expresses a fuller democracy, by attending to civil rights abuses, political persecution, and the unfinished business of Reconstruction. Hansberry saw the threat of nuclear war as a new iteration of a long and familiar American practice of mass destruction. She situated it as a historical extension of the genocide of trans-Atlantic slavery. According to her the government "would not have to compete in any wishful way for the respect of the new black and brown nations of the world" if it fulfilled its democratic ideals.[42] She saw what this nation had done to her father. Lorraine had context for crisis.

1959, *RAISIN* OPENED

Youngest child and bookish, Hansberry learned by watching. Her early work as a reporter for Robeson's *Freedom* helped her refine her ability to bear witness. In her development as an artist and activist, she sought out mediums that she could use to tell the truth about Black people. She knew that in order to do so she would have to chip away at preconceived notions about blackness. After *Raisin in the Sun* opened, Hansberry felt the fervor of newfound fame. Although she had worked for a decade writing for Black radical and leftist periodicals, *Raisin* came to signify the totality of her work. In an interview with Mike Wallace (explored in more detail in chapter 2), Hansberry worked deliberately to reframe his perception of her as a naive housewife. He, however, refused to see her. The encounter with Wallace is one among many that shaped Hansberry's ideas about the transformation Americans would have to undergo to become free. Late in her life, she emphasized the importance of liberals becoming radicals; part of that process required liberals see Black people. The challenge Hansberry posed to liberals also served as self-provocation to move past her upbringing into more revolutionary forms of political practice. She left experiences, like the interview with Wallace, exhausted and frustrated.[43] She turned these moments of misperception into art.

In Hansberry's writing, she uses encounters, real and imagined, to disrupt social scripts and cultural protocols between people. The act of encounter shifted the dynamic between the two engaged in the meeting and those watching as well. In Hansberry's work, for the stage or otherwise, she often carved out room for an audience. The added element of witness accounts for and addresses the alienation implicit in being made other or foreign through the look of another. A knowing or understanding look from a spectator disrupts the totalizing effect of another's gaze and mitigates the impulse, if it exists, "to submit to this foreign point of view."

Fanon and de Beauvoir's renderings of encounter depict interaction between two individuals. Hansberry's encounters required witnesses. Witness functions on multiple levels in her work. Philosophically it serves to triangulate the encounter at the heart of subject formation. Hansberry's writing not only draws from de Beauvoir's conception of women as a class, it also taps into Du Bois's well-known rendering of Black consciousness as doubled. Du Bois writes: "The Negro is a sort of seventh son, born with a veil, and gifted with second-sight in this American world,—a world which yields him no true self-consciousness, but only lets him see himself through the revelation of the other world. It is a peculiar sensation, this double-consciousness, this sense of always looking at one's self through the eyes of others, of measuring one's soul by the tape of a world that looks on in amused contempt and pity. One ever feels his twoness,—an American, a Negro; two souls, two thoughts, two unreconciled strivings; two warring ideals in one dark body, whose dogged strength alone keeps it from being torn asunder."[44] In Hansberry's accounting, the doubling acted internally for the individual and externally as a shaping societal force. Witness draws from the Black radical tradition of affirmation often necessitated by racism's power to isolate individuals. Witness also taps into the dynamic at the heart of theater. In Hansberry's realist drama, she not only made use of the audience as witness but also staged witnessing in her plays. Consider the scene in *A Raisin in the Sun* when the Younger family watches as Walter Lee, the son of Lena Younger and brother of Beneatha, rejects an offer to sell their new house. In the scene, Walter Lee makes a point to draw his son Travis into the act of witness, in some productions, placing him in the center of the scene.

Hansberry's drama depicts how interactions shape perceptions of blackness, presenting the encounter as a radical act. She, however, does not present a figure locked in a history of degradation that he is yet to overcome like Fanon, nor does she see the body and material conditions as roadblocks to individual transcendence. Her work draws from that of de Beauvoir. It affirms the human necessity of mutuality in the exchange, which Hansberry depicts as building blocks that structure collective freedom.

In Hansberry's most well known play and in her larger body of work, she used realism as a form of witness. The form offered her an opportunity to draw attention to how representation works to produce what we recognize as "true."[45] For Hansberry, the truth lay underneath belief, history, and desire. Realism sought to call attention to how belief, history, and desire shape how and what we see. Her writing highlighted the distinction between representation and lived reality. Hansberry's work often refuses to submit to the will of the other by drawing on the collective power of witness to reaffirm her perspective as part of a long history of Black insurgency.

For Hansberry, realism sought to redress the political feeling of despair. Her speech in October 1962 functions as part of a continuum of expression that includes essays, plays, short stories, poems, vignettes, journal entries, and newspaper articles. Hansberry's choice to produce in realistic mediums had everything to do with how she experienced life and coped with death. Her

Ruby Dee, Claudia McNeil, Glynn Thurman, Ossie Davis, and John Fielder in the stage production of *A Raisin in the Sun,* 1959 (Photograph by Friedman-Abeles, © The New York Public Library for the Performing Arts)

organizing of the world through her art weaved together political and artistic collaborations with Robert Nemiroff, friends Paul Robeson, Alice Childress, James Baldwin, Nina Simone, and Ossie Davis and organizations such as the Student Nonviolent Coordinating Committee and the Communist Party. Although Hansberry well understood the desire to attend to Black suffering, she refused to let that impulse morph into an indulgent philosophy of despair.

1964, I GOT A DIVORCE

Similar to many of her intellectual peers, Hansberry turned to theater to work through her philosophical ideas. Many of the existentialists engaged with theater or wrote plays, including Sartre, de Beauvoir, and Camus.[46] They believed that human existence consisted of a set of negotiations with the world, "a set of tasks, things we need to do. We encounter routes and obstacles to the actualization of certain goals, and make a map for ourselves of the world which includes these pathways and blocks to these goals." According to Sartre, emotions emerged as a response to human engagement with the world and its assistance or impediments. According to José Esteban Muñoz: "This notion of emotion being the signification of human reality to the world . . . is deeply relational. It refuses the individualistic bent of Freudian psychoanalysis and attempts to describe emotions as emotions, the active negotiations of people within their social and historical matrix."[47] The idea of being in relation to another provides the basis for Hansberry's important contribution to existentialist thought and her understanding of how art facilitates freedom and justice. In art's ability to act as a conduit for "active negotiations of people within their social and historical matrix," it tapped into the desires that motivate human action even against material factors.[48]

Departing from other midcentury existentialist thinkers, Hansberry did not understand the transcendental state of an individual coming to consciousness as freedom. She thought that individuals had the capacity to enact transformation but that each individual act participated in a larger movement within a long historical period—working together, resulting in a totality of action that enabled becoming free. She saw individual action in relation to long histories of insurgency. She also thought that being in relation had resonance with the colloquial term having relations, and that community and communion emerged through political and personal intimacies.

The idea of encounter, confrontational, comforting or sexual, informs how Hansberry depicts freedom as a practice. Her work, as an artist, activist, and intellectual blossomed in community and flourished in the rare moments that she found mutuality. As with most people, the individuals that had a deep understanding of Lorraine were few. Her relationships with Bobby, Jimmy, Nina, and her lover Dorothy Secules shaped and sustained her. Although Hansberry remained legally married to Bobby until 1964, throughout her adulthood she had intimate same-sex relationships that formed part of her understanding with Nemiroff. For Lorraine questions of living and dying were not abstractions. They were ever present dilemmas that shrouded her every day with as much force as the threat of nuclear war did for many Americans during the missile crisis. The unconventional way she lived, a Black, radical, woman artist and self-described "heterosexually married lesbian," reflected her commitment to define living as a set of possibilities and theories yet to crystallize.[49] On March 10, 1964, Lorraine divorced Bobby, but they never had a traditional marriage. Their love blossomed in activist circles and came into full bloom as he curated her artistic work and public image. Bobby gave Lorraine space, support, and feedback, and provided her cover. Her divorce represents a turning point in the public record of her personal life, but (as explored more deeply in chapters 1 and 5) the social designations of the mid-twentieth century did not capture the lived reality of what we may now call her queer community.[50] Encounters became mechanisms in her work and life to not only call forth histories but also to produce futurity.

Each March 10 marks a turning point in Hansberry's life, but not wholly in the way one would think. Hansberry's divorce marked an official end to her marriage, but the public did not learn about it until after she died. Although her public image laid claim to certain forms of respectable womanhood that sought to capitalize on the approximation of power and cover that proximity provides, her public actions often flew in the face of gender norms and drew from understandings of Black womanhood as transgressive.

Distinct from the other two, Hansberry's third March 10 also required negotiation with the state and a reckoning with how it has shaped the family, her family. For the state-authorized transaction, Bobby traveled to Mexico—the site of Lorraine's father's death and a venue for her early education. In the summer of 1949, Hansberry studied in Ajijic, Mexico, in the University of Guadalajara's art program. She traveled to Ajijic, a rural outpost filled with European and American artists, seeking, like her father, a new landscape. While in Mexico, Lorraine studied with a Guatemalan visual artist, Carlos Mérida. Mérida, an assistant to Diego Rivera, drew from indigenous and European traditions to create abstract art and murals. His ability to draw from and merge traditions certainly must have inspired a young Lorraine, still searching for her medium. She also took classes with Ernesto Butterlin, also known as Linares, an abstractionist painter.

During her time in Ajijic, Hansberry must have reflected on Mexico as a site of possibility and loss; Bobby traveling to the country where her father died to end their marriage, an act of familial reconfiguration filled with mourning and the break of a new day. The trip marked a reclamation as well of life lived outside the mandates of American exceptionalism. At the end of her life, Hansberry let go of the social protection that marriage offered, signaling a transformation in the balance between how her private and public selves would inform her work. The circulation of Hansberry's image, and her association with *A Raisin in the Sun,* produced a public identity that seemed to benefit from what Darlene Clark Hine defines as dissemblance. She explains, "By dissemblance I mean the behavior and attitudes of Black women that created the appearance of openness and disclosure but actually shielded the truth of their inner lives and selves from their oppressors."[51] Although Hansberry made several radical statements during her marriage that articulated her leftist politics, her association with *the* Black domestic drama of the period and, subsequently, with domesticity, overshadowed her serious analysis of class and gender oppression. Hansberry's critique of capital accumulation and investments in historical materialism had much to do with the traditional ways women were expected to labor in America.

In Hansberry's intimate relationships she did not take on the role of the wife or the mother. Bobby took care of her in the sense of clearing space for her to do her work, but after *Raisin,* she provided financially. Her home and professional life defied mainstream assumptions. Led by radical thought, her friend Nina Simone described Hansberry as "a girlfriend . . . we never talked about men or clothes or other such inconsequential things when we got together. It was always Marx, Lenin and revolution—real girls' talk . . . Lorraine was most definitely an intellectual, and saw civil rights as only one part of the wider racial and class struggle."[52] Given her fame, race, gender, sexuality, and class, Lorraine keenly understood the complexity of collaboration rooted in intimacy. Her work, nevertheless, offered the idea of human connection as a treatment for alienation and isolation that punctuated her life and what she called the movement. "Daddy died, *Raisin* opened, I got a divorce"—each marked a moment of loss, possibility, and clarity, and each served a vital function in her becoming free.

Chapter 1 Practices of Freedom

The human impulse, if we may believe the obvious in history,
is to produce or to transform nature.
—Lorraine Hansberry

Hansberry knew the life-and-death stakes of living as a Black person with conviction. She watched her father become disillusioned with American politics. At the time of his death, in 1946, he was planning to live in Mexico as an expatriate. A few years later, in 1950, Hansberry moved to New York, during one of the darkest periods in the life of her soon-to-be mentor, Paul Robeson. In the 1920s and '30s, Robeson experienced unparalleled success as an artist, starring in plays by Eugene O'Neill and breaking boundaries in film. In the 1940s, even as his political activities drew FBI attention, Robeson remained a celebrated artist. In 1944, he starred in *Othello* and sang the patriotic "Ballad for Americans," "accomplishments that would earn him the label America's number-one Negro."[1] He also participated in the political activities of the Popular Front era.

Despite his stardom, a series of events in the 1940s led to Robeson's professional and public decline. On July 25, 1946, Robeson met with President Harry Truman to urge the president to advance anti-lynching legislation.

He warned that if Truman did not comply, Negroes would defend themselves.[2] Truman ended the meeting. Three years later, in the spring of 1949,
Robeson took center stage at a peace conference in Paris and talked about
the Double V campaign, the popular movement that sought victory over
fascism abroad in World War II along with victory over discrimination at
home. He knew that winning the first would not necessarily result in the
second, so he was revising Black people's commitment. He stated that Black
Americans would not fight against the Soviet Union in the event that the Cold
War heated up. He contended, "the only alternative to world freedom is world
annihilation—another bloody holocaust."[3] Robeson's statements in Paris
became the fodder that the Department of State needed to transform America's number-one Negro into public enemy number one. His worldwide
renown surely helped to get him a seat at Truman's table *and* contributed to
his state-assisted derision.

Robeson's involvement with the Council on African Affairs, an anti-colonialist
and Pan-Africanist organization that advocated for an independent Africa, and
the Communist-backed Civil Rights Congress also made him a threat to the
more well-established National Association for the Advancement of Colored
People. Walter White, executive secretary of the NAACP, "denounced Robeson.
The American press quoted his comments widely, and the United States
Information Service disseminated them worldwide. White characterized Robeson
as a 'great artist,' but a man ... [that] was being 'shamelessly used by the
lunatic fringe of party liners.' "[4] Robeson represented a split between civil
rights activists and leftists, but as Dayo Gore, Martha Biondi, and Mary Helen
Washington have shown, the political and organizational allegiances remained
fluid during this period. It also enabled leftists, particularly women, to move
nimbly between groups focused on workers' rights and those committed to
civil rights.[5]

In late July 1950, FBI agents, acting on orders from J. Edgar Hoover, found
Robeson in New York City and informed him that his passport had been
canceled. They came to retrieve it.[6] "By the 1950s, with his passport revoked
and living under 'house arrest' conditions, television, the medium that forever
transformed American culture, was an outlet denied to Robeson."[7] He had to
turn to other channels to disseminate his work. In November 1950, Robeson
founded *Freedom,* a monthly journal for a Black leftist readership, and Hansberry joined the staff.[8] She learned from working with and on behalf of Robeson that art opens doors, poses a threat, and makes people listen. It also left
Robeson overexposed and vulnerable. Witnessing the Department of State's
efforts to dismantle his political and social impact reminded Hansberry to

diversify her approaches to securing Black peoples' freedom.[9] During her time spent working with Robeson, she would learn how women's materiality requires a dynamic version of Black liberation that cuts across and creates lines of affiliation among seemingly disparate organizations. She saw American racism eat her father up and moved to New York as it fed on Robeson.[10]

PRACTICES OF FREEDOM

In the summer of 1950, after struggling through four semesters at the University of Wisconsin, Lorraine Hansberry moved to New York City to pursue a career as a writer.[11] Her fierce independence of mind and rearing in a household filled with Black affirmation enabled her to choose to leave the university and still pursue a life as an intellectual. Following the history of Black biography in those early years, she learned how writing served as an act of freedom and self-creation.[12] In her new urban environment, she carried important knowledge: her parents taught her that freedom is a practice rather than a state of being. Carl had won a legal "victory" in the U.S. Supreme Court in the case of *Hansberry v. Lee,* which found he had the right to purchase a specific property in the Woodlawn neighborhood of Chicago but did not find segregation illegal, an important impact that left more work to be done. But the victory itself only occurred through gender specific sacrifice; Nannie protected her household with a Luger pistol while Carl advocated for justice in the courts.[13] Unlike the title of Malcolm X's speech in 1964, "The Ballot or the Bullet," Hansberry learned at an early age the necessity of both. Lorraine also understood that although the history books would chronicle her father's efforts, her radicalism also needed to borrow from her mother's self-determined place in the home.

In addition, Carl and Nannie imparted a lesson about the difference between reform and revolution. Lorraine did not misconstrue liberation for becoming free. Hansberry saw certain practices as necessary intermediate steps toward becoming free but not acts of freedom themselves. These steps, such as voting, helped to secure the nation-state as the fundamental engine of freedom, but Hansberry knew and understood the shortcomings of relying on the state. As Joshua Chambers-Letson explains:

> Freedom, within white supremacist liberal capitalist modernity, is largely understood to be a possession or right: the freedom to own, to enter the market, or to buy and sell one's labor. As Lisa Lowe argues, "Liberal ideas of political emancipation, ethical individualism, historical progress, and free market economy were employed in the expansion of empire [and these] universalizing concepts of

reason, civilization, and freedom effect[ed] colonial divisions of humanity, affirming liberty for modern man while subordinating the variously colonized and dispossessed people whose material labor and resources were the conditions of possibility for that liberty." Following Mimi Thi Nguyen, after a century and longer of US military imperialism, freedom is not only colonized by liberalism; it is a discourse through which liberalism justifies colonial and imperial violence. Freedom, within liberalism, is an impossibility—a cruel joke or what Lauren Berlant describes as cruel optimism.[14]

As an interim step in the meantime, Hansberry saw the importance of negotiating and working with the state. She did not, however, mistake that work for becoming free. Her later articulation of the distinction between being a liberal invested in maintaining and slightly expanding the privileges afforded "exceptional" Americans to a larger proportion of citizens and a radical invested in producing an egalitarian society acknowledges the toxic force of liberalism for becoming free.

Carl and Nannie Hansberry took active measures to transform their reality, to shift the laws, social conventions, and cultural assumptions that structured their lives. Carl, Nannie, and Paul Robeson showed Lorraine that no matter how good you are, as a Negro, the United States would always break your heart. But Lorraine was not one that allowed herself to linger long in heartache. Her move to New York meant she had to figure out what thwarted the freedom struggles of her father, mother, and mentor.

As Margaret Wilkerson writes, Lorraine moved to New York for an "education of a different kind."[15] She participated in active learning as a writer that would shape her art and activism. Hansberry's writing in the early 1950s functions as a series of collaborative experiments with editors and activists in which she refines her practice as a writer, develops her voice, and cultivates her many public selves. In her published writing, she experimented with forms of realism to not only chronicle an underrepresented Black experience but also to show what is possible. Even though the realist writer is "required to operate according to 'rules of reality,' whatever they may be at any given moment[,] [w]hat for one generation may be realistic could be for another the height of artifice," in the words of William Demastes.[16] Realism provided the ground for Hansberry to imagine and show the artifice of reality. Realism always filters reality through representation, assumptions, experiences, and histories that color each person's perspective. The arbiters of truth in political and historical contexts have power on their side. Hansberry experimented with different forms of realism to lay claim to description for personal, historical, and political purposes.

Similar to her childhood in Chicago, living in New York shaped Hansberry's politics both through the people she met and the conditions that structured her life. When she moved to New York in the summer of 1950, she lived in an apartment on the Lower East Side with three other women and worked odd jobs, including in the fur industry.[17] Eventually she moved to Harlem and continued her activist work. "She attended tenant strikes and civil rights protests," according to Imani Perry. She also "lectured about racial and economic justice at the famous Speakers' Corner at 135th Street and Lenox."[18] In 1952, hopping from apartment to apartment, Hansberry lived briefly with the Trinidad-born Marxist Claudia Jones in Harlem, on West 143rd Street, the *Freedomways* editor Esther Jackson reported.[19] Fifteen years Hansberry's senior, "Jones was entrenched in the Marxist tradition . . . [and] included in her vision of socialism 'an anti-imperialist coalition, managed by working-class leadership, fueled by the involvement of women,'" Denise Lynn has written.[20] Jones, Robeson, and Louis Burnham all shared a vision of social transformation rooted in the action of working-class people. Mary Helen Washington adds: "Jones was a part of the group called the Sugar Hill Set, a group of artists and intellectuals in Harlem that included Hansberry, the Robesons, Langston Hughes, and [Alice] Childress."[21]

Although professional success enabled Robeson and Hansberry's parents to engage in the height of governmental action (meeting with the president and having a case argued before the Supreme Court), their access did not result in collective uplift. Peniel Joseph writes, "Hansberry's unusual biography—an upper-middle-class black woman who abandoned a comfortable existence for identification with the racially and politically oppressed—would lead [novelist John Oliver] Killens to describe her as 'a black nationalist with a socialist perspective.'"[22] Understanding this tension between her upbringing and her chosen affiliations informed how Hansberry performed and theorized her work. Following Jones and Childress, Hansberry saw Black women as central to that process of Black liberation and becoming free; as such, she began to consider how her work, her daily practice of writing, fed the slow burning fires of the movement.[23] In July 1952, Hansberry met Nemiroff on a picket line protesting the segregation of New York University's basketball teams. The romance would continue to bloom with their shared political interests. After marrying Nemiroff in her mother's home in Chicago, she returned to live at 337 Bleecker Street in Greenwich Village. She found collaborators that shaped her development as an artist, activist, and intellectual.

Hansberry's cultivation of her writing and her identity as a writer contributed to her public image and reflected her personal conviction to develop a politics that responded to racism's toxicity. She believed that her calling as an artist, activist, and intellectual expressed the idea that "The human impulse, if we may believe the obvious in history, is to produce or to transform nature." She was challenging social categories so familiar that they seem natural. In the 1950s, during the Cold War, the Lavender Scare, and the burgeoning modern civil rights movement, repressive governmental agents and activists alike used "nature" as an excuse to maintain hierarchies of race, gender, sexuality, and class.[24] In much of her writing in the early 1950s, Hansberry depicted encounters that served to animate self-creation and challenge the idea of a static self. Her public and private selves began to emerge in short pieces of writing and sketches. Her work not only conceptualized people and characters, it also accounted for her inability to fit into neat categories. Ultimately, Hansberry developed her public and private selves into two distinct wholes, and separated them, for the most part. Her writing, and the writing about her, offers more insight into the cultivation and curation of her public self than her private one. But her correspondence with her dear friends, and their observations, offer glimpses into the private Lorraine.

Nevertheless, her semi-public position as a Black lesbian radical required understanding the pursuit of freedom as a way of being in the world that she could develop, not based on natural predetermination. In Hansberry's essay "Simone de Beauvoir and the Second Sex—An American Commentary," from 1957, she questioned the "natural" role of women in the home, "chained to an ailing ideology which seeks always to deny her autonomy and more—to delude her into the belief that that which in fact imprisons her the more is somehow her fulfillment."[25] Hansberry's early published writing serves as potent evidence of her commitment to the Black radical tradition and feminism, but that work does not emerge in the mass media representation of the author of *A Raisin in the Sun*. Misperceptions about Hansberry abound. Although her marriage to Nemiroff underpins the public perception of her as heterosexual, it still does not explain why her middle-class childhood overshadowed her almost decades-long history of writing for leftist periodicals. Hansberry's writing is vital evidence in her story.

Full of hope and possibility for world-shifting change, in her *Second Sex* review essay Hansberry called for revolution, transformation, an upending of things as we know them. Reading de Beauvoir's book, she said, set "mind afire at last with ideas from France once again in history, *equalite* [sic], *fraternite, liberte—pour tout le monde!*"[26] Hansberry concluded that writing contributed to how she could transform America and Americans' understanding of society and humans' places in it. For a young writer, such transformation required perpetual and consistent resistance to "nature." By the late twentieth century, thinkers began to accept Hansberry's early insight about the social construction of categories that were once considered biological. But in the mid-twentieth century, her mode of reframing these categories by attending to how their interlocking nature produces economic, social, and cultural exploitation had not yet taken hold. Through an engagement with her writerly practice one may fully appreciate her contribution and challenge to radicals, including Robeson, and Black radical thought. Hansberry called for the Black radical tradition to account for the common experiences of women working toward persistent change. In so doing, she developed a political strategy to confront the slow death of Black people through the infrastructural work of many movements (the civil rights, women's, labor, and gay and lesbian movements). In addition to thinking of revolutionary change as a rupture, her work presents an understanding of revolution as a perpetual spiral.

Hansberry arrived in New York at a time when many of the most visible figures of the civil rights movement were male and when the movement was consolidating and expanding a view of racial equality that focused on "black action in civic space."[27] As Shatema Threadcraft notes, the focus on civic rather than intimate spaces in Afro-Modern thought privileges individual masculine action as definitive of Black freedom. Hansberry's work in the decade of the 1950s challenged both of these cultural mores. Although she participated in public activism, she also pursued freedom through the private act of writing, and that writing often detailed the effects on women of racial violence and freedom struggles. In the 1950s, Hansberry wrote for periodicals that included the Marxist monthlies *Masses & Mainstream* and *New Challenge*, the Black leftist newspaper *Freedom*, the lesbian magazine *The Ladder*, and the gay magazine *One*.

Hansberry's short-form writing of the 1950s—periodicals, poems, letters, and short stories—was a freedom practice that entailed routine, sought to improve, and applied an idea or a method. Hansberry's writerly practice informed how and what kind of artist-activist she became. It functioned as a working through of her ideas and an analysis of the political mentors she was familiar with, which included her parents, Robeson, W.E.B. Du Bois, Louis Burnham, and Childress. Hansberry's writing became the space where she cultivated a political identity that built on the models she knew. Analyzing her writing as both a practice of self-articulation and a political practice produces an intersectional understanding of how to cultivate freedom and the self.

Keenly aware of the Cold War anxieties that specified her identity and limited access to freedom, Hansberry knew that national belonging for a self-identified Black, lesbian, and Communist functioned as a responsibility. These identity traits placed her in a social position to hold the state accountable for what it purported to do as a matter of course, because she often experienced citizenship as the denial rather than conferral of rights. Throughout the 1950s, she made sacrifices and enacted deliberate freedom practices to support and strengthen her chosen affiliations. By the end of the decade, Hansberry's practice prepared her to take center stage in the American theater scene and the international Black freedom movements of the mid-twentieth century.

In the 1950s, New York City, similar to other major American cities, found itself recovering from the world-shifting impact of the Holocaust and the atomic bombings that ended World War II. The city became the headquarters of the United Nations (1952) and maintained its position as the cultural capital of the United States, home to the Broadway theater scene, corporate offices of major music labels, and the center of publishing. New York and its inhabitants struggled to reimagine life in a world shadowed by the imminent possibility of genocide, war, and a world reordered. Peering from a window in the South Side of Chicago, which could also be a flat in Harlem, the speaker of Hansberry's first published poem, "Flag from a Kitchenette Window" (1950), laments the unfinished business of World War II. The poem's speaker describes:

> Southside morning, America is crying
> In our land: the paycheck taxes to
> Somebody's government.
> Black boy in a window; Algiers and Salerno
> The three-colored banner raised to some
> Anonymous freedom, we decide
> And on the memorial days hang it
> From our windows and let it beat the
> Steamy jimcrow airs.[28]

Although Algiers and Salerno mark sites of Allied victories, for the Black boy sitting in the window "the three-colored banner" symbolizes an unknowable freedom on the Black side of town. Freedom denied but taxation for sure, Black residents pay the cost but do not receive the protections and benefits of the state. The portrait of victory abroad without victory at home circulates widely in midcentury African American literature and functions as one of the catalysts for the modern civil rights movement. Hansberry's speaker moves from the gravesite of a fallen soldier, and as the crowd disperses, a war song resounds; "our steps deliberately / Against the beat / Through the streets / Past the tenements."[29] Stepping intentionally toward freedom, the choreography of movement shapes the community gathered to mourn into one determined to move the country toward a form of human rights that protects all lives, even those lived within Jim and Jane Crow segregation. Hansberry places individual community members at the center of this movement to emphasize how routine actions shape political change.

The content and process, or what I am calling "practice," of her early writing has been overlooked by scholars because, in the case of Hansberry, scholarship overemphasizes popular attention. Disproportionate attention to *Raisin* not only limits Hansberry's impact during her life, it also causes misapprehension of her critical contribution to Black feminism as a theory and practice and to Afro-Modern political thought. Additionally, it reveals the difficulty in identifying her as a conceptual problem for theories of blackness that do not allow for the innovation (conceptual and material) at the heart of practice and rather seeks the consolidation central to the categories that install racial hierarchies.

Hansberry's short-form writing confronted physical, rhetorical, and representational violence in the United States and internationally. And, just as practice suggests, the work served as an iteration of ideas that she would return to and later develop in longer works. As a playwright, she often revisited and revised stories and scenarios that she covered as a journalist, like the freedom movements in Kenya and throughout Africa, which became the basis for her play *Les Blancs* (first performed in 1970). Through recurrence, the writing reveals how practice results in the refinement of vision and the reinforcement of her political project. Her short-form writing prepared her for the national prominence that followed *A Raisin in the Sun* and the stakes of being an artist-activist on a national stage. Hansberry's work during the nine years before the Broadway premiere of *A Raisin in the Sun* offers theories of freedom as a set of practices in an effort to sustain what she called "the movement."[30]

Hansberry's political practices foreground quotidian activity as fundamental to freedom movements. Her training as a journalist helped her to articulate her political investments and develop her voice—a voice that shifts from blunt and funny in the 1950s to measured and incisive in interviews following the Broadway production of *A Raisin in the Sun*. The combination of witnessing, reporting, and theorizing the current state of affairs and imagining other possibilities for freedom in blackness informed her coverage of major national and international stories and established her unique contribution to midcentury Black freedom movements.

WOMEN-CENTERED MOVEMENTS

For Hansberry, the press served a vital purpose in national and international Black freedom struggles by providing a framework for understanding the actions of activists as contemporary and historical phenomena. In her case, it also served as an early site of intellectual community, shaping her understanding of collaboration and mentoring. Her work at *Freedom,* which shared offices with the Council on African Affairs in a brownstone on West 125th Street in Harlem, ranged from answering telephones to reporting. Of the building, Childress described watching " 'Paul [Robeson] taking a visitor to the offices of Du Bois and [Alphaeus] Hunton,' hearing their 'deep and earnest conversation about Africa.' . . . She remembers actors and musicians and neighborhood 'Harlemites' dropping in to talk to Robeson, Eslanda Robeson introducing a young artist to Burnham, Du Bois sitting in his office making a plan to complete his dream of *The Encyclopedia Africana,* and a twentysomething 'Lorraine Hansberry typing a paper for Robeson.' "[31] On her early work as a staff member, Hansberry reflected in a letter to her friend Edythe Cohen, that "Freedom . . . in its time in history, ought to be the journal of Negro liberation . . . in fact it will be."[32] She worked as a staff writer for two years, then became an associate editor. Hansberry wrote stories about lynching, civil rights protests, labor organizing, and postcolonial movements. She also wrote theater and book reviews and children's stories. In these pieces, Hansberry reveled in the beauty of Black people while using her position to hold the state accountable for its responsibility to citizens, one of the central functions of the press in a democracy.

The position enabled her to refine her work and vision to display the beauty and joy of Black existence while also calling attention to the necessity of Black radical politics in community with senior staff members, including the editor, Louis Burnham. As a former executive secretary of the Southern Negro Youth Congress, Burnham "had crossed swords with 'Bull' Connor in Birmingham, Alabama, fifteen years before that name became internationally infamous," Michael Anderson has written.[33] Reflecting on the first time she met Burnham and what she learned about him during her employment at *Freedom,* Hansberry recalls: "His voice was very deep and his language struck my senses immediately with its profound literacy, constantly punctuated by deliberate and loving poetic lapses into the beloved color of the speech of the masses of our people. He invariably made his eyes very wide when he said things in idiom and, sometimes, in the middle of a story, he just opened his mouth and howled for the joy of it. I suppose it was because of his voice, so rich, so strong, so very certain, that I never associated fragility with him, despite his slight frame. His voice and the thoughts he expressed with it were so enormous that, all the time, it has been impossible to associate it with—a fragile heart."[34]

Hansberry's description captures the transformative power of the voice to change registers, captivate, and transport the listener. Burnham taught Hansberry how to reorient the position of the audience through a deft use of language. He also personified courage that defied his slight frame, a description that could easily apply to Hansberry. Burnham's courage and joy gave Hansberry a human example of a way of living and working in the face of state interference. His enormous voice and thoughts breathed life into her early writerly practice. In Burnham, Hansberry found joy for and an abiding commitment to Black people. She writes, "The thing he had for our people was something marvelous; he gave part of it to me and I shall die with it as he did. He would say simply, 'They are beautiful, child,' and close his eyes sometimes. I always knew that he could see them marching then. It was an open, adoring love that mawkishness never touched."[35]

Burnham's vision of Black freedom and the practices necessary to obtain it reinforced Hansberry's childhood lessons about time. She deeply understood the expansiveness of freedom as practices developed over time. And she knew that freedom practices organize how activists experience time, recalling the past while calling forth new social, political, and economic relationships in the future. Her awareness of freedom's temporality helped to alleviate her bouts with depression and informed her resistance to the national despair emerging in the aftermath of World War II and in the midst of the Cold War. From her experience, Hansberry enriched her understanding of how to craft a narrative, develop characters, and report about the complexity of human experience, motivations, and actions.

In October 1951, Hansberry traveled to Washington, D.C., to report for *Freedom* on the activities of the Sojourners for Truth and Justice (STJ), a woman-centered protest organization named for the freedom fighter Sojourner Truth. The group saw itself as part of a long history of revolutionary justice that dated back to the nineteenth century. The Sojourners drew from their knowledge of Black nationalist and Popular Front groups to decide how to organize themselves. The organization advanced "a human rights agenda and a vanguard center political approach," Erik McDuffie has written, and "fostered collective identities and an oppositional consciousness."[36] Hansberry described the STJ as a group that had formed to secure "freedom and happiness" for all Negroes and that pledged "to strive unitedly until the walls of racial prejudice come tumbling down."[37] Its members included Dorothy Hunton, Beulah Richardson, Charlotta Bass, Eslanda Goode Robeson, Shirley Graham Du Bois, Alice Childress, and Claudia Jones.[38] STJ offered Hansberry a model of women activists focusing on women's issues.

In the Sojourners' first political action, 132 women traveled to Washington, D.C., in October 1951.[39] They had an appointment with Maceo Hubbard, a Black official in the Civil Rights Division of the U.S. Justice Department, to present evidence of injustice against African American women, and they also intended to meet together for the first time and plan strategies for the future. Hansberry reported on this meeting in a full-page spread in *Freedom* that included three separate articles, each from a different angle.

Hansberry's reporting served a vital function as witness to the encounters she observed. In "Women Demand Justice Done," she described sixty members of the delegation arriving for an appointment with Hubbard, who was an assistant to the director of the Civil Rights Division. "The white guard sitting in the long, high-ceiling hall of the main corridor of the United States Justice Department looked up in amazement at the face of the determined Negro woman before him," she wrote. "The guard fumbled with the phone for a while and then stood up and promptly led them up one flight to the office of Mr. Maceo Hubbard."[40] The women crowded into the office to face Hubbard, a graduate of Harvard Law School who had served as an attorney for the Fair Employment Practice Committee in Philadelphia.[41] As one of the members of the group, Mrs. Dickerson, began to make their case, "a single white government official stood at first with his arms folded in cold arrogance as if he had come to watch a show." With the eye of a developing playwright attuned to movement, voice, dialogue, and feeling, Hansberry wrote, "Mrs. Dickerson turned to him: 'I'm glad you are here. You may not have had a Negro mother, but you are the son of a woman and therefore must have some interest in the protests of women. We invite you to stay and hear our indictments and our demands.' And maybe for the first time in his life, some shade of humility began to creep in that man's face, and he moved closer to the doorway."[42] Hansberry trained her eye on the subtle shifts in facial expression in order to characterize the individuals that she observed and bear witness to the impact of the encounter.

The meeting showcased how an impassioned group of Black women who willed themselves to power through community organizing could demand the attention of a federal official acting as the gatekeeper for Attorney General J. Howard McGrath. The meeting included, in Hansberry's recounting, five testimonies outlining, as Beulah Richardson did in a call to action, the injustices of Jim Crow, anti-Black violence, and material and symbolic disenfranchisement. Calling attention to the operation of communal rather than governmental power, an unnamed "housewife from N.Y. City" asked Hubbard what he would do to alleviate the suffering of Black women and men in the United States. "We negroes are always proud to have our people put in high places, but we like for it to mean something," the woman said. "If a man is going to be a leader then he should lead us forward, or give up his job." Marking a climax of the action, another unnamed woman, tall, handsome, and young, read a letter from Rosa Lee Ingram, a widow who supported her twelve children as a tenant farmer in rural Georgia. "When she finished there wasn't a dry eye in the room, except for the white official who was still standing there. No one could see Mr. Hubbard's eyes; he held them down. Then he said he was from Georgia, too."[43]

At the Justice Department, the Sojourners described to Hubbard many incidences of racial injustice that Black women had experienced, highlighting the specific ways a feminist perspective shifts Black radicalism. Mrs. Pauline Taylor, the mother of a Korean War veteran and the aunt of a soldier who died in the war, had had her passport taken away because she had attended a peace meeting while abroad. A Mrs. Westry's son had been shot to death by police while he lay on an operating table. Mrs. Josephine Grayson's husband had been executed earlier that year after being accused of raping a white woman. Mrs. Amy Macy's husband had been shot for voting. They spoke to Hubbard about lynching and asked him to take them to the office of the U.S. attorney general: "We know he can put people in jail just like that—and that's what we want, the jailing of some of these lynchers."[44] Hansberry emphasized the geographical and class diversity of the group; she reported that the group included PTA members, cab drivers, domestic workers, trade unionists, a poet, factory workers, and students and that they came from New York, Illinois, Ohio, California, and Virginia.[45] Hansberry's reporting signaled that Black women were ready for a new civil rights strategy and were willing to take action. She wrote, "The bitterness of our women is overflowing and the time was ripe to go to Washington—they dried their tears and spoke their minds."[46] This was distinctive: a group led and organized by Black women of all classes that looked to themselves and their own experiences, not to a male leader, for strategies to end the brutal injustice African Americans in the United States experienced. Hansberry's participant-observation exposed her to women's Black radicalism during the Cold War.

Drawing from prior organizing experience, some members of the STJ had participated in the National Committee to Free the Ingram Family, which formed in 1949.[47] In 1947, Rosa Lee Ingram's white neighbor, John Stratford, had come to the land that Ingram sharecropped, ostensibly to confront her about the fact that her animals were grazing on his property. According to Ingram, however, this was just a pretext. Ingram later testified that the animals belonged to a neighbor, not to her, and that Stratford had been harassing her for sex for some time. She said that he came to her homestead that day to inquire about "me giving him a date. I told him I was not that kind of woman."[48] When Rosa Lee refused him again, Stratford became violent and hit her with his rifle. Ingram's sons heard their mother crying out and came to Rosa Lee's aid with farm tools in their hands. During the struggle that ensued, Stratford sustained head injuries that led to his death. Following the altercation, the police arrested Ingram and her sons, charging them with murder. An all-white jury convicted Ingram and her sons and a Georgia judge sentenced them to death.[49]

Rosa Lee Ingram was in jail in October 1951 and was much on the minds of the women who visited Maceo Hubbard in the Justice Department. For the women of the Sojourners for Truth and Justice, the strategies of the past were no longer adequate. They did not provide the means of addressing injustice. Hansberry's reporting emphasized Black women's routine experience of political and physical violence and the need to develop strategies that could address the daily and often bloody erosion of freedom in Black people's lives. In all three articles, she wrote about the STJ's first civic action, stressing Black women's readiness to try new political strategies. Her writing presented the 132 women who went to Washington as calm, dignified, empowered individuals who were ready to speak publicly about grievous crimes at the hands of white citizens. And her writing ensured that their demands would remain a part of the public record.

In the fall of 1951, when Hansberry began covering the activities of the STJ, many African American leaders had emerged as potential rallying points for civil rights activism, but STJ's activism did not coalesce around these obvious figures. Some of them Hansberry knew personally, including Du Bois and Robeson, both of whom the State Department had judged un-American and punished by revoking their passports. Other figures who had not previously been nationally known emerged during the late 1940s and early 1950s, including William Patterson, an African American leader in the Communist Party who was tried under the Smith Act in 1949; the Trenton Six, who were convicted of killing an elderly white man in 1948; and the Martinsville Seven, who were executed in 1951 after being accused of raping a white woman. However, the STJ did not look to these male leaders for counsel or advice.

They focused on the stories of women who had experienced oppression and developed strategies based on that evidence. Through her experience of covering the STJ's sojourn to the nation's capital, Hansberry learned that dismantling the systems that were responsible for the violence Ingram and other Black women experienced required her to work at the intersection of Black women's experiences and Black radicalism, which often emerged through male leadership in the labor movement.[50]

As a part of the first sojourn, on September 29, 1951, some members of the STJ met at the home of Frederick Douglass in Washington to prepare their demands, which focused on their specific positions as women in society.[51] At the meeting, Beulah Richardson asserted some version of the following:

> We, a representative group of Negro women from different sections of the nation, assembled in Washington D.C., on September 29, 1951, at the home of Frederick Douglass, to unite in dedicating ourselves to fight unceasingly for the freedom of our people and for the full dignity of Negro womanhood,
> DO HEREBY PROCLAIM:
> For too long has the Government of this land turned a deaf ear to our plea for justice. For too long have we tolerated the double anguish of being both victim of the mob and victim of the Government. . . . We refuse any longer to watch our children die a thousand deaths by mobs, hooded or unhooded, by starvation and disease. We are sick and tired of being second class citizens in this our country which denies us dignity and honor in any of its 48 states.[52]

(Because the archive captures the speech through its reenactment in a pageant Hansberry and Childress wrote, rather than from news coverage of the event, the exact wording may have varied somewhat.) Hansberry's early experiments in writing would form the basis of her realist aesthetic, which took shape in drama, essays, fiction, and screenplays. Her investment in realism stemmed from her understanding, via de Beauvoir's *Second Sex,* that identity categories are constructed and that discrete acts of authorship participate in reinforcing individual identity. Hansberry knew that individual acts emerge in relationship to historical strictures that encourage normative manifestations of identity. In other words, when individuals encounter someone new, they draw from their historical knowledge to categorize the person (as in the description of Hansberry in newspaper coverage following the production of *A Raisin in the Sun* as a housewife). While individual acts and historical knowledge function as the tributaries that feed normative identities, blackness often appears contrary to the individual act or historical evidence. It disrupts what it means to be a housewife or a citizen. Through writing, Hansberry sought to offer more complex representations of the realities of blackness.

Offering a different perspective than classic theories of Black visual culture and identity (Du Bois's double consciousness or Frantz Fanon's description of Black ontology), Hansberry used realism to show how blackness challenges the legibility of social roles. When she described *A Raisin in the Sun* as a play that "tells the truth about black people," Hansberry made a profound statement. She said this knowing that Black stereotypes are the legible mode of blackness to Broadway audiences. Her description of *A Raisin in the Sun* qualifies the depictions of status quo stereotypes as lies and the nuanced depictions of Black family life as a form of truth telling. In Hansberry's work from writing for *Freedom* to her collaboration with the Student Nonviolent Coordinating Committee on the photo essay *The Movement* to her last plays, she experimented with forms of realism in order to shift the shape of Black people as an American idea. In American expressive culture, particularly the theater, Black people took the routine shapes of, for example, minstrels and mammies. Hansberry's work shifts that shape.

The STJ articulated how racial injustice, government policy, and international relations eroded Black women's experience of citizenship and challenged the premise of U.S. democracy. On February 29, 1952, Richardson recited the scripted speech in a staged reading of the demands to celebrate *Freedom* and Paul Robeson. Richardson's speech insisted that protection from the federal government was a key facet of citizenship. Indicting governmental and nongovernmental agencies, the speech called for the equal protection of the federal government in order to eradicate the practices that supported the subordination of Black women. The group demanded voting rights, justice for families of lynching victims through the prosecution and sentencing to death of vigilante murderers, representation in the U.S. government, an end to Jim Crow, passage of a fair employment law, the freeing of Ingram, the end to persecution of great leaders, and the formation of an international coalition for peace.

Hansberry's work as a correspondent for *Freedom* enabled her to engage with earlier generations of Black freedom fighters, both men and women, and learn from them, her orientation toward practicing freedom through writing pushed her toward different strategies for enacting freedom than the legal ones her father and his generation pursued. Her artistry required that she capture the visionary rhetoric of the STJ in dramatic form. Hansberry had witnessed Richardson's speech in 1951 and captured it for the *Freedom* celebration in 1952 in a pageant about Black life from the time of slavery to the present. Her work as a reporter served as the basis for artistic work that situated the activism of STJ in a long history of Black insurgency—a history that, as Carole Boyce Davies argues, often places women "outside the black radical intellectual tradition."[53] The pageant focused the extension of that Black radical tradition through the work of women. In the pageant, Hansberry and Childress offered a vision of freedom from interference and presented Black women as active participants in the work of carving space for African Americans to become full citizens.

Hansberry's early creative work established her understanding of the writer's responsibility to expose state-authorized violence. In July 1951, the Marxist periodical *Masses & Mainstream* published Hansberry's poem "Lynchsong." Like an open door, the first line of Hansberry's poem invites you in with a single word, "Laurel," a plant with a "name sweet like the breath of peace."[54] Instead of the typical association of laurel with Olympic crowns, however, Hansberry links it to lynching grounds, one of which was Laurel, Mississippi, where on October 17, 1942, a mob stormed the jail where Howard Wash was being held and took him to a local bridge, where they hanged him. It was the third lynching in Mississippi that week.[55] Nine years later, the pain of that event, which Hansberry selected to stand in for all violence against African Americans, still informed her work. She accused both church ("black robes") and state ("a / Cross in front of City Hall") for the continuing violence and made clear that it is not limited to the South ("cross in Chicago"/ "cross . . . in New York City"). She inserts an elegiac lament in the center of the poem:

> Lord
> Burning cross
> Lord
> Burning man
> Lord
> Murder cross

Although "Lynchsong" refers to specific past events and to the national scope of lynchings, a particular case was on Hansberry's mind in July 1951. Willie McGee, who had been sentenced to death for ostensibly raping a white woman, had been executed two months earlier in Laurel, Mississippi. Hansberry writes, "I can hear Rosalee," the woman thought to be McGee's wife, and can still see the "eyes of Willie McGee."[56] Hansberry may have heard of the woman who called herself Rosalee McGee; in 1950, after McGee's trial and conviction, Rosalee had traveled to New York to raise money for McGee's family.[57]

"Lynchsong" mourns loss of life through the impending execution of McGee and for the long history of racialized execution. In 1945, Willette Hawkins, a white housewife, accused McGee of rape. McGee was tried and an all-white jury found him guilty. The Civil Rights Congress appealed the case twice, both times resulting in a new trial. Following his second trial and conviction, McGee allegedly told the district attorney, Paul Swartzfager, that he was having an affair with Hawkins and that the sex was consensual.[58] Instead of admitting to the affair, Hawkins claimed that McGee had raped her. Hansberry's poem ends by marking time for the act of mourning:

> sorrow night
> and a
> sorrow night[59]

"Lynchsong" mourns systematic killing by depicting a spectrum of violence from vigilante justice to state-sanctioned execution. It portrays how women play a crucial role in this history, the speaker describing in the poem "My mother told me about / Lynchings."[60] The stories Black women told each other about their experiences, across generations, across classes, across geographical distance, informed the work of groups like the STJ, and Hansberry's poem acknowledges this gender-based circulation of knowledge even as the poem suggests that it is not enough to stop a state-sanctioned legal lynching. The state of Mississippi executed McGee on May 7, 1951.

"Lynchsong" mourns the systematic killing of Black people, which resonates with the appeal the Civil Rights Congress made to the United Nations in "We Charge Genocide" (October 1951), "for relief from a crime of The United States Government Against the Negro People."[61] This paper petitioned the United Nations for redress and, in so doing, called on a body of nations to police the United States for its excessive and deadly use of force against a targeted population. The United Nations was established in 1945 to prevent atrocities like those enacted during World War II. The Civil Rights Congress (CRC) appealed to the U.N. on the basis of the international organization's Universal Declaration of Human Rights, and more specifically the Convention on the Prevention and Punishment of the Crime of Genocide.[62] CRC's book-length essay called on the U.N. to protect Negro citizens on the basis of their human rights. World War II taught activists and the world the impermanence of states; a reality further exemplified in the ongoing independence movements in Africa and the Caribbean. Hansberry shared with the CRC the guiding principle that individuals have the capacity to change the organization of the state and that the United States is not the final arbiter of human rights.

SELF-DEFENSE FOR PEACE

As a writer for *Freedom*, Hansberry honed her ability to bear witness to acts of Black insurgency that challenged socially agreed upon conventions. These moments of social change would help her to better understand what movements made possible *and* what types of people could appear within more expansive democracies. Although not explicitly stated as such, Hansberry's later writing would reveal her understanding that realist writing "never reflects but instead reconstitutes its object."[63] Her writing in the 1950s seems compartmentalized, but she pushed publishing conventions during the period by focusing on the international scope of Black freedom movements and how they intersected with burgeoning feminist and gay and lesbian movements.

Hansberry's relationship with Du Bois furthered her understanding of Black internationalism. She read his work and studied African history and culture with him at the Jefferson School. In 1953, she mounted her own class at the school on "the Literature of the American Negro People."[64] Hansberry was Du Bois's "favorite pupil," according to Shirley Graham Du Bois, and he was "exceedingly fond and proud of her."[65] Building on the work of her mentor, Hansberry considered how Black internationalism accounted for women's labor.

She turned to Africa for inspiration in reporting for *Freedom* on the Mau Mau Uprising in Kenya and an essay in 1955 on Black child labor in South Africa. In 1952, after decades of British policies that had destroyed nearly every aspect of their culture, the Kikuyu people of Kenya began to defend themselves against incursion. Hansberry wrote "Kenya's Kikuyu: A Peaceful People Wage Historic Struggle Against British" four months later, in December 1952, in an effort to combat British characterizations of the Kikuyu warriors as terrorists or as practitioners of witchcraft. She presented the Kikuyu as people who over the previous five decades had tried every peaceful strategy to persuade the British government to protect their rights. "Today the Kikuyu have been driven to fight back in the only way they can—with force," she wrote. "In our papers, the efforts of the Kikuyu and Masai people of Kenya to gain freedom—just as we gained freedom in 1776—is called 'terrorism.' During the Nazi invasion of France and Holland and the Soviet Union we did not call the heroic retaliation of the Free French or the Dutch underground or Soviet partisans—'terrorism.' No, we correctly understood that they were patriots fighting for the freedom of their lands and peoples. So it is today in Kenya, and all Africa."[66] Hansberry's writing makes the case that rather than distinguishing the acts of "the heroic retaliation of the Free French" from the armed resistance of the Kikuyu, the distinctive factor when assessing such practices should be whether they safeguard human life and work to ensure freedom from interference and the right to self-govern. Hansberry's reporting captured practices of freedom that sought, in the case of Kenya, to produce new modes of governance. Her work also participated in the post-colonial project by highlighting the uneven implementation of democracy for Black people. Likening the Kenyan independence movement to that of the United States situates insurgency as fundamental to the democratic process.

Tony Bogues explains that consideration of the history of Black people from the Haitian Revolution to the civil rights movement produces freedom as a practice. Through action from armed insurgency to cultural and spiritual practices, Black people have redefined their relationship to the state and states through movement. In Western thought, Bogues clarifies, freedom operates in two ways: negative and positive. "Negative freedom is about a *freedom from,* an absence of interference . . . positive freedom is about a *freedom to* and includes issues of self-realization and mastery."[67] Hansberry's advocating for the Kenyan independence movement presents the necessity of freedom (in its positive and negative operation) as fundamental to democracy through daily actions that recall Black insurgency.

She illustrated her point with a fable. A man befriends an elephant. Being kind, the man allows the elephant to put his trunk inside his hut during a storm to keep it dry. The elephant, seeing no reason for the rest of his body to get wet, decides to push himself completely into the hut. The man, forced out into the storm, seeks redress from an Imperial Commission of the other animals. After hearing both sides of the case, the commission finds the elephant's testimony most credible. Having no other choice, the man builds another hut, only to have another animal occupy it. Repeatedly the man builds huts and loses them to animals that claim them. After suffering many losses, the man decides to build a huge hut. "As soon as the animals saw the new hut, they ran to take it from him." Once they were all inside, they began to argue about who owned the hut and fighting ensued. "While they were fighting the man made a fire and burned down the hut, jungle lords and all. Then he went off to build himself another hut in peace."[68]

When the Kikuyu had protested, the British ignored them. When they resisted, the British slaughtered them. Now they had no other option but to destroy the system that was destroying them. And she added a warning to all colonizing European nations in Africa: "So it is today in Kenya, and all Africa."[69]

Studying the insurgency in Kenya informed Hansberry's writerly practice in her children's story and later in the play *Les Blancs.* In 1952 Hansberry also published a short story under the pseudonym Elsie Robbins that describes the dehumanization of Black South African children by the Dutch settlers of South Africa and the mechanisms the children create to defend themselves. The byline gave Hansberry an opportunity to experiment with her public presentation, using a name that she would deploy again when she authored other children's stories. The story begins with a question: "Did you ever hear of a baby carriage that had legs instead of wheels, one that walked instead of rolling?" This is how she introduces the topic of abuse of Black South African children who take care of white children and are forced to carry them on their backs. Hansberry tells the story of eleven-year-old Mina, a South African girl who is a nursemaid to a Boer boy. Mina's living conditions suggest that she is less valuable than livestock: she lives "in a rough shack behind the house where she worked. It wasn't even as good as a chicken coop." Mina's three-year-old charge exacerbates her fraught circumstances; he rides Mina like a horse, kicking her to go faster as they travel through the neighborhood. As Mina crawls down the sidewalk, she sees a group of children that are turning the tormenting of human "baby carriages" into a sport by stepping on the bare feet of the African children who are carrying white children. When she sees this, Mina attempts to turn back, but the little boy riding on her back kicks harder and screams to urge her forward. Just as Mina feels the jolting kick of her charge to move her forward, she sees a group of protesters that includes her parents coming down the street. "They marched silently, their heads held high." Seeing the procession, "suddenly she cast the hateful load from her back and ran to her parents." Mina's observation and then action transforms her from service animal to citizen and repositions her charge from child to object of oppression. Shocked by Mina's action, the boy lay on the sidewalk as the protesters "smiled and took her hands. . . . They too were throwing the burden of white rule from their backs and claiming their country for themselves."[70] For the reader, the encounter depicted between the children and the adults helps to cultivate and incubate activism. Writing the story prepared Hansberry for when she would take center stage in public encounters about art and politics.

In the form of a children's story, Hansberry locates resistance to state-authorized oppression in a refusal to accept the daily conditions that dehumanize Black people. She demonstrates that resistance to the systems of oppression that structure Black people's lives requires, as Threadcraft argues, freedom practices that women *and* men enact, children *and* adults. Hansberry understood the act of refusal as a learned behavior that shapes citizens. The refusal may be jarring, disorienting, and violent, but it is nevertheless necessary.

Both of these pieces about Africa used fiction to explore what becoming free might entail. They present a spectrum of responses to systematic oppression, from armed rebellion and "burning down the house" to a peaceful march of men and women, parents and children. Hansberry clearly understands the

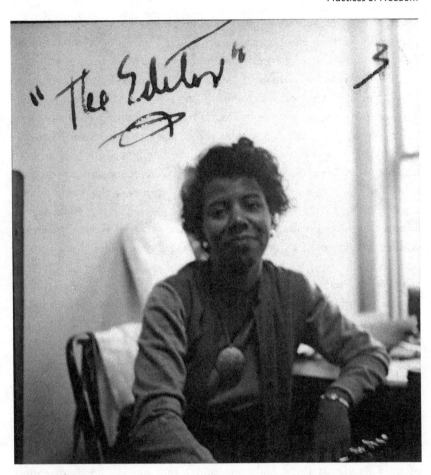

Lorraine Hansberry, the Editor (Photograph courtesy of Joi Gresham)

former response and warns that colonialist oppression carries the seeds of its own destruction. And in her short story just as powerfully, she imagines a young girl who is ready to embrace freedom the moment that possibility presents itself. It is easy to imagine U.S. parents reading this short story to children who just a decade later would become the freedom fighters of the civil rights movement. Hansberry's depictions of freedom in these two pieces from 1952 do the cultural work of creating space in the imagination for a refusal of oppression and new strategies for drawing freedom into reality.

Hansberry's investments in self-rule coincided with her dedication to covering leftist organizing as a reporter for *Freedom*. She participated in political activities (conferences, marches, and writing) organized by communist groups and worked with communist organizations beginning in 1950.[71] Her affiliation and work sought to end police violence against Negroes by drawing support from an eclectic group of friends who functioned as political allies. In a story Hansberry wrote for *Freedom* in May 1952, she quoted African American lawyer and later judge and congressman George W. Crockett's response to allegations that "so many Negroes in Detroit were Communists. In this instance, 'Communist' meant any Negro who fought against police terror." Crockett responded, " 'I don't know anything about the Communists in Detroit, but I do know a lot about Negroes, and anytime a Negro boy is shot down on the sidewalks, you are going to find hundreds of Negroes in the streets protesting.' "[72] Although the Cold War had a devasting impact on Black leftists, Hansberry's political voice drew from the radicalism of her parents' generation and her own vision of a world yet to come that foregrounded Black women's liberation.

Following President Harry Truman's speech in 1947 before a joint session of Congress in which he outlined the impending threat of Soviet aggression, he implemented a foreign policy known as the Truman Doctrine. The policy had implications for practices at home and abroad. On March 21, 1947, Truman signed an executive order that required federal employees to participate in a loyalty program. "According to the order, 'complete and unswerving loyalty' on the part of federal employees was of 'vital importance,' and therefore the employment of 'any disloyal or subversive person constitutes a threat to our democratic processes.' " In June 1947, Congress passed the Taft-Hartley Act, which required officers of labor unions to swear that they were not members of the Communist Party. Following suit, school districts began to require teachers to sign loyalty oaths. The primary investment of the federal government to fight communism equated any critique of government action or inaction with communist infiltration. In the early 1950s, print publications and radio functioned as the central modes of mass communication. Due to its mass and international influence, print became a contested mode during the Cold War.[73] The press had the difficult position of checking U.S. governmental power without appearing to aid communism.

As a part of Hansberry's professional responsibilities to *Freedom* and personal investments, she traveled to Montevideo, Uruguay, in March 1952 to serve as a U.S. delegate for the Inter-Continental Peace Congress Conference, in place of Robeson. Hansberry's participation in the conference clarifies how her guiding belief in the distinctiveness of humans as a species coincided with her political theory and practice. In "The Negro Writer and His Roots: A New Romanticism," Hansberry argued:

That man is unique in the universe, the only creature who has in fact the power to transform the universe. Therefore it did not seem unthinkable to me that man might just do what the apes never will—impose the reason for life on life. That is what I said to my friend—"I wish to live, because life has within it that which is good, that which is beautiful and that which is love. Therefore, since I have known all of these things, I have found them to be reason enough and—I wish to live. Moreover, because this is so, I wish others to live for generations and generations and generations and generations . . ."[74]

Hansberry's commitment to life underpinned her description of the Kenyans' resistance to British imperialism as a fight for life. Similarly, the Inter-Continental Peace Congress Conference, which was organized to protest the Korean War, sought to develop anti-imperialist policies. Achieving peace, a political state that furthers life, requires the dismantling of imperialism. It may seem antithetical for Hansberry to advocate for the Kikuyus' armed resistance one month in *Freedom* and in the next issue to describe her participation in the Inter-Continental Peace Congress Conference; however, when state governments wage war against citizens because of their ideologies and citizens defend their lives, the defense is in furtherance of life and, therefore, peace. Violence, when enacted in the continuance of life, is a mechanism necessary for peace.

Moreover, violence is only antithetical to peace in a system in which peace is operative. Under the U.S. Cold War policy, civil rights extended to Black Americans and human rights to colonial subjects had been suspended. In such a context, the very apparatus responsible for maintaining the law and protecting citizens—the state—exacts violence; it precludes peace. In a nation that truly allows for peace, there would be no need for self-defense. The very provocation of self-defense renders peace a political state that Hansberry was trying to move toward, an ideal political state, rather than an immediate political outcome or personal choice. Meaning, if the Kikuyu decided not to resist the British, Kenya would not be at peace, because colonialism disallows peace. Hansberry's coverage of the conference challenged U.S. Cold War ideology as a master narrative that attempted, unsuccessfully, to separate physical aggression against Negroes in the United States and North Koreans in Korea. Hansberry's experience at the Inter-Continental Peace Congress Conference showed her that achieving peace required responding to imperial violence through armed resistance and diplomacy. The wide array of tactics harkens back to her parents' different roles in supporting the desegregation of housing in Chicago.

The U.S. State Department found the conference threatening and worked to have it canceled. The organizers of the conference had originally scheduled

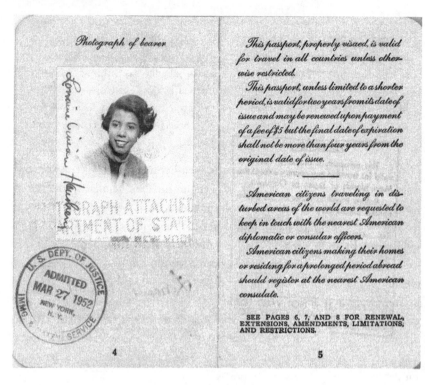

Hansberry's passport (Photograph courtesy of Joi Gresham)

it to take place in Buenos Aires, but under pressure from the State Department it was moved to Montevideo.[75] Even so, Uruguay officially banned the conference. The proceedings were held covertly, behind drawn curtains, with instructions to a pianist to begin playing if the police arrived and the participants to begin dancing.[76] "If it was true that the Congress was held under conditions of hostility, then it must be understood that it was only the hostility of the government and the police. The people of Uruguay were glad to see us, in that country where one could see the words: No Uruguayans to Korea! written in the streets and everywhere posters announcing and greeting the coming of the congress of peace."[77] Called by the members of the congress from countries in the Americas and the Caribbean who suffer from colonialism and would gain the least from a third world war, there were 250 delegates from nine countries: Paraguay, Brazil, Venezuela, Argentina, Puerto Rico, Chile, Colombia, Uruguay, and the United States.[78]

Hansberry's participation in the Inter-Continental Peace Congress Conference taught her about perceptions of the U.S. military and government in

South America. During the conference delegates described how the United States exploited their countries' material resources: copper in Chile, cotton in Paraguay, land for a military base in Puerto Rico. Embedded in the participants' resistance to furthering the Korean War was an abiding investment against "Yankee Imperialism."[79] Hansberry's coverage of the conference described how sessions focused on the mutuality of national independence and peace and reminded her of her responsibility to the world as an American.[80]

The conference revealed to Hansberry that delegates from member nations understood her position as a U.S. citizen without the protections of citizenship, creating a feeling of collectivity and expanding her understanding of activist collaboration from historical commonalities to personal relationships. Hansberry's Americana echoes, as she reported about the conference, "every cry of outrage and anger that is uttered by anyone of 15,000,000 voices" for people "subject to violence at the least whim of white supremacy in the form of a southern lynch mob," "a black robed judge," "or a university cop." The resonance "is heard throughout the Americas. And with each handshake and embrace and gift they said to me: When you go home, tell your people, that we are allies!" In her speech to the conference participants, she explained:

> All my life I have been proud that I belong to a people who have answered their oppression with militant resistance and magnificent dignity. A people who have indeed put some of the richest chapters of heroism in the history of the United States. Our oppressors, who distort our history, defile our culture, laugh at our beauty and deny our courage try desperately to make all the world believe their empty lies about us. And one grand experience of my life, was that at this congress I learned firsthand—how miserably they have failed.[81]

Following her return, the State Department revoked Hansberry's passport. The FBI also opened a file on her, introducing Hansberry to what Robeson and Du Bois already knew about state surveillance. Unlike her male mentors, however, the state, like the public, deemed her work unthreatening. As a result, her popularity increased as her FBI file grew.

In 1954, Hansberry became the associate editor of *New Challenge*, the organ of the Labor Youth League. Pushing the periodical to consider the mutuality of race and class struggles, Hansberry continued her coverage of independence movements in Africa, particularly Kenya, and the burgeoning modern civil rights movement. The magazine expressed its ideological investments in Marxism with the goal of enriching society for future generations of youth. The magazine stated: "We try to give expression to the activities and ideas of all young Americans striving for a more democratic and prosperous land in a world at peace." Hansberry's reporting on the Supreme Court's school desegregation decision in *Brown v. Board of Education* (1954) and the murder of teenager Emmett Till (1955) reinforced her contention that civil rights function to maintain human rights. Therefore, Hansberry's writerly practice oriented her toward advocating for systems of governance that protect the lives of Black people and depicted freedom practices as local and diasporic in nature.

Hansberry called for civil rights protections in the United States as a necessary step in Black people's exercise of positive freedom. In 1954, following the Supreme Court's decision in *Brown v. Board of Education,* Hansberry argued in the pages of *New Challenge* that resistance to school desegregation served to obscure the primary investment of segregationists in maintaining property rights and class hierarchies. She connected the Court's desegregation ruling to the lynching of Emmett Till. On August 28, 1955, fourteen-year-old Till was murdered in Money, Mississippi, for allegedly whistling at a white woman. Following his death, Hansberry charged, "Negro and white teen-agers going to Southern schools together could mean Negro and white adults joining unions together, working together for better conditions, voting together for liberal State and Congressional legislators. This is behind the violent campaign against the Supreme Court decision and against the Constitution, which led to the brutal murder of Emmett Till."[82] Bracketing the plausibility of the cause and effect relationship between desegregation and labor practices, Hansberry's assertion drew attention to a fundamental breakdown in the primary function of the state to first guard human rights and then enforce the protection of civil rights. The retaliatory violence against Till demonstrated a rupture in U.S. democracy that spread through the state of Mississippi. Following the acquittal of the men who murdered Till, Hansberry reported on a world turned upside down: "TWO WERE MURDERED IN THE FRONT LINES—they tried to vote. In our civic classes we were taught it is a duty for every citizen to vote, that murder is the worst crime. In the South it works the other way around: for a Negro to try and vote is a crime and to murder him is 'legal.' "[83]

The violent contexts of Black freedom movements, both in the United States and abroad, remained a prominent feature in Hansberry's understanding of herself as an activist and a writer. She must have reflected on her experiences during childhood of violent reactions to her parents' attempts at desegregation when she considered the responses to the Supreme Court ruling in *Brown.* As Hansberry's reporting reflected, the violence that erupted following the Court's decision reaffirmed her understanding that freedom practices must entail legal *and* extra-governmental modes of becoming free.

Hansberry's involvement with the Communist organization the Labor Youth League through writing for its organ complemented her employment in the summer of 1954 at Camp Unity, an integrated camp in Wingdale, New York, founded for the working class to enjoy culture and to support the Progressive Movement, which Hansberry was affiliated with since her years as a college student in Wisconsin. She saw the camp as a space in which participants could actively experience the principles of anti-fascism and democracy that drew them there.[84] Serving as lawn program director, Hansberry invited W.E.B. and Shirley Graham Du Bois to visit. She also facilitated performing arts and cultural experiences at the camp. As a member of the staff, she worked with Philip Rose, who later produced *A Raisin in the Sun*. Rose said that Hansberry worked at the camp as a waitress but told him she dreamed of being a writer. "And he said to her, 'I hope you do become a writer, because you're a lousy waitress.' "[85] Although an unsatisfying experience, Hansberry's involvement in the camp evidenced her investment in interracial political coalitions and communities as yet another mode of freedom work and her becoming free.

PERSONAL AND POLITICAL

As Hansberry's professional life advanced, so did her personal life. In a letter to her beau Robert Nemiroff dated December 26, 1952, Lorraine declared the three things she was sure of:

1. I am a writer. I am going to write.
2. I love you, problems be damned.
3. That it is possible that our sharing a life together would be a rather beautiful thing.[86]

On June 20, 1953, Hansberry married Nemiroff, a white Jewish activist and graduate student at New York University. Following their marriage, she resigned from *Freedom* but continued to write occasionally for the paper. In the early years of their relationship, Lorraine wrote about Nemiroff with affection and love, referring to him as "Roberto Mio," and "Mon Chere" [*sic*] in one letter.[87] In a letter dated Christmas 1955, Lorraine gushed, "All these marvelous creatures whom I love! Family! Husband! Comrades! Friends!—I have my special strange moments when it does seem quite worth it."[88] Four years later she described herself as a "heterosexually married lesbian" in an anonymous letter to *The Ladder,* the publication of the Daughters of Bilitis, the first organization for lesbians in the nation.[89] In the late 1950s, Hansberry was exploring her sexual identity and working through how loving a woman might influence her thinking about the movements she was working to build. Her multiplicity (investment in Black feminist nationalism and interracial coalition; her deep connection with Nemiroff and queer desire) did not register in the public perception of her following *A Raisin in the Sun,* and therefore resulted in perpetual misreadings of her and her work. The work itself, however, retains the complexity of her vision.

The ambivalence that ends her proclamation, "I have my special strange moments when *it does seem* quite worth it," reveals more about Lorraine than her loved ones. Her uncertainty marks a distinctive contrast from her measured, assertive and deliberate public presentation in interviews and speeches following the production of *A Raisin in the Sun.* Lorraine suffered with perpetual uneasiness, anxiety, and depression. The complexity evidences her guiding belief in the human capacity to will oneself into defying restrictions and how it informs her life and the cultivation of her public self through daily practice. The letter also offers insight into a private world in which she did not compartmentalize parts of herself.

During the Cold War years, lesbians and gay men faced regular oppression and discrimination. Both groups were labeled as perverts and as national security risks, and gay and lesbian bars were subject to frequent police raids. Masculine lesbians and male-to-female transgender individuals were at high risk because of their clothing; when police raided a bar, they automatically arrested any woman who wasn't wearing at least three items of female attire.[90] The names of those who were arrested were published in local newspapers, and people frequently lost jobs as a result.[91] Even when there was no raid, lesbians were at risk on the street and in parking lots: any show of affection between two women could trigger homophobic attacks that typically included beatings. Black lesbians faced double jeopardy: they were targeted for their race and for their sexuality. So it was no small step for Hansberry to begin thinking about the lesbian world just as her career was gaining some momentum.

Lorraine's personal writing often expresses a sense of anticipation that informs her worldview and political project as a perpetual action of becoming free. While she was at Camp Unity, Nemiroff visited on weekends and brought along their dog Spice. In her letters to him, she showed affection for Bobby, but she also wrote in a letter on July 8, 1954, of her longing and same-sex desire: "I know what I have always known before consciousness even that most important it has to be Her—I mean The Woman. It apparently simply will not be The Man for me. I almost wish that could make me sad, but it never has it doesn't now. It is too beautiful just thinking about Her and

Lorraine Hansberry and
Robert Nemiroff, 1954
(Photograph courtesy of
Joi Gresham)

looking forward to meeting her and letting everything begin and all this ugly
waiting over with."[92] Lorraine describes a lover that will let her life begin and
end her perpetual state of anticipation. Meaning, even as Hansberry understood freedom as a practice, she longed to be free and to live without fear in
the full flourishing of her desire.

Hansberry used letters as a way of connecting across geographical and philosophical differences. She used them to build community, particularly given
the constraints on interracial and lesbian gatherings. Through her letters, she
found ways of producing encounters that she needed or desired, expressing
anticipation of a not yet available moment of intimate connection or political
possibility.

Explicitly linking her personal struggles to her political investments, in a
letter dated August 1954, Unity, Wingdale, Lorraine talked about her depression as her "chief characteristic" and described it as a political contradiction
given her critique of despair earlier in the letter. She spoke of her personal
challenge to overcome this contradiction that "pervades my entire relationship

with life."[93] She saw depression as antithetical to the dream-filled world of the imagination that motivated her art and activism. Nevertheless, Lorraine lived with the feeling of depression and, what she characterized as a fundamental contradiction.

Months after Hansberry finished her duties at Camp Unity in December 1955, an act of civil disobedience by Rosa Parks, refusing to yield her seat on a crowded bus in Montgomery, Alabama, to a white patron, invigorated the modern civil rights movement. Although Parks is most well known for the single act of defiance, as Danielle McGuire chronicled it in *The Dark End of the Street,* her history as an activist began with her work as a field secretary for the NAACP, investigating cases of rape in the South. The fundamental lack of state protection for Black people from violence and death that invigorated activists following World War II ordered Parks's steps and Hansberry's political practice. In an essay titled "Notes on Women's Liberation—1955," Hansberry offered an intersectionalist argument about women's oppression well before Kimberlé Crenshaw coined the term "intersectionalism." In the essay, Hansberry also warned against the impulse to create hierarchies of oppression and invited men to work with women as comrades.[94] Her essay drew from her observations of the women of STJ centering women's activism in the movement.

Hansberry's overlapping commitments produced complicated and nuanced political criticism. Her work as a reporter slowed down after her marriage to Nemiroff in 1953. The sale of his song "Cindy, Oh, Cindy" in August 1956 provided the couple enough economic security for Hansberry to start focusing on her creative writing full time. In 1957, she completed her first full draft of *A Raisin in the Sun.*[95] Even though her contribution to periodicals decreased, she continued to submit fiction and write letters to engage in public debates.

Through her friendship with Baldwin, who was openly gay, Hansberry would have become familiar with many of the issues the gay and lesbian communities were contending with in the late 1950s.[96] She met Baldwin in the winter of 1958 when she visited a workshop reading of a theatrical adaptation of his novel *Giovanni's Room* at the Studio Theatre. Many members of the audience found fault with the play, based on a novel that focuses on a white gay American man living in Paris and his difficulty in finding fulfillment in his relationships. Hansberry, a virtual unknown to the Broadway theater executives at the reading, defended Baldwin's work from "up in the bleachers." He remembered, "I was enormously grateful to her, she seemed to speak for me; and afterward she talked to me with gentleness and generosity never to be forgotten. A small, shy, determined person, with that strength dictated by absolutely impersonal ambition: she was not trying to 'make it'—she was trying to keep the faith."[97] Hansberry had the ability to shape shift—to change the way she appeared depending on the audience. Although she often described herself as shy, an assessment that Baldwin agreed with, friends experienced her as gregarious, the life of a party, and having a dominating personality. Replicating this twoness, in her journals she often expressed uncertainty, trepidation, and lack of confidence. In public, particularly in debate, she exhibited confidence and a steely determination. These multiple sides of Hansberry—public and private, personal and communal—informed her intellectual life, which comes to the forefront most forcefully in her written work.

As she worked on *A Raisin in the Sun*, Hansberry wrote two letters to *The Ladder*, a magazine the Daughters of Bilitis (DOB) had founded in October 1956.[98] In the first letter (May 1957), signed L. H. N., Hansberry praised the magazine's unique focus. She offered an incisive and nuanced response to the organization's goal of advocating "a mode of behaviour and dress acceptable to society." Hansberry explained that as a Negro she was familiar with the language of and rationale for respectability politics. Questioning the political project of assimilation, she asserted, "The most splendid argument is simple and to the point, Ralph Bunche, with all his clean fingernails, degrees, and, of course, undeniable service to the human race, could still be insulted, denied a hotel room or meal in many parts of the county. (Not to mention the possibility of being lynched on a lonely Georgia road for perhaps having demanded a glass of water in the wrong place)."[99] Hansberry's example of Bunche, a top-level diplomat at the United Nations who was also Black, urged the DOB to think about the implications of race but also how an intersectional perspective fosters new political practices. As a Black professional woman, Hansberry understood the limits of attempting to shape one's body to conform to social norms. Her point was twofold: assimilation reinscribed norms that were historically grounded in a limited understanding of what it means to be human, and even those who assimilated most successfully would never be physically safe.

In addition, naming Ralph Bunche called attention to how Cold War politics subjected gays and lesbians as well as people of color to persecution. By 1957, the FBI had followed Hansberry for five years. The surveillance of Black writers coincided with that of gays and lesbians.[100] By referring to Bunche, she was invoking not only respectability but also Americanness, for he served as an official representative of the United States in all its paradox. He stood as a demonstration of American exceptionalism and democratic possibility and a potential threat. Hansberry's point, his ability to gain traction with the former, did not diminish the latter. As such, she proposed a different strategy to transform society.

Instead she elaborated a radical understanding of human existence that had the potential to expand the political possibilities for gays and lesbians in the future. In so doing, she untethered assimilation from self-determination. She wrote: "the homosexual HAS to . . . assert to the world that no crime is committed in his sexual habits. . . . To raise the question thus is automatically to insist on thinking of the homosexual as a human being among human beings, which means that it is a question of human rights and not special rights for 'degenerates' or the willfully incorrigible."[101]

It may seem odd that Hansberry used rights-based discourse at a time when the state was sanctioning persecution that limited the activities of the Mattachine and the DOB. Following her logic closely, though, it is clear that she did not cede the protection of rights to the state but called for an understanding of the equal status of humans to claim their rights. She made the distinction that laws as an articulation of the state help to secure power but they do not create hierarchies. Additionally, activists should claim rights on the basis of their humanity and not within the current structures of governance.

In Hansberry's second letter (August 1957), which she signed with the initials L. N., she identified herself as a "heterosexually married lesbian" in response to an article that considered how to navigate same-sex desire in the context of a heterosexual marriage. Hansberry struggled with the moral position of a married woman who realizes that she desires women. She described the social and economic challenges for women that "have been taught all their lives . . . was their 'natural' destiny." But she also said that answers to these questions that counseled women-loving women to grit their teeth and "make a 'happy marriage' " ignored the complexities of the situation.[102] She contended that women must attend to the social pressures and laws that prohibit same-sex coupling and account for the financial precarity that accompanies divorce. Hansberry understood that social transformation would require shifting women's material conditions. "Among women born between 1921 and 1930, a greater percentage married than any previous cohort." The social and financial pressure of marriage loomed large for Hansberry's generation. Her familial class privilege, however, enabled a form of autonomy that many women did not share; it helped support her political vision and her sense of isolation.[103]

Hansberry's public self-making as a freedom writer occurred within the geopolitical climate of the Cold War and the burgeoning modern civil rights movement. These contexts shaped the power dynamics she had to negotiate and help explain why she foregrounded different aspects of her identity in certain moments. Like the practice of having different user names for social media platforms, Hansberry used pseudonyms, initials, and her legal name in different venues and forms of writing. On one hand, Hansberry's writing in leftist and civil rights periodicals helped clear space for Black women to take center stage in political struggles. On the other hand, she signed her work in gay and lesbian journals with pseudonyms or initials, which had the effect of shielding her from the persecution other gay civil rights activists, including James Baldwin and Bayard Rustin, faced. Hansberry's work as a freedom writer cultivated a public self that both obscured and helped the development of her private self. Her choices strategically loosened the social constraints on blackness as a historical and gender-specific category in the short and longer term.

The letters in *The Ladder* solidify Hansberry's ongoing investment in considering social positioning as multifaceted and constructed, directly taking on understanding of blackness that leads to the erasure of difference in sexuality. While identity categories certainly have important political and institutional purposes, understanding Hansberry's unique political and artistic contribution requires attending to the specificity of her writerly practice, which often challenged or complicated contemporary understanding of race, gender, sexuality, and political affiliation.

Her semi-public correspondence in *The Ladder* functioned in ways similar to her writing about the STJ to mark the expanse of freedom as a practice that includes, to quote Hortense J. Spillers, "the potential to name."[104] As Lisbeth Lipari explains in "Intersectionality: Lorraine Hansberry's 1957 Letters to the *Ladder*": "Lorraine Hansberry, who, while widely regarded as a signifier for racial justice for close to fifty years, was not constructed as a queer signifier until after her death in 1965. The 'revelation' came about in 1976 when Barbara Grier, former editor of the lesbian periodical the *Ladder*, publicly identified Hansberry as the author of two public letters published in the *Ladder* in 1957."[105] As a public figure, Hansberry's private life certainly has political stakes if you follow Threadcraft's argument that the intimate sphere is political ground. But so too does the public writerly self that she cultivated by asking the readers of *Freedom* and *Masses and Mainstream* to focus on women, the readers of *New Challenges* to focus on Black people, and the readers of *The Ladder* to consider Black women. Hansberry's initialing rather than signing the letters in 1957 certainly enabled her prominence as a key figure in the civil rights movement following the Broadway production of *A Raisin in the Sun*. Nevertheless, Grier animates a practice Hansberry set in motion and chose not to continue as the work on her public self after *A Raisin in the Sun*.

Although Hansberry identified as a lesbian and should be understood as such, her daily acts of freedom constituted her politics and offer more nuanced insight into her investments, allegiances, and desires than an identity category can communicate. In Lipari's biographical entry about Hansberry for *Writers of the Black Chicago Renaissance,* she asserts Hansberry attended at least one DOB meeting. In Elise Harris's article about Hansberry's life for *Out* magazine she claims Hansberry never attended a DOB meeting. The controversy over Hansberry's official affiliations coincides with a motivation to pin her down.[106] Labeling demarcates the subject's position, sets expectations, and categorizes the individual among similar kinds of people. One does not learn much by assigning an identity category to a person, although investigating the circles of Hansberry's affiliates does offer some evidence of her possible influences, mentors, and collaborators. But naming her interlocutors, friends, and guides differs from categorizing her, which serves the political purpose of containment rather than insurrection. Categorizing Hansberry as a Black lesbian member of the Communist Party enriches a genealogy but does not challenge the social categories that constrained women in the 1950s.

Hansberry published two short stories in *The Ladder* and two in *One,* using the pen name Emily Jones, that explore same-sex desire through encounter. The stories offer insight into how Hansberry used realism to imagine what is possible.[107] The main characters in "The Budget," "Chanson du Konallis," "The Anticipation of Eve," and "Renascence" are white women who attempt to control their desire for their own sex because they fear the costs of expressing their desire in public. As Hansberry wrote her career-defining play, she also used fiction to explore the unwieldy impact of making private desire public. In "Renascence," a title that refers to a poem by Edna St. Vincent Millay, Hansberry contemplates the very idea of "pure existence" that does not contain within it the shadow of death. The story establishes her understanding of reality as contending with loss. Her realism, again, served as a mode to explore the "rules of reality."[108] In "The Budget," the protagonist laments, "Spring has always been my enemy."[109] The blooming blossoms and new beginnings traditionally associated with spring antagonize Hansberry's protagonist. The story equates the protagonist's refusal to buy flowers, because they are not in the budget, with her resistance to making eye contact with a woman walking down the street.

With the woman, the protagonist's strict practice of expending only allocated emotional resources falls short and demonstrates the unpredictability of desire. The protagonist turns "to look back at her . . . because of that really outlandish outfit, well, one would stare. And, as a matter of fact, and I trust you will understand how sometimes the *bizarre* can be charming—well, she was a very lovely girl . . . In any case, when I turned to look around at her the second time—she was following me with her eyes! And—smiling! They have no shame! Right there in the public street—she smiled at *me!* In broad daylight!"[110] The protagonist accuses the woman of "following her" with her eyes, although the protagonist turns "around and looks back at her the *second time.*" The easy misattribution of blame draws attention to the danger of trafficking in forbidden desire, which often leaves the least empowered individual responsible for breaking the law. The story uses the financial restrictions of a budget as a metaphor for emotional limits. Desire does not, however, operate in the same way as currency. Hansberry's useful rhetorical device helps communicate the fallacy of the protagonist's self-policing because desire has a way of spilling over and exceeding containment. Desire colors the way we experience the world and motivates action. Hope for freedom from constraint figures prominently in Hansberry's writerly practice.

Through the character of Konnie, Hansberry describes the feelings of a married woman who is beginning to realize that heterosexuality is not enough to meet her needs. The insurgent quality of desire informs looking in Hansberry's story. "Chanson du Konallis" describes an encounter in France among a white couple, Konalia Martin-Whiteside Heplin (Konnie) and her husband Paul, and a Negro singer, Mirine Tige. Konnie and Paul, out for a night on the town, watch Tige perform. Tige sings a song about her adoration for women, which causes Konnie to reflect on her own history of desire. Konnie becomes overwhelmed with the memories Tige triggers and the narrator explains Konnie's state of mind: "This thing of allowing the mind to do what it would lately—well, it was really just too much! She must go to the ladies' room and adjust her makeup and look at herself and quiet it all down." However, she does not leave. Paul, who had arranged the evening because he had seen Tige perform before and was attracted to her, asks the manager of the club to introduce them to Tige. Konnie feigns affront at Paul's suggestion of an introduction, but she is already aware that she is drawn to the singer. As Tige holds Konnie's look ("Mirine Tige did not let go of Konnie's eyes"), Paul asks the singer why she speaks in French when she is among Americans. She responds, " 'Then, Monsieur Heplin, why not speak it when you *feel* like it.' She looked to Konalia, 'and all else you enjoy. One might learn *that* from the French.' " Tige's invitation to enjoy permeates Konnie's sensibility. As Tige stands to leave, "Konalia felt that the woman's body swayed in front of her suddenly as when she sang; then she realized that they were merely waves of loveliness that shimmered in front of her. She longed to close her eyes."[111] Her exploration of the gaze contrasts with Frantz Fanon's analysis in *Black Skin, White Masks* (1952). While Fanon investigates how Black maleness informs looking, Hansberry takes up the intersectionality of the gaze among women of different races and sexual interests to demonstrate the flow of power within an encounter.

As she did in the children's story "This Little Piggy Got Dumped on the Sidewalk," in "Chanson du Konallis," Hansberry imagines a scenario in which the object (in this case of desire) claims power by repositioning herself. In a conversation with Konnie and Paul, Tige reveals that she grew up as the child of sharecroppers in Georgia. Tige directs both the conversation and Konnie's gaze: "Mirine Tige did not let go of her eyes and Konnie felt she was almost smiling behind the insolent lips."[112] Tige then begins to code switch, speaking in French with Konnie to exclude Paul from the conversation. While early in the story Konnie laments that she cultivated reserve just as her family had done, Tige actively revels in the pleasure of entertaining desire. In the exchanges between Konnie and Tige, one may see Hansberry examining her family history of self-control as a means to achieving social political goals; her mother and father were Republicans and her lawyer father ran for Congress. But the story makes space for a contemplation of shedding that reserve in the name of desire, of achieving freedom from the constrictions of family mores. In the story, Hansberry's focus on the animation and recalibration of the gaze suggests how feelings can mobilize political practices as they spill over into how one sees the world.

The circulation of desire that colored Hansberry's life in 1958 animates the relationships in "The Anticipation of Eve." The story depicts a young woman, Margarite, known as Rita, attempting to share with her cousin Sel and Sel's husband David that her roommate, Eve, is actually her lover. The anticipation of the title speaks to Rita's descriptions of waiting for Eve to come home from work as a theater actor, waiting for the perfect time to share with her cousin that she is in love, and waiting for a time when their love would produce the same joy as a heterosexual marriage announcement. On the night depicted in the story, Rita has mustered the courage to tell Sel and David about Eve, but before she has the chance, Sel explains to Rita that it's time for her to marry and that she has fixed her up with a man named Kevin. Sel then leaves the room to tend to her crying baby and David explains that Rita cannot date Kevin because Kevin is gay. David's expressed disgust about Kevin's presumed sexuality undercuts Rita's plan. She eventually escapes the apartment and, as she walks home, she reflects, "Someone had spoken to me of something they thought was unclean and sick and I could think only of beauty and spring nights and flowers and lovely music . . . Someday perhaps I might hold out my secret in my hand and sing about it to the scornful, but if not, I would more than survive."[113]

The story depicts a desired and foreclosed encounter. It depicts the failure to connect across difference. And although Sel and David understand themselves as liberals, asserting that housing should be integrated and fighting against the policing of appearance, they are both homophobic. Additionally, they invest deeply in the cultural currency of marriage despite Rita seemingly having no economic impetus to wed. The story surfaces registers of being that exceed the normative everyday social structures. Rita longs for a time when she will be able to share her love with her family, but if not, she "would *more* than survive."[114] The ability to carve out something more than survival in the spaces that exceed normative structures, the underground, undisclosed spaces, points to another kind of freedom practice that eludes governmental reform and social regulation.

In the 1950s, Hansberry explored and advocated for both types of freedom. She unflinchingly described the physical, rhetorical, and representational violence Blacks were experiencing in the United States and Africa, but she also wrote about the freedom to create new worlds. She used her short-form writing as a space for intellectual and emotional exploration. This laid the groundwork for her later work. As a playwright, she returned to stories and scenarios she had covered as a journalist in the 1950s. During the nine years before the Broadway premiere of *A Raisin in the Sun*, Hansberry explored and developed a theory of freedom as a set of practices that could sustain a new movement for civil rights.

Describing Hansberry's writing as a practice calls attention to its configuration as rehearsal through repetition and routine. Her unwillingness to yield to the conventions, restrictions, prohibitions, or expectations for a Black woman in the 1950s enabled her to cultivate freedom practices in solidarity with calls for Black liberation both within and beyond the restrictions of what Afro-Modern thought imagined as Black political life. Through rehearsal, Hansberry's practice challenged the seeming uniformity of blackness. Not all Black leaders were middle-aged men: some were young women. Not all Black women were straight: some were exploring other sexual identities. Not all Black social movement builders were middle class: some were women who cleaned houses and worked in factories. Each of these observations opened new social spaces that welcomed and encouraged other Black women. In each case, Hansberry approached issues through an intersectional lens: Black and female, Black and sexually questioning, Black and young. These multiple perspectives opened new spaces in her imagination, and her writing captured those spaces so others could enter them.

Her work in the 1950s reveals that the decade was not as moribund and conformist as many have described it. For Hansberry, despite the dangers and risks of the positions she was taking, this was a time of fertility and intellectual blossoming. The worlds she imagined in that decade presaged many events. Children participated in the civil rights movement alongside their parents. Working-class Blacks took to the streets and broke the back of Jim and Jane Crow. Black women birthed third-wave feminism and began applying that analytical lens to everything they encountered. Gays, lesbians, bisexuals, and transgender people embraced the idea of rights and pushed for laws that would enshrine them.

Analyzing Hansberry's writing as both a practice of self-articulation and a political practice produces more nuanced and intersectional understanding of how to cultivate freedom and the self. Fully grasping Hansberry's impact demands attending to how her early writing paved the way for her later work and how doing that early work constituted a mode of doing freedom that remains unfinished.

EVERYTHING CHANGED, EVERYTHING REMAINED THE SAME

On March 1, 1959, ten days before *A Raisin in the Sun* premiered on Broadway, Hansberry gave a lecture, "The Negro Writer and His Roots," that clarified and reiterated her chief investments as a writer and an activist.[115] The lecture, at the American Society of African Culture, considered how the Negro artist could disrupt the national feeling of despair and the policies of destruction. In the talk she explained, "If the world is engaged in a dispute between survival and destruction, involving the most fundamental questions of society vs. the individual—in a dispute between the champions of despair and those of hope and glorification of man—then we, as members of the human race, must address ourselves to that dispute." Hansberry offered a historical argument to support her contention that the Negro's experience in the United States gives insight into the limits of despair: "It is a curious thing, but I am not the first to note that when hope begins to die, reason is often swift to follow."[116] As a remedy for despair Hansberry put forward life and love, but she did not present them in a vacuum.

She turned to the now familiar late twentieth-century symbol of the blues man as the embodiment of hope in the midst of despair. "They do not see," she argued, "even yet, in the 'black and unknown bards' of whom James

Weldon Johnson sang, the enormous sound of a great and incredibly courageous people who have known how to acknowledge pain and despair as one hope."[117] For Hansberry, the imagination provided a possibility for "the future itself." She ended her speech with words of encouragement: "Let us take courage. Once physics overwhelmed the minds of men. And it came to pass, that he who had no wings came to command the air at speeds no bird can manage. Surely then, as we turn our full attention to the hearts and minds of men, we shall see that if man can fly—he can also be free."[118] Hansberry's practices of freedom not only required persistence, they also demanded defiance. Her unwillingness to yield to the conventions, restrictions, prohibitions, or expectations for a Black woman in the 1950s enabled her to cultivate freedom practices in solidarity with calls for Black liberation from Chicago to Mississippi, from New York City to Kenya. Although Hansberry's life changed forever after the New York premiere of *A Raisin in the Sun*, her solidarity remained steadfast.

Chapter 2 The Shaping Force of *A Raisin in the Sun*

"... it is our dreams that point the way to freedom"
—Audre Lorde

I have given you this account so that you know that what I write is not based on the assumption of idyllic possibilities or innocent assessment of the true nature of life—but, rather, my own personal view that, posing one against the other, I think the human race does command its own destiny and that that destiny can eventually embrace the stars.
—Lorraine Hansberry

In Nina Simone's hit song from 1964, "Please Don't Let Me Be Misunderstood," she sings, "I'm just a soul whose intentions are good / Oh Lord, please don't let me be misunderstood." Simone and Lorraine Hansberry had a fierce friendship. According to Simone, Hansberry radicalized her.[1] Their shared vision as friends, artists, and activists also led to misunderstanding by the publics and people they served and loved.[2] Both women were before their time, advocating for gender, racial, and sexual equality as a function of human rights. Hansberry came to national prominence in 1959 through the Broadway production of *A Raisin in the Sun,* and the accolade of the New York Drama Critics Award. Her success with this domestic drama shaped her public image. She became known as a young housewife simply wanting access to the American dream. And, as much as the public loved casting her in that role, it never fit.

In the months leading up to the Broadway production, Lorraine struggled with all the bits of her life that would not fit her public image—the Black playwright and an American beauty.[3] During her employment at Camp Unity, she said to Philip Rose that she wanted to be a writer. According to Rose, "She was told, 'You can't write about black people. Nobody's going to read that.' She wrote a play about three white girls in the Village. It was beautiful writing, but there was no passion in it." He encouraged her to abandon her writing about the Greenwich Village scene. Hansberry returned to the drawing board and, after taking time to primarily focus on creative work, she finished a draft of *A Raisin in the Sun*. In the summer of 1957, with Nemiroff, she invited Rose for dinner at the apartment on Bleecker Street. They served spaghetti for dinner and banana cream pie for dessert, and read the play. " 'She read for me and three other people who were there,' Rose recalls. 'She read about half of the play. I left at 2 in the morning.' "[4] Five hours later, with the play still on his mind, he called Hansberry and told her that he wanted to produce it. In November 1957, she finished her first full draft of the play and then refined it in collaboration with Phil and Bobby.

The pieces began to fall into place. Sidney Poitier read the play and shared it with a young Black director, Lloyd Richards, who also began to give Hansberry feedback. Born in Canada and raised in Detroit, Richards read the play and immediately saw its potential. According to him, " 'I used to meet with Lorraine once a week to work on the play.' "[5] The collaboration would prove historic. After months of revisions while Rose busily tried to raise money, they decided to take the play to New Haven for tryouts and then on to Philadelphia. The turning point in the production history came when Johnny Shubert, of the Shubert family that owned the theater chain, saw the play in Philadelphia. Shubert promised Rose the Barrymore Theatre in New York, in five weeks. In the interim Rose took the play to Chicago, where it received rave reviews. Hansberry, meanwhile, received an arrest warrant. The story of the play usually fast forwards at this point to opening night in New York. In Hansberry's becoming, however, the warrant in Chicago marks a break that shaped her public image and reinforced her political commitments.

In 1958 the City of Chicago filed a lawsuit against Carl, Perry, Lorraine Hansberry, and others for forty-two cases of alleged building codes violations. The city had previously sought civil action against Carl A. Hansberry, Perry Hansberry, M. L. Hansberry, and C.A. Enterprises for overcharging rent to

Black people living in their properties.[6] Worried about the impact the case would have on Lorraine's burgeoning career, her brothers signed an affidavit testifying that she was wrongfully named as a defendant in the case.[7] The wrangling over the properties in Chicago would cause Lorraine to relinquish her share of the estate. In giving up her inheritance, she opened the door for a kind of political striving distinct from her father and siblings. Ironic perhaps, since *A Raisin in the Sun* considers how Black freedom in the United States becomes intertwined with property rights, particularly land rights, that the legacy of Lorraine's father would reemerge in the midst of her run-up to Broadway. His life and death shaped her most profound accomplishment, but on her terms. By Hansberry's volition she continued to draw from her father's impulse to challenge oppressive structures, but she did not cling to the romance of capitalism.

Although *A Raisin in the Sun* reflects Hansberry's radical ideas about what marriage, family, community, and the practice of freedom entail, her public image and the form of the play (a domestic drama) obscured the public's recognition of her views. Similar to Hansberry's public life, her marriage had all of the trappings of a traditional 1950s union, besides being interracial. She and Bobby wed on June 20, 1953, in Chicago in front of dozens of guests.[8] The day before her wedding, however, the couple protested the execution of Julius and Ethel Rosenberg. Bobby recalled, "We spent Saturday night picketing the courthouse in Chicago and we married on Sunday . . . they were executed Saturday night. And we had no heart for the wedding. I mean, we had heart for the wedding, but . . ." Hansberry remembered, "Our voices above the champagne glasses, our eyes questioning one another between the fresh fragrant flowers in their gleaming pots on the coffee tables of the wedding house, festive house. The Chicago heat in the vast living room suddenly overpowering the senses, some grim terrible fire within suddenly making it more awful, more stifling—the desire to fling the glass into the flowers, to thrust one's arms into the air and run out of the house screaming."[9] Lorraine and Bobby shared ambivalence on their wedding day and would come to find that the tension between their political commitments and being a traditional family could not hold. They would have to remake their union into a marriage of a different sort.

From 1953 to 1957 Lorraine and Bobby continued to try to balance their political and personal commitments. In her letter from Camp Unity in 1954 described earlier, anticipating "The Woman" she expected to find, she went on to describe the woman's physical characteristics and personality with great care and detail. "I like to think that she will be beautiful in the way I think of beauty."[10] The anticipation coincides with resolution to meet Her.

Although Lorraine moved back to Chicago in 1954 after her stay at Camp Unity, by October 1956 she had returned to her apartment in Greenwich Village, where she described the vicissitudes of her domestic life: "Yesterday I rose at eight and brushed my hair and rushed out to move the car before I should get a ticket. I returned and watched Robert wash and shower and shave and listen to disk jockies at that strange hour. . . . Then I vacumed [*sic*] the rug and the corners of the house where the dog hair collects in pounds between times when I am finally moved to clean. . . . And then I scrubbed, not well at all, the bathroom and the kitchen and spread paper on the floor . . . I did not answer the telephone, except once before ten thirty, that was Joan about an apartment . . . and then I read Simone in frustration again and slept."[11] Her intellectual journey from 1953 to 1957 encompassed her longstanding critique of capitalism, and the possessiveness it requires, nuanced by her engagement with the work of de Beauvoir, or she references "Simone." Hansberry's restlessness with women's roles continued for the rest of her life. But the commonality she found with Bob would help her come to greater intellectual and political understanding of how to become free within the given structures as one worked to dismantle them. By 1957, Lorraine and Bobby began a new iteration of their marriage, still premised on mutual respect but less dependent on the possessive protocols of monogamy.

During the months leading up to the New York production of *A Raisin in the Sun,* Lorraine privately and semi-publicly came to terms with what her marriage could and would be.[12] In 1957, Hansberry had a relationship with a photographer, Molly Malone Cook. In an extended letter to Cook, Lorraine contemplates the limitations of labels such as "homophile" or "homosexual" and attributes to Cook the phrase "queer beer," which Hansberry used as the title for an essay. Later, Cook became partners with Mary Oliver, and they lived together in Provincetown, Massachusetts.[13] The public visibility of that relationship, like her contemporaneous letters to the *Ladder,* emerged in the independence of the character Beneatha in *A Raisin in the Sun,* but for the most part remained invisible to the public until after her death.

As Hansberry put the pieces of her personal life together, her professional life took a historic turn. From New Haven to Philadelphia, to Chicago and New York, the reviews of *A Raisin in the Sun* were positive. They focused on the ways Hansberry's art and its politics fit into mainstream norms. Read against her contemporary Malcolm X, with whom she shared a birthday, and the organization he came to personify, the Nation of Islam, depictions of Hansberry's version of Black freedom struggles proved much easier for mainstream American audiences to swallow, particularly as the winds of Cold War nationalism continued to pick up speed. At the same time, scholarly criticism described her work as an extension of Richard Wright's naturalism without accounting for how *A Raisin in the Sun* contributes to a global vision of Black freedom predicated not only on what is but also on what is possible.

Set in a cramped apartment on the South Side of Chicago, *A Raisin in the Sun* depicts three generations of the Younger family buckling under the pressure of their deferred dreaming. The family reflects a long history of Black people's foreclosed desires and denied opportunities. Similar to many Black families in America, the Youngers had become accustomed to waiting for change to come. The death of the family's patriarch, Big Walter, however, results in an insurance payment to his widow, Lena Younger (also known as Mama), that has the potential to change each member of the family's life.

Lena's son, Walter Lee, dreams of becoming an entrepreneur by opening a liquor store. His sister Beneatha aspires to attend medical school. Ruth, Walter Lee's wife, shares with Lena the vision of buying a home so that the family can escape the cramped quarters of their small apartment. Each dream is personal, seemingly individual, and in line with what we have come to call the "good life" in American society.[14] Higher education, entrepreneurship, and home ownership: all stepping stones on the family's ascension to the middle class. In addition, the set, style, and narrative of the play domesticates the Youngers' dreams and deemphasizes the way their yearning participates in a global movement for Black freedom.

Much of *A Raisin in the Sun* features characters discussing, debating, and arguing over competing interests. Ultimately, Mama entrusts her son with $6,500 of the insurance money. She has already used $3,500 to make a down payment on a home. She instructs him to save a portion of the money for Beneatha's education and to use the rest for whatever he desires. Before the Youngers have a chance to move, because of Walter Lee's bad investment they lose the $6,500 and must choose whether or not to leave their South Side apartment and move into the house. The possibilities for a Black family to live the "good life" in Chicago in the 1950s come starkly into view when we learn that buying the home also will entail the Youngers desegregating a neighboring community. By tying their home ownership to desegregation, Hansberry calls attention to the global systems that structure their civic exclusion and material poverty. Hansberry's early work as a journalist and associate editor for *Freedom,* covering African independence movements, as well as her membership in the Communist Party, informed her understanding of how local acts of justice fed global Black freedom movements. Hansberry understood that the regularity and routineness of domestic life and aspirations conceals how they perpetuate and participate in reinforcing, or in the case of Hansberry's play, disrupting power structures. The same everyday maintenance of power ensures the proliferation of minor harassments that specify living while Black. Hansberry's education in Marxism, Black radical thought, and existentialism taught her that domination does not erupt onto the scene. Individual state actors structure it. Individuals must, then, exercise freedom practices on a daily basis to restructure it.

Moments like these in 1959 produced Hansberry's public self, the critical contexts for its emergence, and the ways it has hidden her radical vision, which is at the heart of *A Raisin in the Sun* and continues to unfold in her later published and unpublished works. Hansberry's choice to depict neighborhood desegregation as a linchpin in the global battle for spatial justice strategically situates women's desires and roles as central to Black freedom movements. Although as Edward Soja has argued, "justice and injustice are infused into the multiscalar geographies in which we live, from the intimacies of the household to the uneven development of the global economy," in the 1950s the private properties of the domestic sphere set it apart from pursuits of public justice. The home remained the province of women, and the ideal of home ownership reflected an expansion of democracy through property rights. Home ownership promised a locale of relative autonomy for any American who could afford it.[15] Following state desires, many civil rights organizations encouraged Black women to aspire toward white ideals of domesticity and leave the battle for civic inclusion to men operating in the public sphere. In an interview in 1959, Hansberry asserted: "The most oppressed group of any oppressed group will be its women, who are twice oppressed. So I should imagine that they react accordingly: As oppression makes people more militant, women become *twice* militant because they are twice oppressed."[16] Hansberry's militancy translated into her understanding of women's liberation not only requiring a restructuring of property relationships but also the matrix of desires that singularly associated them with domestic space.

THE PLANTATION AND THE GHETTO

At the heart of *A Raisin in the Sun* is a radical vision for spatial justice that relies on the geographical and historical relationship between the plantation and the ghetto. I use the term "ghetto" here, following Hansberry and Tommie Shelby, to mean a geographical location with unequal access to civic inclusion, which disproportionately impacts Black people. My use of the term does not hold the stigma of its deployment in the late twentieth century. For

Hansberry, the ghetto and the violence that it installs elaborate a power dynamic instituted in the eighteenth and nineteenth centuries in U.S. and Caribbean plantations. The state's spatial arrangements extract resources from communities of color while supplying little to no services or protections, and yet require from them taxation equal to their white counterparts. In "Justice, Deviance, and the Dark Ghetto," Shelby makes a distinction between civic obligations and natural duties to question the justness of civic participation without civic inclusion or benefits. He writes, "Civic obligations are owed to those whom one is cooperating with to maintain a fair basic structure. They are the obligations that exist between citizens of a democratic polity as defined by the principles of justice that underpin their association. . . . By contrast, natural duties are unconditionally binding, in that they hold between all persons regardless of whether they are fellow citizens or are bound by other institutional ties. Both civic obligations and natural duties are moral requirements. The key difference is that one has civic obligations qua citizen and natural duties qua moral person."[17]

The distinction helps to clarify the difference between what Hansberry presents as useful tactics in the furtherance of freedom and her governing principles. For Hansberry, furthering civic obligations (such as by voting) often functioned as a useful tactic but did not operate as a principle because civic obligations usually support structures that administer unfreedom (the U.S. government). According to historian Arnold R. Hirsch, "The most distinguishing feature of the post–World War II ghetto expansion is that it was carried out with government sanction and support."[18] In an interview following Hansberry's well-documented meeting with Attorney General Robert Kennedy, she asserted, "We need legislation to guarantee any right a person can be denied. . . . The first thing that must be achieved is equal job opportunities for Negroes, then equal housing. When unemployment is six percent nationally, it is as high as thirty percent among Negroes. . . . Negroes are the last chosen for any job, skilled or unskilled. Negroes are starving to death."[19] Hansberry understood that strategic and tactical engagement may serve a necessary and worthwhile purpose, but a fundamental understanding of spatial justice enabled her to apprehend the formation of working-class urban Black communities as necessary for the extraction of resources and not participatory engagement within a capitalist democracy. This understanding limited her investment in civic participation as the ultimate terrain for freedom struggles.

The end of *A Raisin in the Sun* stages a critical political decision. The only white character in the play, Karl Lindner, visits the Youngers' apartment, at

Walter Lee's request, to reverse the deal that Mama made and repurchase the Youngers' house in Clybourne Park. This is the second time in the play that Lindner visits the Youngers' apartment. The first time, he arrived uninvited with an offer to purchase the house, at a financial gain for the Youngers, in order to keep his community segregated. Although Walter Lee had voiced his intent to strike a deal with Lindner, instead he states that they will not sell the house. Lindner, confused by what he understood as Walter Lee's willingness to accept his offer followed by the assertion that the family will not accept it, seeks clarification. He asks, so "you have decided to occupy"?[20]

The use of the word "occupy" resonates with twenty-first-century class-based movements for inclusion and expresses a tactic deployed by civil rights activists in the mid-twentieth century to desegregate public spaces. The word choice helps to establish the stakes of the move within a long and ongoing history of urban hyper-segregation. "Occupy" suggests an invasion, an act of holding space that runs the risk of seizure. Occupation functions as a tactic in the meantime, a stepping stone in the movement toward freedom from inter-ference. As an occupation, the Youngers' move also draws attention to Black people's limited property rights in the 1950s.[21]

Since the play's first performances, audiences have debated whether the Younger family should move at the end of *A Raisin in the Sun*. The choice to move, which in some reviewers' minds translated to touting the virtues of assimilation rather than integration, sparked several subsequent plays that ponder the prudence and aftermath of the Youngers' relocation, with the most acclaimed being Bruce Norris's Pulitzer Prize winning *Clybourne Park* (2010). For Hansberry, the ending of the play presented a problem as well. In a version that preceded the text for the Broadway production in 1959, the play ended with the family huddled in their new home, armed and awaiting the vigilante violence of their neighbors. Hansberry had previously explored inter-racial violence as result of integration in her unpublished stories from the 1950s. Similar to the work she published in *Freedom,* her experimental writing revealed preoccupations that take center stage in her dramatic works.[22] Hans-berry changed the ending and the final scene in the Broadway production to focus on the Youngers' leaving their apartment.

The debate over the implications of the ending of the play assume Hans-berry adopts a notion of freedom akin to the American idea of freedom as property rights. The equation of property rights and citizenship first emerged, according to Soja, in ancient Greek city-states, then continued through feudalism, and reemerged in the United States and Europe after the American and French revolutions. American democracy functions in two ways. One is an individual's ability to express rights based on property ownership, as guaranteed by the Fourteenth Amendment. Second is a collective expression of communal consensus structured through elected representation. An important example is the development of capitalist democracy in the United States through slavery. "What became legitimized if not sanctified," according to Soja, "was the inalienable rights to own property as the central principle in defining the capitalist nation-state, its system of laws, and its revised definition of citizenship. Human rights in general and such specific claims as the right to the city become subordinated to the primacy of rights to property."[23] During the civil rights movement, activism focused on producing equal access to public spaces.

A more radical vision, Hansberry's play draws into question the regulation of private property that is an intimate space, figuring intimate space as the realm for rethinking the operation of democracy as property rights. Questioning the very notion of freedom as property rights redirects the debate over whether or not the Youngers' should move because the move amounts to a strategic reclamation of power not an affirmation of capitalist possibility. Therefore, whether or not they encounter violence in Clybourne Park, the move functions as an occupation. As Lena Younger says in the play, "Once upon a time freedom used to be life—now it's money. I guess the world really do change."[24]

Situating property rights and their protection as the basis of citizenship requires the correlation of property accumulation with greater freedom. As such, critics interpreted the purchase of the Youngers' home as an expression of possibility in the conceptual world of freedom as a state of being. Philosophically, however, Hansberry challenges the property ownership model of democracy in the play before the Youngers decide to occupy. In a conversation between Beneatha and her suitor, Asagai, that follows Walter Lee losing the majority of the insurance money, Asagai draws attention to the processual dimensions of freedom as a practice. Audiences of the 1959 production of the play saw an abridged version of the speech, limiting Hansberry's comment on the connection between domestic spatial justice and public claims for space through boycotts in the United States and independence movements abroad.[25]

At the beginning of the play, Beneatha has decided that she will be a doctor—an unlikely choice for a Black woman living in a Chicago kitchenette apartment in the mid-twentieth century, but Beneatha is unconventional. She yearns to reposition herself in society and sees education, not marriage, as her means for social transformation. Hansberry's choice to make Beneatha an aspiring doctor challenges gender conventions of the time and presents a profession that demonstrates the ability to transform the material conditions of the body. Asagai, an exchange student from Nigeria, courts Beneatha and exposes her to the politics of Black internationalism. After hearing about the family's financial loss, he attempts to comfort Beneatha; unassured, she asserts, "you are still where I left off. You with all your talk and dreams about Africa! You still think you can patch up the world. Cure the Great Sore of Colonialism—(*Loftily, mocking it*) with the Penicillin of Independence!" Unbothered, he responds, "yes!" Beneatha then calls into question the effort of independence movements that result in the installation of the same tyranny, but with Black actors, and asks "where does it end?"[26]

The notion of an "end," which Asagai refuses, exclaiming, "I live the answer," taps into a central philosophical thread that underpins Hansberry's political investments in freedom as a practice. The question of "What happens to a dream deferred?" shaped Hansberry's political consciousness from the writing of *A Raisin in the Sun* until her death in 1965. The question resonates profoundly because it calls to mind personal, familial, communal, and national aspirations and their disruption. Does a dream deferred "dry up like a raisin in the sun," losing its force and potential, or does it "explode," multiplying its impact and dispersing its power? From 1957 through 1965, the national mood toggled between hope and despair, between the dissipation of political fervor and the eruption of passionate resistance. Beneatha questions the operation of freedom, but she misses Asagai's point that an ultimate result, "an end to struggle," would require an installation of freedom in unfreedom because such a status would depend on having rather than doing.

In a slight shift in the direction of the conversation, Beneatha explains that, like thieves in the night, people stole her future from her. Asagai asks, "But did you earn it? Would you have had it at all if your father had not died?" He continues, "isn't there something wrong in a house—in a world—where dreams, good or bad, must depend on the death of a man?" Inhabiting freedom, in a property ownership model, requires death and exploitation. The system of inheritance, the legal structures that protect it and the property rights that install it, demand not only the death of the one that bequeaths but also the extraction of resources from all of those that lead to the accumulation of wealth. Asagai's question begs for dreaming that does not necessarily require the installation of despair. He explains, "In my village at home it is the exceptional man who can even read a newspaper . . . or whoever sees a book at all. I will go home and much of what I will have to say will seem strange to the people of my village. But I will teach and work and things will happen, slowly and swiftly. At times it will seem that nothing changes at all . . . and then again the sudden dramatic events which make history leap into the future. And then quiet again. Retrogression even. Guns, murder, revolution. And I even will have moments when I wonder if the quiet was not better than all that death and hatred. But will look about my village at the illiteracy and disease and ignorance and I will not wonder long."[27]

Asagai is describing the uneven pace of social change. His emphasis lands on dissatisfaction with the feeling that "nothing changes at all," but his description also supports the idea of freedom as a practice. Practice enables the innovation of new political and racial roles because it enacts a vision through the routine efforts usually associated with the infrastructural work of women during the civil rights movement. According to the Black feminist theorist Audre Lorde, "Interdependency between women is the way to a freedom which allows the *I* to *be,* not in order to be used, but in order to be creative. This is a difference between the passive *be* and the active *being.*"[28]

The conversation between Asagai and Beneatha functions as a turning point in the play and, therefore, affects how we understand the ending. Asagai recontextualizes the Youngers' choice to move, placing it in the context of a global movement for Black freedom. The notion of escaping the trap of the ghetto, as he describes, requires understanding the geographical and historical relationship between the ghetto and the plantation. As Hansberry explained in 1959 during an interview with Studs Turkel, Asagai "gives the statement of the play."[29] His speech establishes a context to understand the Youngers' decision as both radical and incremental, a necessary part of ongoing and unfinished business.

HANSBERRY'S PUBLIC SELF

For most of the American public, Hansberry burst onto the national theater scene with the Broadway production of *A Raisin in the Sun.* Although she had worked as a journalist for years and published dozens of pieces of writing, this was her first published and produced play. As a result, Hansberry emerged in the spotlight as a young Negro housewife who told the "truth" about Black urban life.[30] According to *Ebony* magazine, her work pictured "Negroes honestly and objectively as completely human types facing the challenging implications of their position in a changing society."[31] The description of Hansberry's honesty, from reviews in *Ebony* to the *New York Times,* acknowledged her ability to craft characters rather than the caricatures familiar to most U.S. theater audiences. And her work seems to distill a version of domestic and familial aspirations common in popular presentations of mainstream

American desires in the mid-twentieth century. The play, however, subverts national desire. After Mama places the down payment on the house, Lindner, the head of the Clybourne Park Improvement Association, pays the family his first visit. He makes his pitch to repurchase the home and Walter Lee asks him to leave, Mama returns and the children, with a humor born of a life steeped in racism, explain to her what has transpired. Beneatha wonders, "What they think we going to do—eat 'em?" Ruth responds, "No, honey, marry 'em."[32] The joke takes on particular irony given Hansberry's marriage to Robert Nemiroff and the way their relationship helped to facilitate the financing of the play.[33] Hansberry's personal relationships challenged the national desire for interracial sexual domination and, instead, enacted coupling and coalition that remained prohibited nationally until 1967 in the Supreme Court's decision in *Loving v. Virginia.*

Hansberry's public image, which emphasized her youth, marital status, class privilege, and, according to *Ebony Magazine,* education, certified the authenticity of her narrative. *Ebony* erroneously reported of Hansberry's education, "A 28-year-old graduate of the University of Wisconsin, she is one of a slowly growing group of Negro dramatists who learned their craft through study and diligent labor in university and community theaters. After moving to New York in 1950 and marrying songwriter Robert Nemiroff in 1953, Miss Hansberry wrote four plays as 'exercises in writing' before settling down 'to write a play about the contemporary Negro in full dimension.' "[34] Hansberry did attend the University of Wisconsin, but she did not graduate. And although she did spend much of her time in New York refining her craft as a writer through practice and formal education at the New School and engagement with community theater, the article misplaces emphasis and does not account for the role activism played in her development as a thinker and a writer. Hansberry's politics infused her art and private life.

The mainstream press couched Hansberry's distinction in familiar tropes of middle-class womanhood. In an interview in May 1959 with Mike Wallace, who was on the cusp of breaking a career-defining story about Malcolm X and the Nation of Islam, a tension emerged between the image of Hansberry as an overnight sensation *and* the writerly self that she crafted through a decade-long history of publishing and participating in grassroots organizing.[35] Wallace began the interview with the following description: "One night, Lorraine Hansberry, a girl who had dabbled in writing, made a brash announcement to her husband. She was going to sit down and write an honest and accurate drama about Negroes."[36] The introduction presents Hansberry as a novice in terms of her writing, making her success that much more unpredictable.

Although she was only twenty-eight when *A Raisin in the Sun* premiered on Broadway, and it was her first major work, she did have all of the seriousness of an established artist, having studied art and activism all her life. She didn't dabble; she made a concerted effort to refine a craft as a part of freedom movements that she connected to the slave revolts of the eighteenth and nineteenth centuries (such as the Haitian Revolution) and pan-Africanism of the 1930s. The historical thrust of her work accounted for the well-known (W.E.B. Du Bois) and lesser-known (STJ) strands of Black intellectual history. She read Du Bois and took issue with Richard Wright and also studied the work of women and leftist thinkers, which also clarifies her repeated statement throughout the interview that she wrote an "honest" work.[37] For Hansberry, "honest" means fidelity to a history of ideas and not the believability of being able to see Black people as human beings. Her play not only changed the shape of America's dramatic canon, it also broadened the scope of commercial theater. *A Raisin in the Sun* demonstrated the profitability of realist Black narratives when only melodramas and musicals had been popular in the past.

The interview, although released posthumously, reflects the misperception of Hansberry that would shape her public image. Her ascension in spite of her association with the internationalist left demonstrates a delicate dance of Cold War civil rights. Just days before *A Raisin in the Sun* opened at the Ethel Barrymore Theatre, Hansberry offered the keynote address at the American Society of African Culture (AMSAC) conference in 1959. Nemiroff later published the address under the title "The Negro Writer and His Roots." The society sought to create " 'links between culture and politics in Africa and America.' " The conference featured speakers that spanned political ideologies, from leftists to more conservative civil rights advocates to "U.S.-government sponsored spy operations (John Davis, the CIA, the FBI, and Harold Cruse, working undercover), authorized to monitor and contain black radicalism."[38] Hansberry's speech exuded a challenge to Black writers and political operatives that extended the work of her short-form writing in the 1950s and would stand in contrast to many contemporary critics' reception of *A Raisin in the Sun*.

In the speech Hansberry challenged illusions that she argued govern art making in the mid-twentieth century, illusions particularly about the relationship between art and society and how the artist depicts society. She took square aim at the Cold War politics that undercut the Popular Front and shaped the civil rights movement. With an urgency fueled by leftist Black internationalism, she charged:

Which brings me to the last great illusion that I would think still clings to the cultural fabric of the country like dampness to wool on a rainy day. This is the all-important illusion in America that there exists an inexhaustible period of time during which we as a nation may leisurely resurrect the promise of our Constitution and begin to institute the equality of man within the frontiers of this land.

The truth is of course that a deluded and misguided worldwide minority is rapidly losing ground in the area of debating time alone. The unmistakable roots of the universal solidarity of the colored peoples of the world are no longer 'predictable' as they were in my father's time—they are here. And I for one, as a black woman in the United States in the mid-twentieth century, feel that I am more typical of the present temperament of my people than not, when I say that I cannot allow the devious purposes of white supremacy to lead me to any conclusion other than what may be the most robust and important one of our time: that the ultimate destiny and aspirations of the African people and twenty million American Negroes are inextricably and magnificently bound up together forever.[39]

Hansberry's depiction of shared fate occurred in a conference funded by the Central Intelligence Agency.[40] Her assessment of "unpredictability" served as a warning to operatives in the room that the time for gradualism had expired. Hansberry's depiction of insurgency echoes in the words of Asagai in her play and harkens back to her work with STJ, which she also referred to in the speech.

The Cold War contexts intensified the political impact of Black celebrities, including artists. The U.S. government could showcase them as unofficial ambassadors and examples of American exceptionalism (such as Jackie Robinson) or public enemies (Robeson, Josephine Baker, William Patterson).[41] The impulse to quiet artists that Hansberry addressed in her speech demonstrates the two-pronged attack of the federal government, to encourage artists to create art that does not engage with the pressing political issues of the day, and to disrupt artists' ability to share work that foregrounded progressive politics. According to Mary Helen Washington, it was a time "when being on the Left or in the Communist Party guaranteed literary extinction."[42] Hansberry's comments and commitments to realism reflect her understanding of how state actions intertwined aesthetics and politics. She said, "all art is ultimately social: that which agitates and that which prepares the mind for slumber. The writer is deceived who thinks that he has some other choice. The question is not whether one will make a social statement in one's work—but only *what* the statement will say, for if it says anything at all, it will be social."[43] Her comment also reflects an understanding of theater as integrated into the social sphere and not separate from it. The words and worlds presented on the conference or theatrical stage have an impact on how audiences understand the distinction between the possible and impossible. In both venues, Hansberry sought to expand the realm of the possible.

The following year Hansberry's speech did not appear in the volume John A. Davis, president of the AMSAC, edited of selected papers from the conference. "It seems . . . likely that Hansberry's use of terms like 'white supremacy,' her critique of 1950s civil rights strategies, and her direct references to the Cold War, lynching, the 1955 Bandung Conference, and 'paid informers' so alarmed Davis and his CIA sponsors that he" decided not to publish the speech.[44] Even if the speech had been published, it would have appeared after Hansberry's hit play. In terms of the historical record, the speech offers insight into how to read Hansberry's drama, and, just as importantly, how to understand the misreading of her through an almost singular focus on her play. Hansberry's searing and incisive political critique did not wane, but her public image of middle-class Black respectability gave audiences a chance to misunderstand her as a liberal and not a radical.

The lasting impact of Mike Wallace's interview took shape when he asked Hansberry about a quote in which she allegedly critiqued negro dramatists for their inability to transcend racial categories. Transcendence would include presenting a nuanced depiction of race relations and disentangling art from protest. Wallace quoted Hansberry saying in a *New York Times* interview, "Negro dramatists burn to fight the cause. They show the Negro as all good and the white man as all bad. That isn't truth. Compared with Negro poets who have transcended the color question and present it in sophisticated terms, most of our playwrights are retarded."[45] Hansberry has denied using the language in the quote. According to her, there is "no contradiction between protest and good art." The misquote in the interview helped produce a reading of Hansberry's play as transcending racial categories and embracing universal themes. The interpretation does not account for her correction that the universal exists within the particular. As a result, the criticism depicted her politics as provincial, assimilationist, and accommodating.

Hansberry's play makes a clear distinction between assimilation and integration. While assimilation requires the subordinating of one culture to another and the adoption of the dominant culture's views, integration maintains the discrete characteristics of each group. The conversation between Beneatha and Asagai offered a model of "relating across human differences as equals"—the ability to build community within difference, "not shedding of our differences, nor the pathetic pretense that these differences do not exist," but a clear acknowledgment that democracy *requires* collaboration that resists exploitation and domination.[46] The colonial model of extraction of resources at the heart of the spatial logics of major U.S. cities impoverishes democracy because it denies individuals the opportunity to meet as equals and collaborate and rather places them in competition for resources and defense of positions.

The quote from the *New York Times* also serves to diminish the reach of Hansberry's work. On one hand, the power of Hansberry's practice resides in its appreciation of how daily acts serve as the constitutive work of freedom movements, while the interview attempts to constrict her vision to the realization of a single family's integration into a segregated neighborhood. In severing the tie of the family's action from other acts of Black insurgency, Wallace tries to contain Hansberry, which also makes her work consumable.[47]

According to Nemiroff, the misquote took on a life of its own. In the same *Times* interview, the reporter, Nan Robertson, quotes Hansberry saying, "I told them this wasn't a 'Negro play.' It was a play about honest-to-God, believable, many-sided people who happened to be Negroes."[48] Giving evidence of Hansberry's objection to this characterization, Nemiroff explained:

> In her scrapbook, beside a clipping of this interview, Lorraine wrote these words: "Never said NO such thing. Miss Robertson goofed—letter sent posthaste—Tune in next week" ... The letter of correction was never printed. A month later, in a second profile ("Her Dream Came True" 4/9/59), presumably by another writer, the alleged statement was repeated. And from there it spread like a prairie fire. In short order, a second "quote" was mysteriously appended to the first to complete the equation: "I'm not a Negro writer—but a writer who *happens* to be a Negro." And now nothing could stop it, for it seemed to solve the problem for white Americans—how to classify the author of "The Best Play of the Year" while, at the same time, avoid honoring the special qualities that made her what she was. By the time Lorraine died, the phrase had undergone, in the *New York Times* obituary, a further metamorphosis: "The work was described not as a Negro play but one about people who happen to be Negroes. And its author, too, *insisted throughout her short lifetime* that she was not a Negro playwright, but" ... etc. [italics added].[49]

The words that Hansberry contested publicly and privately served to mold her public image and the scholarly criticism of her work. Hansberry's work requires scholars to account for the complex web of relationships that she presents, depicting desegregation as a civil rights, human rights, and women's rights issue. Foregrounding any one of the aforementioned rights placed Hansberry within a school of thought that diminishes the expansiveness of her vision.

As Margaret Wilkerson details in her analysis of the twenty-fifth anniversary edition of *A Raisin in the Sun,* the version of the play originally staged on

Broadway cut or truncated some of the more politically charged scenes, including the conversation between Beneatha and Asagai at the heart of this chapter. In response to the truncated version of the play, critics from Harold Cruse to Amiri Baraka questioned the work's political vision. Cruse dismissed the play as " 'the artistic, aesthetic and class-inspired culmination of the efforts of the Harlem leftwing literary and cultural in-group to achieve integration of the Negro in the arts.' In other words, it is a 'most cleverly written piece of glorified soap opera,' a 'second-rate' play about working-class Blacks who 'mouth middle class ideology.' "[50] Cruse's comments take on richer meaning when understood as a continuation of the antagonism Hansberry produced in her AMSAC speech. His vitriol may have also been based in a personal affront. "According to legend, Hansberry had turned down his request to read one of his proposed musical plays," Peniel Joseph has written.[51] One wonders if critics would have found Hansberry's class critique as unfathomable if they understood how her personal life served as a reflection of her feminist materialist approach to art and activism. Given Cruse's governmental affiliations, however, learning about Hansberry's queering of the Black family would have likely added fuel to his flame.

In cultural criticism more generally, the struggle of the play has often been staged as an antagonism between protest art and formal intervention. The play, throughout its history, has served as a perfect staging ground for an examination of what practices of fugitivity may exist within dramatic realism. Or, how do practices of fugitivity proliferate in the trap.

I borrow the colloquial term "trap" to refer to geographies of fugitivity within larger social structures and to the protocols of meaning making that formal devices produce. Desegregation requires understanding freedom practices within unfreedom, practices of freedom within the trap. Trapdoors, tunnels, and undercommons preserve such activities and the practices themselves function as space clearing exercises that allow more room to maneuver. Geographies of fugitivity acknowledge as Stefano Harney and Fred Moten argue that "all modernity will have at its heart, in its own hold, this movement of things, this interdicted, outlawed social life of nothing."[52] I focus, here, however, on the possibilities Hansberry's thought provides for what Harney and Moten call outlawed social life.

In *Black Movements: Performance and Cultural Politics*, I argued that Black women of the late-twentieth and early twenty-first centuries often cultivated freedom practices from within constricted environments. These women artists, Coco Fusco, Suzan-Lori Parks, and Beyoncé Knowles, use strategies of indirection to free up space to define themselves, situate themselves in time, and claim the power of chosen affiliations. Hansberry's freedom practice accounted for the association of women with domestic space and how the burgeoning civil rights movement needed to advocate for spatial justice in public and intimate environments. The literary criticism of the 1959 production of Hansberry's play and the critical debates over whether the play argues for and succeeds because of its investment in integration of neighborhoods and financial resources miss the larger issue of how the Youngers' move functions as one tactic among many that Hansberry explored in her writing.

A Raisin in the Sun begs the question as to how the home, the domestic scene of civil rights struggle, a scene that predominately figures as women's space, participates in the global pursuit of Black freedom that emerges when the Younger family must reconsider its willingness to move after Walter Lee loses the majority of the inheritance money. The move does not solve the Youngers' problems or the larger social ills of Black Chicago. As Michelle Gordon astutely argues, "Acutely aware of the social organization and violence at the center of Chicago's near-absolute segregation, Hansberry stages a revolutionary intervention into the cyclical systems of ghettoization, proffering *Raisin* as a dramatic prelude and challenge to the racialized rituals of ghettoization, desegregation, and organized white resistance."[53] The move functions as a significant moment of disruption given that most large U.S. cities in the 1950s and today suffer from hyper-segregation. Black people living in northern urban areas in the 1940s and 1950s experienced overcrowding, confinement, and cramped quarters. From 1910 to 1970, millions of Black people moved from southern rural environments to northern cities. The mass movement of northern migrants transformed the demographics of America's states. As a result, many northern states that had small populations of Black people experienced rapid increases. The Great Migration resulted in the racial integration of many northern states, but did not impact the integration of neighborhoods.

In response to the influx of Black migrants, northern real estate agents, including Carl Hansberry, reconfigured dwellings designated for one family to accommodate two or three families. The segregation of cities encouraged property owners to increase the amount of housing without increasing the amount of land allocated for housing. Therefore, "after 1950 . . . Blacks and Whites came to reside in wholly different towns and cities" even though integration increased at the state level, according to Douglas Massey. "From 1950 to 1970, the move toward integration at the state and county levels continued as Black out-migration from the South accelerated after World War II. . . . As a result, from 1900 to 1970, macro-level segregation largely disappeared from the United States. Indices of Black segregation and racial isolation at the state level were cut in half."[54]

The story of the Great Migration demonstrates a tension at the heart of American culture in the mid-twentieth century. Black people fled the south in the early twentieth century to escape racial violence in the forms of rape and lynching and to pursue economic opportunities in the north. However, northern migrants found new challenges marked by a deep investment in the doctrine of racial segregation. "At the neighborhood level . . . Black segregation continued to increase from 1950 to 1970, although at a decelerating pace that reflected the high level of racial segregation already achieved."[55] By 1970, most Black people living in northern urban areas lived in neighborhoods that were two-thirds Black.

In terms of integration in the twenty-first century, the experience of many urban dwellers parallels those of their white and Black racial counterparts in the mid- and late twentieth century. "The extreme segregation of Blacks continues unabashed in the nation's largely metropolitan areas, and is far more severe than anything experienced by Hispanics or Asians." Although the popular perception propagated by twenty-first-century network television shows (*Blackish, Scandal, This Is Us* . . .) and media suggests that class and race work together to inform rates of integration, census data show that "segregation can in no way be attributed to class" and that "as a result of segregation, poor Blacks are forced to live in conditions of intensely concentrated poverty."[56]

The entrenchment of segregation at the neighborhood level results in many Black and brown-skinned people lacking equal access to education, public facilities, including libraries and parks, and state services. According to census data, levels of segregation are not likely to abate in the near future, Massey explains: "At the rate of change observed between 1970 and 1990, the average level of Black-White segregation in northern areas would not reach the lower limits of the high range until the year 2043. At the slower rate of change prevailing from 1970 to 1980, it would take until 2067. As of 1990, no large northern Black community approached even a moderate level of residential segregation."[57] In other words, large cities in the United States are not only segregated, they are deeply segregated and are showing little signs of change.

Separation in urban environments from the Great Migration of the early twentieth century to the present has been totalizing. The impermeability of integrating neighborhoods as a means to redistribute resources marked a rupture in the social design that would and historically did not occur without violent recompense, and nevertheless, "Hansberry does not offer desegregation as the ultimate answer to segregation, but rather as a necessary step toward what she envisioned as 'a socialist organization of society as the next great and dearly won universal condition of mankind.' "[58] In a letter, Hansberry wrote: "You see, our people don't really have a choice. We must come out of the ghettos of America, because the ghettos are killing us; not only our dreams, as Mama says, but our very bodies. It is not an abstraction to us that the average American Negro has a life expectancy of five to ten years less than the average white. You see, Miss Oehler, that is murder, and a Negro writer cannot be expected to share the placid view of the situation that might be the case with a white writer."[59] Although the version of *A Raisin in the Sun* that appeared on Broadway served to restrict critics' perception of Hansberry's project, she clarified in interview after interview the larger stakes of her work.

In her interview with Wallace she stated that no freedom practices are off the table. We "must embrace all causes, must embrace all methods," she asserts:

> For me this is one of the most affirmative periods of history. I am very pleased that those peoples in the world whom I feel closest to, the colonial peoples the African peoples the Asian peoples they're in an insurgent mood and are in the process of transforming the world, and, I think, for the better. I can't quite understand pessimism at this moment unless of course one is wedded to things that are dying out, which should die out, like colonialism, like racism and so forth. Walter Lee Younger and his family are necessarily tied to this international movement whether they have consciousness of it or not they belong to an affirmative movement in history. Anything that he does that is the least positive has just implications that embrace all of us. I feel that his moving into the new house, his decision, is, in a way, a reply to those who say, that you know, all guilt is equal, all questions lack clarity, that it's hard to know what you should fight for or against, that there are things to do, that the new house has many shapes. And that we must make some decisions in this country as this man does.[60]

Hansberry was articulating a political stance rooted in Black internationalism. She linked Black Americans' pursuit of freedom to post-colonial struggles in Africa and Asia to affirm a collective struggle. She also drew attention to the dying European empires as a warning for the growing American one, suggesting that the United States had hitched its train to a dying political model. And, even though Hansberry used the character of Walter Lee to challenge the emancipatory possibilities of a capitalist model, she affirmed: "Anything that he does that is the least positive has just implications that embrace all of us."[61] She also clarified that freedom requires decisive action.

Hansberry's comment resonates with contemporary debates about the limitation of political action and activism in the context of necropolitics—"contemporary forms of subjugation of life to the power of death," as J. A. Mbembé wrote, arguing that weapons of mass destruction create *"death-worlds,* new and unique forms of social existence in which vast populations are subjected to conditions of life conferring upon them the status of *living dead.*"[62] Mbembé challenges Michel Foucault's genealogy of the Holocaust as the historical antecedent of these death-worlds. Rather, Mbembé argues, the plantation and the colony functioned as the geographical model.

Hansberry's response calls for the anxiety and despair of life lived in the shadow of the Holocaust's mass death *and* the longer history of the plantation and the colony. She troubles the historical and spatial boundaries of Wallace's question. Her assertion that "this is one of the most affirmative periods of history" draws attention to how the modern civil rights movement functions as a second reconstruction, an opportunity to reimagine Black freedom as a global endeavor. Although Hansberry's play focuses on a local context, she cautions against understanding the domestic drama and intimate space as separate from a world system that creates camps, holds, and traps. Hansberry also cautions against the totalizing rhetoric of liberalism, "a reply to those who say . . . all guilt is equal," which consumes our present and threatened mid-twentieth century freedom practices. Hansberry learned from her parents the impossibility of home if we understand home as an enduring and secure set of property relations that persists as a result of one's citizenship. In Hansberry's unpublished story "Homecoming" (1950) she depicts soldiers returning to Harlem after World War II. One soldier has a damaged eye. Although he has returned to the United States, the soldier has an abiding sense of danger. His dread soon finds just cause, when he dies at the hands of a police officer. His mother tries to convince friends to attend a meeting to organize around her son's murder but neighbors fear being branded communists. One neighbor, however, decides to go with the eyes of the lynchers watching.[63] As Imani Perry details in *Looking for Lorraine,* Hansberry's short stories anticipate concerns that she explores in greater depth in her drama and reflect her interior life; her private working through of personal experiences. Carl's decision to move to Mexico informed Lorraine's understanding of how geographically disparate freedom practices could produce political webs of affiliation among activists across the globe. She offers a set of relations that "displaces the already displaced impossibility of home."[64] By the end of the play, the Youngers do not leave their apartment to find a home in Clybourne Park. Their relocation itself functions as the disruption.

As the interview with Mike Wallace reveals, Hansberry's race, gender, marital status, and age led to misreading of her play and ideas. Literary and cultural histories prescribed readings of Hansberry and her work. In the mid-twentieth century realism, naturalism, and modernism dominated literary and dramatic production and informed her position generationally, in terms of American theater and African American arts. Hansberry's play draws from the naturalism of Richard Wright's groundbreaking novel *Native Son* (1940) but, distinctively, does not take on the socially produced fatalism of his narrative and therefore reflects realism more strongly than naturalism. Nevertheless, in Walter Kerr's assessment of the play for the *New York Herald Tribune,* he concludes, "Not one of these vital, restless, decently ambitious members of a chauffeur's family really has a choice about anything: about scrambled eggs, the house he will live in, the share of the world he might hope to own."[65] Brooks Atkinson similarly wrote of "the knowledge of how character is controlled by environment."[66] The analysis of Kerr and Atkinson works *against* the spatial justice argument that Hansberry's play makes because they understood the play as following in the tradition of naturalism that *Native Son* popularized. In the case of *Native Son,* the will of the protagonist, Bigger Thomas, becomes subordinate to the environment rather than, in Hansberry's case, individuals participating in crafting structures that produce neighborhoods, geographies, and global networks. For Wright, the individual is a victim of his circumstance, but for Hansberry, the individual is a participant within structures that can harness power by realizing his or her relation to people across the world working for liberation.

The play's thematic interests in political and social issues also align with the tenets of realism. According to Lawrence Jackson: "In private correspondence with ranking Communist William Patterson, she wrote, 'My play was an effort to say that principle decisions are not abstract style but are the very fabric of existence.' "[67] Unlike Wright's book, Hansberry's play ends not in death but with the promise of more justice work left to be done. Similar to the ending of Baldwin's *The Fire Next Time,* Hansberry's play ends by asking its audience to make a choice about political possibility, despair or hope. These daily choices, within the trap, produce freedom practices and serve as the threads that stitch together freedom movements.

HOUSING AND DESEGREGATION

The theme of hope and despair packs a particular punch, according to critic Harold Cruse, if one accounts for the working class of the Younger family and the middle-class background of the playwright. Cruse lambasts Hansberry in *The Crisis of the Negro Intellectual,* charging that she values integration because of her personal investment in being in an interracial relationship and living in Greenwich Village. Similar to my method, Cruse uses Hansberry's biography to examine her work, but rather than as a source of illumination, he deploys his interpretation of her life to undercut the validity and political potency of her play. He claims that Hansberry abandoned the values she developed while living and working in Harlem once she moved to the Village.[68] According to Cruse, if Hansberry demonstrated fidelity to the working class, she would understand and concede to the existential crisis of Black life for families like the Youngers that must endure generations of poverty. Cruse, similar to Malcolm X, misunderstood Hansberry's investment in interracial coalition as a betrayal of Black freedom movements. Her life in the Village enabled her to conceptualize a more expansive understanding of Black womanhood that would challenge the predominance of masculinity in Black radical thought.

In Hansberry's interview with Wallace, he asked her about choosing a working-class background for the Younger family, since she grew up in a middle-class family. She responded: "I deliberately chose the class background of the people who are the characters in *A Raisin in the Sun* because my own particular point of view is that most of what we hope for as a people, most of what we hope for, our ultimate stature as a people, is going to come from these people who are the base the backbone of our people."[69] Hansberry asserted the necessity of looking to working-class people as the basis for achieving the goals of freedom to determine one's outcomes, although she did not say why. Her larger body of work reflects, however, her investment in collective liberation as the basis for becoming free. The disproportionate number of working-class Black people required that freedom work begin there.

She made a clear and elaborate case for representing the working class in her AMSAC speech, which Wallace may not have known about but Cruse certainly did. She argued: "I say that foremost are the villainous and often ridiculous money values that spill over from the dominant culture and often make us ludicrous in pursuit of that which has its own inherently ludicrous nature: acquisition for the sake of acquisition. The desire for possession of 'things' has rapidly replaced among too many of us the impulse for the possession of ourselves, for freedom."[70] This line echoes a critique Mama articulates in *A Raisin in the Sun* of the conflation of money with freedom, although Mama's comment has a different implication. In the context of the play, her words also signal a generational divide between her and Walter Lee. Hansberry's speech asserts an unequivocal moral position.

Later, in a self-reflective turn, she insisted: "The war against illusions must dispel the romance of the black bourgeoisie. Nor does this imply the creation of a modern kind of buffon [*sic*] dressed up in a business suit, haplessly trying to imitate the white counterpart. On the contrary. These values have their root in an *American* perversion and no place else. The man in pursuit of the idle dreams is a man in pursuit of idle dreams. His color does not confound this to the point of absurdity—it merely makes it complex."[71] Hansberry defined the artist's job as correcting illusions produced by the U.S. government as a part of its Cold War propaganda. Artists also must create new visions.

In the interview, Wallace continued the line of questions about class and referred to E. Franklin Frazier's acclaimed sociological study *Black Bourgeoisie* (1957). Frazier made two pertinent points: questioning the existence of a Black middle class as defined by a group of citizens that exerts economic and political power, and lamenting the idea of the Black middle class or bourgeoisie, which he calls a myth, because it does not exert any power and isolates itself from working-class Black people and their traditions as a way to establish its distinctiveness. Wallace said: "You mentioned the sociologist E. Franklin Frazier, who obviously is a man you respect. He said that the middle-class Negro is less competent than his white counterpart 'because he doesn't have to compete with whites. The Negro professional makes excuses for his deficiencies. He likes to complain to white people, work for a raise, trying to get up in the world you shouldn't expect us to measure up to your standards.' " Hansberry responded: "Yes, well Dr. Frazier of course is speaking from within the veil and he's speaking within an intimacy that you might not as readily understand. It's impossible to discuss the Negro as an abstraction unto itself in this country. So that what he is saying is basically true that because of the isolation and separation that our people are forced to endure, this particular group cannot come face to face with some of the more acute realities of what they are trying to overcome because they just don't get there, they don't become bankers. They don't get an opportunity to deal with those actual things. That has nothing to do with not having their sights on it."[72] Wallace tried to make the case for Black people's cultural pathology, but Hansberry did not allow it, arguing that the racist structures shape Black people's position in society.

Similar to Wallace, Cruse asserted that Hansberry and other artists exist on an island separate from the everyday realities of Black people. Frazier, however, drew attention to the statistical improbability of such separation, given the small number of Black people in the United States: 0.3 percent in the highest income bracket in 1949. "In 1949 the median income of Negro families in the United States was $1,665, or 51 percent of the median income of white families, which was $3,232. Only 16 percent of the Negro families as compared with 55 percent of the white families had incomes of $3,000 or more."[73]

Hansberry offered a similar analysis in an interview with Studs Terkel in 1959, estimating "at this time the Negro middle class—the comfortable middle class—may be from five to six percent of our people, and they are atypical of the representative experience of Negroes in this country."[74] Given the minuscule number of Black people in the middle class and Hansberry's relationships with activists and community organizers, evidence suggests that her community consisted of individuals from different economic classes.

At the same time, Hansberry's work calls into question Frazier's assertion that "In escaping into world of make-believe, middle-class Negroes have rejected both identifications with the Negro and his traditional culture. Through delusions of wealth and power they have sought identification with the white America which continues to reject them. But these delusions leave them frustrated because they are unable to escape from the emptiness and futility of their existence."[75] Both Frazier and Cruse saw the desire for assimilation plaguing Black people in the mid-twentieth century, and although assimilation may drive the pursuit of integration, they are not necessarily tied. Hansberry saw integration as one practice of freedom among many that furthered an ongoing investment in Black internationalism. In response to Wallace questioning her about the discussion of assimilation in *A Raisin in the Sun,* she responded, "Since the 30s what we want is a recognition of the beauty of things African and a beauty of things black."[76]

The public presentation of Hansberry's political and personal desire complicated her asserted investment in "a recognition of the beauty of things African and a beauty of things black." In Cruse's analysis of Hansberry and Wallace's interview, both question Hansberry's relationship to the Nation of Islam and its beliefs. Cruse claimed that Hansberry told a *Village Voice* reporter, "Those Muslims 'are anti-white, reactionary separatists.' "[77] As chronicled earlier, Hansberry had an ongoing issue with being misquoted in mainstream media. In the conversation with Wallace she asserted the importance of "black nationalists," which at the time would have included the Nation of Islam. He went on to say that in community meetings in Harlem there was "talk of black supremacy, there's talk of any kind of integration, there's considerable anti-Semitic talk that takes place in these street corner meetings."[78] Hansberry clarified that she had not heard any expression of anti-Semitism in the meetings and explained the distinction between being anti-Semitic and anti-white. She challenged anti-Semitism but refused to call Black nationalists racists. She said:

> We are talking about oppressed peoples who are saying they must assert themselves in the world. Now personally, I hope that I believe most of all in humanism. I'm not interested in color. I've fought against color prejudice all my life.

I'm not interested in having white babies murdered any more than I can counte-
nance the murder of Kikuyu babies in Kenya. I hate all of that kind of thing. But
let's not equalize the oppressed with the oppressor and saying that when people
stand up and say we don't want any more of this they are now talking about a
new kind of racism ... My position is that we have a great deal to be angry
about, furious about. You know it's 1959 and they're still lynching Negroes in
America and I feel, as our African friends do, we need all ideologies which point
toward the total liberation of the African peoples all over the world.[79]

Hansberry offered a complicated and nuanced political position that
Americans still have trouble understanding decades later. She did not identify
as a Black nationalist, but she understood the necessity of their existence
because, similar to Malcolm X, she believed that liberation from colonial rule,
which differs from freedom practices that maintain self-governance, requires
any means necessary. In addition, Hansberry did not advocate for racial hierarchies *but* she did require an accounting for how power dynamics inform an
individual's position and ability to maneuver over time. The political acts of a
group that has been historically oppressed, therefore, must differ from the
options open to the oppressor. In the interview, Wallace tried to equate Black
nationalism with segregation but his analysis did not account for the historical
extraction of resources from Black communities to support white communities. Segregation requires subordination of Black communities while Black
nationalism entails self-governance.

Wallace's misreading of Hansberry's political allegiances reflects a tendency
to evaluate actions without accounting for the history that situates, precedes,
and calls them forth. Malcolm X similarly misunderstood Hansberry's investment because he so fervently believed in Black separatism. In a 1963 interview
with Louis Lomax, Malcolm X asserted integration reflects a primary desire
for interracial intimate relationships. He said: "Check out these integration
leaders, and you will find that most of them are either married to or hooked
up with some white woman. Take that meeting between James Baldwin and
Robert Kennedy; practically everybody there was interracially married. Harry
Belafonte is married to a white woman; Lorraine Hansberry is married to a
white man; Lena Horne is married to a white man. Now how can any Negro,
man or woman, who sleeps with a white person speak for me? No black
person married to a white person can speak for me!"[80] Ironically, as Manning
Marable's groundbreaking biography demonstrates, Malcolm X had a same-
sex relationship with a white man, so it is noteworthy that his initial assertion
privileged patriarchy and heteronormativity. Equally as important, Malcolm
equated interracial desire with racial self-hatred.

According to Ossie Davis, Hansberry's friend and cast member of the 1959 production of *A Raisin in the Sun* (he served as Sidney Poitier's replacement during the run of the show), Malcolm made several statements questioning Hansberry's politics because of her marriage. According to Davis, Hansberry confronted Malcolm about the statements, and "He said, 'I said that because that's what I thought at that time. But I'm sorry that I said that because I see now that that's wrong and I hope you will understand and forgive me because you know I've changed my thinking and I'm, you know, I'm bold enough to say that I've changed my thinking. I'm sorry about that but that's what I believed at that moment.' And she was prepared to forgive him."[81] In 1965, Malcolm X attended Hansberry's funeral and asked Ossie Davis and his wife, Ruby Dee, to introduce him to Paul Robeson. Although Malcolm came to acknowledge the necessity of justice workers committed to interracial coalition formation aimed toward the liberation of Black people, the reception of Hansberry's most well-known work remains haunted by the equation of integration with assimilation.

"THAT MONEY WAS MADE OF MY FATHER'S FLESH"

In the conversation between Beneatha and Asagai that serves as a turning point in the play, Beneatha communicates the stakes of Walter Lee losing the money. She charges, "That money was made of my father's flesh." Property rights, personal properties, and people as property become intertwined in the histories Beneatha calls forth through this line. To understand the relationship between Black people as property and as private property owners requires attending to the intricate and competing impulses, following emancipation, to maintain racial and sexual hierarchies *and* uphold the "sovereign choices of the property-holder."[82] Different from battles for public space, equal access to private property—either through inheritance or purchase—has proven a stumbling block in Black freedom struggles. For example, Martin Luther King Jr.'s Chicago housing desegregation campaign in 1966 was one of his only unsuccessful major civil rights projects.[83] Well before King's campaign, however, advocating for equal protection and access to accumulating private property proved a stubborn terrain for abolitionists and Black freedom fighters. As Adrienne D. Davis outlined in "The Private Law of Race and Sex," in the years leading up to and following emancipation, attempts to transfer private property in wills from white men to Black children and the Black women with whom they shared a sexual relationship required courts to examine how to maintain Black people's position as property and, therefore, property-less and support "the *power of the testator* to direct disposition of his property after his death."[84] The investment of U.S. courts in upholding the transfer of private property within families as an expression of citizenship helped to produce the sexual economies: the overlap of intimate relationships with economic ones.

Davis clarifies that courts had to balance competing material and ideological interests in order to decide how to bequeath the estates of white men that had willed their property to Black children and the Black women with whom they shared a sexual relationship. The essay establishes how the court's rulings serve to reinforce a racist "sexual economy." The term "sexual economy," she explains, "collapses the boundary still often drawn between the intimate and market (economic) spheres of human life." Although under a different racial configuration than explored in Davis's essay, Hansberry's play depicts the ongoing salience of sexual economies' impact on freedom struggles. *A Raisin in the Sun* demonstrates how a father's property functions as the catalyst for transgressive social relationships because it requires his legacy as property— flesh—transform into Mama's "economic personality," her "legally enforceable market relationships."[85]

By 1959, the courts settled the legality of the transfer of private property through estates from one family member to another one. The courts, however, still had not ruled definitively on the transfer of property between racial groups. In 1940, the Supreme Court heard the case of *Hansberry v. Lee,* brought by Carl Hansberry, with the aid of the NAACP, in response to a dispute over a home he purchased in a Chicago subdivision called South Park, a neighborhood that bordered Woodlawn. The neighborhood separated Black Chicago from Woodlawn and Hyde Park.

The Woodlawn Property Owners association established a housing covenant in 1928 to ensure that the neighborhood remained segregated as the Black population in Chicago exploded during the Great Migration. Almost a decade later (1937), Carl Hansberry, a successful attorney and real estate investor, purchased a home from James T. Burke in the South Park subdivision at 6140 Rhodes Avenue through a white broker. The neighbors first sought to remove the Hansberrys with force, gathering as a mob in front of the residence and only dispersing through the encouragement of the Hansberrys' gun. The home owners' association next sought an injunction to remove the Hansberrys from their house, arguing that James Burke violated the housing covenant stipulating that the owner " 'Does hereby covenant and agree with each and every other of the parties hereto, that his said parcel of land is now and until January 1, 1948, and thereafter until this agreement shall be abrogated as hereinafter provided, shall be subject to the restrictions and provisions hereinafter set forth, and that he will make no sale, contract of sale, conveyance, lease, or agreement and give no license or permission in violation of such restrictions or provisions' . . . that 'no part of said premises shall in any manner be used or occupied directly by a negro or negroes.' " Ironically, the association sought relief based on a ruling in the case of *Burke v. Kleiman* from 1934, in which Olive Ida Burke, James's wife, filed suit to enforce the covenant. In 1939, the Illinois Supreme Court heard the case of *Lee v. Hansberry* and held that "*Burke* 'was a class or representative suit.' Thus 'other members of the class are bound by the results in the case unless it is reversed or set aside on direct proceedings.'"[86] In response, Hansberry petitioned the U.S. Supreme Court to review the case, arguing that the covenant did not meet the stated legal requirements for a class action and that restrictive covenants violated the Fourteenth Amendment.

In *Hansberry v. Lee*, Carl won the battle but not the war. After hearing the arguments and reviewing the facts of the case, the Supreme Court found that the body represented in the *Burke* case could not stand in for the body seeking relief in the *Lee* case because an individual, James Burke, functioned as de facto complainant in one case and de facto defendant in the other one. The court did not rule restrictive housing covenants unconstitutional until 1948 in *Shelley v. Kraemer*. Nevertheless, following the 1948 ruling, the federal government continued to participate in deeming neighborhoods with Black people financially risky and therefore disqualified from federally backed mortgages. As a result, government policy continued to prevent the transfer of private property from white people to Black people for ideological reasons.

A Raisin in the Sun complicates the story of Chicago's midcentury and ongoing housing segregation by calling attention to "the racial economies of sexual relationships," in this case through marriage.[87] Ta-Nehisi Coates's ground-breaking essay "The Case for Reparations" offers a narrative history of an average Black family, the Ross family, and their battle to obtain fair housing in Chicago from the 1920s to the early twenty-first century. The central figure of the tale, Clyde Ross, describes how he migrated from Clarksdale, Mississippi, to Chicago in 1947. Like many veterans of World War II, Ross used the benefits that he earned through the GI Bill to purchase a home. Unlike white veterans, however, he had experienced the racial domination of growing up as the seventh of thirteen children in Mississippi and, as a northern migrant, would face the restricted housing covenants imposed on Black home buyers in Chicago. Coates writes, "From the 1930s through the 1960s, black people across the country were largely cut out of the legitimate home-mortgage market through means both legal and extralegal. Chicago whites employed every measure, from 'restrictive covenants' to bombings to keep their neighborhoods segregated."[88] The deregulation around lending policies enabled white sellers to swindle Black home owners which produced great wealth for owners and perpetual debt for buyers.

Hansberry's play intervenes midway in Coates's story and serves as a productive detour because it raises the question of how marriage informs the ability for Black people to make intergenerational transfers. Coates's essay focuses on government-regulated markets that require Black people's labor to become property for exchange rather than of exchange. His incisive and thorough engagement demonstrates the ways government intervention ensured that Black people remained poor. His essay, however, leaves out a part of the ideological picture by overlooking how private property houses intimate relationships and therefore serves as the perfect nexus to affirm individual rights and economic personality as belonging almost exclusively to white men.

In *A Raisin in the Sun,* Hansberry explored how the material inheritance the father leaves his children amounts to an ideological disruption of midcentury U.S. sexual economies. Motivated but not limited by her father's legacy, Hansberry produced the shadow figure of Big Walter to personalize the physical losses that accrue through freedom movements to emphasize that transfer of property does not amount to liberation. In Hansberry's play, the transfer of property functions as a freedom practice that positions the Youngers to struggle in a complicated terrain. Unlike public space, intimate space governed by the laws and ideological investments of private property more readily conveys the history of racial domination as sexual domination. *A Raisin in the Sun* calls for a radical spatial justice project that accounts for everyday forms of racial domination practiced in private. These intimate moments that structure the meaning of family also inform the policies and laws that govern the transfer of wealth and the movement from property to property-holder, from freedom deferred to freedom through practice.

Chapter 3 Origins: Black Radicalism as a Shapeshifting Pursuit

By 1960, Lorraine Hansberry was a household name—an international superstar who was sick of the play that made her famous. Her flourishing career gave her a sense of security, which emboldened her politically and personally. She found herself still married, yet enamored with her long-term lover Dorothy Secules. As Hansberry gained greater clarity about her vocation as a freedom writer and her public and private selves, she wrote a series of origins stories of race (*The Drinking Gourd* and *Toussaint*), sexuality and gender ("Queer Beer" and "Myself in Notes"), and citizenship as a result of settler colonialism (*Laughing Boy*). These stories helped establish the historical trajectory of what she called "the movement" and served to anchor her Black radicalism and feminism. Neither term's use during the period totally captures Hansberry's philosophical investments. Dayo Gore, Jeanne Theoharis, and Komozi Woodard argue in the introduction to *Want to Start a Revolution*, "One of the most lasting definitions of black radicalism emerged in Harold Cruse's book *The Crisis of the Negro Intellectual* (1967), which drew a rigid distinction between nationalist and integrationist politics and sharply critiqued black communists."[1]

Cruse's retrospective analysis, which took direct aim at Hansberry, questioned interracial collaboration. In addition, feminism did not become associated with women of color until later in the twentieth century. As with other Black women activists of the Cold War era, Hansberry accounted for the material histories that conditioned and crosscut the lives of Black men *and* women. Therefore her writing, a practice of becoming free, drew from seemingly disparate traditions (Black radicalism and existentialism) to stave off the death-bound alienation of blackness in its usual and exceptional manifestations. Hansberry understood the isolation that resulted from her fame as the flip side of anti-Black alienation, so she forged historical connections. Similar to her short-form writing in the early 1950s, the origins stories focus on the triangular dynamic of observing, being observed, and witnessing to establish a history of responses to being captured by a glance or a social structure.

Lorraine's writing helped to produce a world freer from the deathly forces of racial domination, colonialism, homophobia, and sexism *and* cultivated her identity as well. In a series of notes popularized by a Brooklyn Museum exhibit in 2014, "Twice Militant: Lorraine Hansberry's Letters to *The Ladder*," she takes stock of herself. The notes reveal the complexity of her political investments and her multifaceted personality. They also show the youth, beauty, charisma, and insecurity of a woman living in New York City in the midst of world-shifting change. In anticipation of her twenty-fourth to thirty-second birthdays, Lorraine listed her likes, dislikes, wishes, fears, and hopes. On the cusp of her twenty-fourth birthday, she wrote that she liked being alone. As reflected in the other lists, loneliness would continue to torment her, often proving tiring and debilitating. In 1953, she also noted that she despised "masculinity in women" and was indifferent to "money, somewhat." Her ambivalence about certain forms of gender presentation and disregard for money persisted throughout the notes and draws attention to a nuanced understanding of class and gender. In a letter penned in 1957, she reflected, "it has been interesting to me that for one who is so acutely interested in the status of woman as a social question, something of a Feminist even, that I encourage, celebrate rebels in the x sex, that what I am most excited by, attracted to is the rather disgusting symbol of woman's oppression itself: *femininity*. Woman has been imprisoned in her skirts and there are few who can hold forth on the damnation of the dress longer than I—and yet I prefer them on those I am interested in . . . because I am fond of being able to watch calves and ankles freely."[2] Wrestling with the distinction between personal desire and gender categories, Lorraine understood the dominant pressure for women to appear only in one way, unlike the dynamic multiplicity of gender presentations available in the twenty-first century.

Hansberry's political investments accounted for and made demands on her personal interactions. Her friendship with Baldwin proved enduring. The two artists shared a political bond that drove their art. They also understood the intimate alienation of being a gay person in a still racially segregated and homophobic society. On April 11, 1959, Hansberry documented that she liked "conversations with James Baldwin, *Juno and the Paycock,* slacks, Eartha Kitt's eyes, voice, legs, music, and the genius of Shakespeare."[3] Only months after *A Raisin in the Sun* premiered, she said she was bored with the play as well as with "loneliness and most sexual experiences." Although the play came to define Hansberry, her self-inventory, a freedom practice, cleared room for the figure she had prepared herself to be since her days at *Freedom.*

Her private life and personal struggles present a more complicated figure than public assessments in newspapers and magazines, pointing to the difficulty in shifting how one is perceived. She appeared before the public a young, beautiful, articulate, middle-class wife who affirmed Black people's desires for normative American ideals. In 1960 Hansberry bought a house at 112 Waverly Place and became neighbors with Secules.[4] In the same year, she affirmed her admiration of Eartha Kitt and expressed her vanity, noting "I like getting dressed up" and "being admired for my looks." She also revealed her adoration for Dorothy, her neighbor and lover, her "homosexuality," and her desire to "feel like working."[5] Lorraine both embraced the solitude brought by and felt embattled by the pace of her writing. Similar to her early years in New York after *A Raisin in the Sun,* she wrote volumes of material, but much of it went and remains unpublished. Her comment registers a recurring frustration between her public presentation and her personal battle for productivity and happiness. At the same time, Hansberry understood observing and being observed as a process of doing and undoing history. Therefore, her archive functions as an important site to see her anew.

The interrelation of racial, sexual, and economic liberation could not have been more personal for Hansberry. In 1960 she affirmed, "I AM BORED TO DEATH WITH *A RAISIN IN THE SUN!,* Being a Les, Lesbians (the capital L variety), the Race Problem, the Great American money obsession, My own loneliness, SEX," and "Being a 'Celebrity.' " Although she "wanted to be in love! and Dorothy Secules (at the moment)" she also recognized that Bob brought stability and productivity to her life and writing.[6] He not only served the practical function of encouraging her to get work done, he also helped her to ward off the depression that dogged her when she could not write. Anxiety and depression emerged in her contestation with her own visibility. She wanted to be admired for her physical beauty and anonymous, able to exert influence and be a comrade. These desires, expressed through her routine creative process, demonstrate Hansberry's complexity, not her contradictions. Hansberry brought that complexity to her practice and radicalism.

Soon after the premiere and fanfare of *A Raisin in the Sun*, NBC Studios commissioned Hansberry to write a screenplay in honor of the centennial of the Civil War. The commission offered her an opportunity to contemplate a civil war in the midst of a second one, the world again on the brink of wreckage or redemption. The screenplay, titled *The Drinking Gourd*, tackled a question that she pondered since childhood: "who and what a 'master' might be." In an introduction to the screenplay, Hansberry is quoted describing a trip she took to Kentucky to meet her maternal grandmother for the first time. She writes, "My mother first took us south to visit her Tennessee birthplace one summer when I was seven or eight. I woke up on the back seat of the car while we were still driving through some place called Kentucky and my mother was pointing out to the beautiful hills and telling my brothers about how her father had run away and hidden from his master in those very hills when he was a little boy. She said that his mother had wandered among the wooded slopes in the moonlight and left food for him in secret places. They were very beautiful hills and I looked out at them for miles and miles after that wondering who and what a 'master' might be."[7]

Even for Hansberry's child self, the idea of one human being holding complete dominion over another one seemed unfathomable. Lorraine's childhood teemed with moments that signaled her parents' distinctive position, operating outside the racial norms that constricted many Black people. In an effort to explain the childhood origins of her cross-class allegiances, she recalls a story of being given a white fur coat for Christmas. "She was the only child who did not come from the 'Rooseveltian atmosphere of the homes of the thirties.' "[8] When she wore the coat to school, the other children roughed her up. Instead of having disdain for her attackers, Lorraine yearned to understand what set her apart from them. At home she developed a double consciousness that deepened her love for Black people and reminded her of their diverse experiences. What might a "master" be, given Hansberry's resistance to a uniform understanding of blackness and therefore what it meant to be enslaved? What might a master be, given Hansberry's exposure to Black resistance struggles and ability to pose ethical challenges to tyrannical displays of power? What might a master be given the flow of anti-blackness among white and Black people alike? What might a master be given the propensity for domination inter- and intra-racially? What might a master be given the persistence of Black freedom movements above and underground?

Hansberry's early experiences helped her to conceptualize what it meant to be Black outside the structure of Jim Crow. Blackness did not present an impermeable barrier to opportunity or possibility. Nor did it erode value or carry a historical stigma. Instead of distancing herself from the legacy of slavery and the *Gone-with-the-Wind* degradation that typified popular understanding of the institution, she challenged renderings of blackness in the mid-twentieth century through a sober depiction of the slave past. Her drama shows how those who exercise power to further systems of oppression become dehumanized in the process. And those systems, even with the stubborn efforts of powerholders, will not necessarily last. Signaling the impermanence of oppressive structures in the past and present, Hansberry sets *The Drinking Gourd* on the cusp of the Civil War, at a turning point in history. As she faced turning points in her personal and professional life, she thought about historical connection and structural change as the basis for sustaining movements even during dark times. Hansberry intervened in historical narratives to shift the shape of the body and the structure of institutions that embodied practices support.

DRINKING GOURD

In the three years following *A Raisin in the Sun,* Hansberry created work that sought to invigorate once-degraded identities (Black, woman, lesbian) with potential. Her pursuit had personal consequences, as she continued to learn to live with her competing desires and commitments. "One isn't born, but rather becomes, a woman," according to Simone de Beauvoir. In Hansberry's book review of de Beauvoir's *Second Sex* in 1957, she described how American women (Irish, Polish, Jewish, and Black) emerge as a response to and in fulfillment of the nation's democratic ideals: "We have been . . . the black slave woman paradoxically assuming perhaps the most advanced internal freedom from a knowledge of the mythical nature of male superiority inherent in our experience as chattel. We have been the Jewish woman finding liberty in picketlines [*sic*]. We have not voted long, but we have a freedom in our gaits on the pavement that suggest almost an intuitive awareness of how the franchise was won. It is this multi-experienced class from which American communist women be drawn."[9] Against the grain of patriarchy and as a fulfillment of the idea of America, freedom emerges in her walk. Depicting the history of slavery expands possibilities for feminism, coalition formation, and activism because the history reveals the limits of what a master might be. The totalizing power associated with a master does not account for networks of desires and modes of unregulated exchange. It also does not account for the enslaved who defied regulation because of their dual status being subject to but unrecognized by the law.[10]

Two images contextualize Hansberry's screenplay *The Drinking Gourd.* One is an obfuscation that focuses on white women victims; as Hansberry explains, "it has been perfectly popular, admirable, the thing to do, all of my life since *Gone with the Wind,* to write anything you wanted about the slave system with beautiful ladies in big fat dresses screaming as their houses burned down from the terrible, nasty, awful Yankees."[11] The "tragic" impact of the Civil War justifies isolating Black Americans. The second image is of a social plan, as Hansberry describes Black Chicago: "I think you could find the tempo of my people on their back porches. The honesty of their living is there in the shabbiness. Scrubbed porches that sag and look their danger. Dirty gray wood steps. And always a line of white and pink clothes scrubbed so well, waving in the dirty wind of city. My people are poor. And they are tired. And they are determined to live. Our Southside is a place apart: each piece of our living is a protest."[12] In many ways both images are apart, separate from the lived reality and a portion of what insulates white America in the mid-twentieth century. The act of representing reality encapsulated Hansberry's work as an artist-activist. Understanding the Civil War more fully and its impact on becoming an American, a woman, a Black person, invigorates "each piece of" Black Chicagoans "living" which "is a protest."

The Drinking Gourd tells the story of two overlapping families split apart by slavery. One family, the Sweets, finds itself facing the challenge to modernize the plantation to maximize profits. The other family, composed of the Sweets' enslaved, uses every resource at its disposal to challenge the institution of slavery through the daily maintenance of the Sweet plantation. As is the case with most depictions of the brutal institution, both families pay a steep price for their investments.

But the payback of Hansberry writing this drama for television in 1959 also speaks to the shifting culture of America, or what Manning Marable calls the second reconstruction.[13] The writing of the screenplay coincides historically with the movement from a world of separate but equal to the painful battles for civic inclusion through blood-stained lunch counters, sidewalks, and churches. In as much as the civil rights movement functions as a return to the unfinished business of abolition, Hansberry's screenplay speaks to her time as it does to the past. In a journal entry Hansberry noted about the time, "Some scholars have estimated that in the three centuries that the European slave trade flourished, the African continent lost one hundred million of its people. No one, to my knowledge, has ever paid reparations to the descendants of black men; indeed, they have not yet really acknowledged the fact of the crime against humanity which was the conquest of Africa. But then—history has not yet been concluded . . . has it?"[14]

Hansberry's screenplay participates in the national project of reconstruction. It produces a relationship to the past, those on and off the record, that provides grounds for addressing contemporary wounding. As Lisa Lowe argues of Hazel Carby's theory of reconstruction in *Reconstructing Womanhood,* "It also established a method of *reconstruction* in which the study of Black women's intellectual work required more than mere retrieval; Carby showed us that reading lost histories required the *deconstruction* of liberal institutions and ideologies that had worked to render them illegible."[15] Reconstruction names modes of production that emerge through interpretations of the past in the service of drawing forth new answers to contemporary problems by accounting for the material histories that shape Black people. From the built environment to the body, material conditions serve as potent signs of slavery's ongoing legacy. Reconstruction requires reimagining embodiment, bodies, and the categories that name them (race, gender) as a negotiation with the past rather than an expression of accumulation or a break from accrued meaning.[16] While all modes of cultural production have the potential to impact the material world, theater focuses on the physical transformation of bodies, places, and objects as one of its distinctive attributes as a genre. Hansberry's work in radical leftist circles positioned her to frame *The Drinking Gourd* as a challenge to understandings of slavery as Black people's traumatic legacy rather than the trauma that organized the Western world. Although she describes in her reading of *The Second Sex* the impact slavery has on how Black people experience gender, in *The Drinking Gourd* she clarifies that the institution shapes gender in general.

With a name that anticipates a setting of Toni Morrison's *Beloved,* the Sweet plantation emphasizes the brutality of slavery through the relative benevolence of its owner, Hiram Sweet. In the opening moments, the beleaguered patriarch questions the future of slavery over dinner with his wife, sons, and family physician. His son, Everett, and the physician, Macon Bullet, think the family needs to modernize the plantation, but Hiram wonders, "Then what happens, Macon, if it's all a lie—the way we live, the things we tell ourselves?"[17] Hiram's words echo Asagai's questions in *A Raisin in the Sun.* Both men suggest that even in the midst of thinking one is on the right side of history, the contexts that shape our choices may shift, challenging one's deepest commitments and rendering one disposable. Hansberry's deep investment in grassroots mass organizing helped her conceptualize freedom practices, including writing, as impermanent. She understood that they required daily maintenance and that the goals could shift. She also understood that context and position mattered. So in shaping a meditation about slavery that unsettles the moral consensus, she offered room for her audience to explore ambivalence about the racial domination that structured contemporary society.

The Drinking Gourd presents the potential for a world turned upside down through the voice of a patriarch that has lost the power to govern his family and plantation, a crisis of patriarchy and the patriarchal. Hiram's physical weakness translates into an opportunity for his overzealous son and estranged wife to secure their reputed rightful places in the world as master and mistress. Everett makes room for himself on a plantation where the shadow of his father looms large by taking over the day-to-day running of the fields and unleashing an overseer, Zeb, who will do irreparable damage to the enslaved and, by extension, Hiram. Maria, the wife of Hiram and mother of Everett, encourages her son's ambition out of jealousy over the sexual relationship between her husband and Rissa, the matriarch of the enslaved family depicted in the screenplay.

The impermanence of slavery, and therefore things as they "always" have been, poses a challenge for the three central enslaved characters in *The Drinking Gourd* as well. While they all thirst for physical freedom, Rissa also desires to protect her son, Hannibal, and his love interest Sarah. Sarah shares Rissa's concerns about the prospects of fleeing the Sweet plantation. She asks Hannibal, "H'you know it's so much better to run off? (*A little desperately near tears, thinking of the terrors involved*) Even if you make it—h'you know what's up there, what it be like to go wanderin' 'round by yourself in this world?" Disrupting the notion that freedom entails adopting a progressive posture that moves Hannibal from point "A" to point "B" in a straight and efficient manner, he instead embraces the unpredictability at the heart of fugitivity. Clear that the devil he knows is not better than the one he does not, Hannibal responds, "I don't know. Jes know what it is to be a slave!"[18] Through the conversation, the characters participate in the act of reconstruction at the heart of the screenplay, which intercedes in history through a return that destabilizes power dynamics in order to affirm the unfolding of a second reconstruction in the present. As Aida Levy-Hussen argues, "the history of slavery is an affective density that resists *telling*—or narrative apprehension—that is retrievable only through performative re-encounters with the past that etch their meaning on the body and mind through the sensory register of pain."[19] Through the retelling, Hansberry explodes the given to be seen of her mid-twentieth-century world's conventions of race, gender, and sexuality. She stages historical return as an embodied disruption that challenges the shape of the body.

The screenplay's challenge to what it means to be a master replaces the site of return as singularly one of injury and supplements it with fugitivity.[20] *The*

Drinking Gourd does not dodge the irredeemable suffering of slavery, but it also does not locate that pain singularly within the bodies of the enslaved. Hannibal explains, "Whatever you hear Master say 'bout slavery—you always believe the opposite. There ain't nothin' hurt slave marster so much—(*Savoring the notion*)—as when his property walk away from him. Guess that's the worst blow of all. Way I look at it, ever' slave ought to run off 'fore he die."[21] It challenges the notion that Black subjects work to reclaim their humanity and instead shows how slavery produces the fundamental loss of America, which only reconstruction may repair. As Hansberry's writing for *Freedom* establishes, she sought to call forth histories through her work that served as the foundation for structuring new worlds. As an artist-activist, Hansberry set ideas and concepts in motion; she animated freedom. The space she creates in her writing serves as a site of return but one that does not presume the stability or reliability of what we think we know about the slave past; one that instead seeks to apprehend how changing locations upsets social arrangements, even ones as calcified as those at the heart of such a peculiar institution as slavery.

In a conversation between Hannibal and Rissa, Hannibal questions the assumptions that organize slave society and support racial and gender hierarchies. While Rissa tries to assert Hiram's relative generosity, Hannibal challenges the comfort of liberal relativism. He exclaims, "I am the only kind of slave I could stand to be—a *bad* one! Every day that come and hour that pass that I got sense to make a half step do for a whole—every day that can pretend sickness 'stead of health, to be stupid 'stead of smart, lazy 'stead of quick—I aims to do it. And the more pain it give *your* marster and more it cost him—the more Hannibal be a man!"[22] Hannibal refuses to concede. He resists slavery in all its manifestations because he understands concession feeds slavery's corrosive power. His acts of resistance also display a form of masculinity that the Sweets find particularly threatening. By the end of the screenplay, he and his family pay for his being "a man."

The most striking sequence of the screenplay depicts the impact of Hannibal's unwillingness to tolerate oppression. His stance demonstrates how slavery induces the enslaved to become complicit in the institution. Hannibal refuses to adjust to the institution of slavery. Martin Luther King Jr. asserted in a speech in London in 1964, "I never intend to adjust myself to segregation and discrimination. I never intend to become adjusted to religious bigotry. I never intend to adjust myself to economic conditions that will take necessities from the many to give luxuries to the few, and leave millions of people perishing on a lonely island of poverty in the midst of a vast ocean of prosperity. I never intend to adjust myself to the madness of militarism, and to the self-defeating effects of physical violence."[23] Hannibal pays a high price for his ethical commitment to what King called maladjustment. In the climactic scene of the screenplay, Everett learns that Hannibal has been stealing away to learn to read. Corrupted by power, Everett instructs Zeb to blind Hannibal because the "ability to read in a slave is a disease" so "one cuts out the disease." Unlike twenty-first-century film depictions of slavery, Hansberry does not show the scene of mutilation. Instead she focuses the camera on Everett. The screenplay directions read, "Everett turns on his heel away from the scene, and with a traveling shot, we follow his face, as he strides through the woods and as, presently, the tortured screams of an agonized human being surround him."[24] Through the focus of the camera on Everett, Hansberry associates the screams, the violence of slavery, with the white body. The horror and injury belong to him. Everett too must carry the physical manifestations of slavery.

Hansberry's directions draw attention, once again, to the corrosive force of slavery on white America as well as Black. Her intention reaches a final conclusion when Hiram learns what his son commanded and goes to Rissa's cabin to make amends. Rissa's diplomacy has reached its limit. She no longer has the capacity to stomach Hiram. When Hiram enters the cabin, the two have an encounter uncharacteristic of their relationship: "She looks at the master with uncompromising indictment and he returns her gaze with one of supplication, and drops his hands in a gesture of futility." Hiram begins to explain that he did not give the order to blind Hannibal and that Everett acted without his permission. Unmoved, Rissa retorts, "Ain't you *Marster?* How can a man be marster of some men and not at all of others—."[25] Hiram, realizing an irreconcilable breach has occurred, leaves the cabin. Suddenly, the illness that has plagued him throughout the screenplay returns and he falls to the ground. His body manifests the illness he has cultivated through omission and commission. The disease he nurtured will consume him. Hiram calls for help, but his cries land on deaf ears. He dies alone, outside Rissa's cabin. Spreading the physical impact of slavery, the violence overwhelms Hiram's physical body.

Although Rissa found ways to function with Hiram, she also moved around him. Her ability to leverage the hypervisibility and simultaneous invisibility of blackness enabled her to gather information. Early in the screenplay, Rissa stands off to the side as Hiram and Everett have a heated exchange. Everett leaves, and Rissa, "Coming out the shadows as all of the servants seem to do when they are called or needed," responds to Hiram's call for her.[26] Following Du Bois, Hansberry's description of Rissa as a "servant" troubles the common understanding of the enslaved as completely outside capitalism and positions them instead as fundamental to it. Rissa's movement early in the screenplay anticipates the last sequence where she sets Hannibal, Sarah, and Joshua free. After Everett mutilates Hannibal and Hiram dies, Rissa takes Joshua to meet Sarah and Hannibal in a clearing. Recalling the role of protector Hansberry saw her mother take on with pistol in hand, Rissa shoves the gun that she has stolen from the Sweets into the hands of Sarah, and the three take off into the woods.

Hansberry's screenplay complicates our understanding of slavery as a rupture that Black Americans can never get over or past. All of the characters in the screenplay attempt to exercise their roles without fully attending to the external forces, those of the impending war in this case, that frame their actions. At one point the stage directions indicate "Rissa . . . is cut from the same cloth [as Hiram] in her individualism."[27] The lure of self-possession limits their ability to perceive changes in what is possible. The comment establishes the necessity of collaboration as a function of encounter. Hansberry understood that individual transformation would not result in Black people becoming free.

At the same time, Hansberry deeply felt the allure of access through her newfound fame and understood the limitations of subscribing to a system of inclusion based in capitalism. In two conversations with secondary characters, Hansberry explicates mastery. Before Everett discovers that Hannibal has learned to read, Coffin, a name that befits a Black slave driver, confronts Hannibal about his perpetual absence from the fields. Hannibal questions, "Coffin, how you get so mixed up in your head? Them ain't my fields yonder, man! Ain't none of it my cotton what'll rot if I leaves it half-picked. They ain't my tools what I drops and breaks and loses every time I get a chance. **None of it** *mine*." Coffin's investment in protecting the Sweets' profits results in his subordination. Slavery makes him a slave driver rather than a property owner. In his effort to safeguard the institution he forecloses becoming free. Everett has a similar exchange with Zeb. Everett reminds his employee, "you had better reckon on knowing who is master here and who is merely overseer. Let us be very clear. You are only an instrument."[28] Both exchanges tap into the desire for self-possession through a misplaced allegiance to the structure that limits agency. Instead of understanding that protecting the plantation system ensures the perpetual domination of Coffin and Zeb, both men cling to their relative privilege in the pecking order as an indication of possible ascension against all evidence to the contrary. The screenplay reveals that being a master means grasping to protect the structures that degrade you. That mastery not only applies to those in positions of dominance but also those that seek to occupy them as well.

Although Hansberry enjoyed the privileges of her class position, her experiences as a child and young adult confirmed that her bourgeois status would not protect her from the embodied realities that structured her life. Although NBC commissioned *The Drinking Gourd* and deemed it superb, they never produced it, finding it too controversial. Hansberry, having had a similar experience with the film adaptation of *A Raisin in the Sun*, faced the abundant pressure of limited access. In 1959, she sold the film rights of *A Raisin in the Sun* to Columbia pictures for $300,000, and as a condition of the sale she insisted that she would write the screenplay.[29] In two drafts of the screenplay, Hansberry attempted to expand its world by depicting the Youngers' interaction with their community. She added scenes that built on the themes of systematic racism, Black nationalism, and Marxism. Eager to see a return on their investment, Columbia executives "wished to censor any uncomplimentary comment about colonial Britain and France and any trace of anti-colonialist sentiment." The final version of the film closely resembled the play and curtailed Hansberry's desire to use mass media to expand and further disseminate her radical vision. Nevertheless, she knew that her early success and relative freedom could distract her from the work her fame and wealth enabled. As a result, she focused attention on the working-class Black people, mass movements, and grassroots organizing as a way to disrupt the lure of fame and financial prosperity.

LOCATING A USABLE PAST

In "Me Tink Me Hear Sounds in de Night," an essay she wrote in 1960, Hansberry explicated how the blight of slavery infected Europeans and white Americans alike. The essay, similar to the speech "The Ground on Which I Stand" (1996), which August Wilson offered decades later, explains the absence of "the Negro in the American theatre." To pinpoint the cause, Hansberry drew a connection between racism, which she argued developed as a result of seventeenth-century colonial conquest, and transatlantic slavery. Racism as a concept, she argued, "made it possible to render the African a 'commodity' in the minds of white men, and to alienate the conscience of the rising European humanism from identification with the victims of that conquest and slave trade."[30] Although much of midcentury literature focused on how racism informs Black people's self-perception (*Native Son, The Street, Notes of a Native Son,* and *Black Skin, White Masks*), Hansberry carefully stipulated "in the minds of white men," to resist understanding racism as totalizing or all-encompassing. She also used the phrase to challenge the regulation of white perceptions of gender. Even as she struggled with her newfound fame and the isolation it produced, Hansberry also knew that she had an underground community that supported her. In his memorial essay to Lorraine, Baldwin wrote:

> This country's concept of art and artists has the effect, scarcely worth mentioning by now, of isolating the artist from the people. One can see the effect of this in the irrelevance of so much of the work produced by celebrated white artists; but the effect of this isolation on a black artist is absolutely fatal. He *is,* already, as a black American citizen, isolated from most of his white countrymen. At the crucial hour, he can hardly look to his artistic peers for help, but they do not know enough about him to be able to correct him. To continue to grow, to remain in touch with himself, he needs the support of that community from which, however, all of the pressures of American life incessantly conspire to remove him. And when he is effectively removed, he falls silent—and the people have lost another hope.
>
> Much of the strain under which Lorraine worked was produced by her knowledge of this reality, and her determined refusal to be destroyed by it.[31]

The power dynamics that made certain modes of community and communion legible shaped Hansberry's work and, ultimately, her archive. The encounters staged in her writing and facilitated through her papers offer an asynchronistic opportunity for connection.

Hansberry's writing practice necessarily intervened in the space between realism and reality to remake both. Her relationship with her uncle, African Studies professor William Leo Hansberry, produced a pride in her African heritage before Black pride emerged as a rallying cry during the Black Power and Arts Movements. Based on her international understanding of blackness, in "Me Tink Me Hear Sounds in de Night," instead of depicting the concept of the human as encompassed by European philosophy, Hansberry particularized that conceptual frame as one among others: "In order to accommodate programs of commerce and empire on a scale never before known in history, the Negro had to be placed arbitrarily outside the pale of recognizable humanity in the psychology of Europeans and, eventually, of white America."[32] She deftly connected the conceptual framing of "the Negro," a term that stands in for a group referred to earlier as Africans, to the development of capitalism and empire. The economic system emerges alongside the ideological one and depends on representational support.

For Hansberry, the theater and other modes of cultural production served a vital purpose to economic and ideological systems of domination. She argues that the fanciful negro operated outside of fathomable humanity. "He was to be—and, indeed, *became,* in a created mentality of white men—some grotesque expression of the mirth of nature; a fancied, static vestige of the primeval past; an external exotic who, unlike *men,* would not bleed when pricked nor revenge when wronged."[33] The notion of becoming, which Hansberry explored in her analysis of *The Second Sex,* reemerges here to denaturalize racism and trouble the hold it has on cultural production. Hansberry also sheds light on her choice to depict Hiram as a benevolent slave owner in comparison to Everett's brutality. The impending storm of the Civil War, which closes the screenplay, challenges the ideal of Negro compliance and demonstrates the operation of racism in an audience's ability to celebrate Shakespeare's Hamlet seeking vengeance but question the motivations for redress of Hansberry's character Tshembe in her play *Les Blancs.* Similarly, Hansberry ends her screenplay with Sarah taking up arms as a way to defend herself against the quotidian and grotesque violence the enslaved experienced. The violence moves from public to private spaces, and, as *The Drinking Gourd* depicts, has the potential to invade any aspect of life. The desire for civility does not address the routineness of violence, only its gross manifestations. Hansberry understood, however, the everyday incidents served as a training ground for white and Black subjects alike.

Hansberry's writing and role as a writer pose a challenge to the notion of social permanence and the resistance to imagining a new configuration of freedom. For example, she disagreed with theories and literary depictions of the built environment causing racism rather than perpetuating it. She maintained that humans created structures and, therefore, could recreate them. "Stanley Gleason and the Lights that Need Not Die," an essay she wrote for the *New York Times* in 1960, could be read as a response to Wright's *Native Son.* The essay, part bildungsroman, part social history, depicts the personal development and societal diminution of an African American young man named Stanley Gleason. Riffing on W.E.B. Du Bois's description in *The Souls of Black Folk* (1903), Hansberry figures Stanley, from the beginning of the essay, as a problem. In elementary school, white adults teach Stanley that his being is a thing apart, unworthy of using the same restrooms or extending from the same branch of the human tree as his white counterparts. In response, he develops a defiant gait: "There is about his walk something which suggests that, somehow, Stanley knows that his ancestors did survive the middle passage voyage and that he, for his part, has survived a climate which includes tuberculosis, rats and some of the most insidious hatreds on the face of the earth. His bouncy figure seems to be an act of defiance: a symbol of almost omnipotent awareness that he has played a telling trick on somebody by sticking it out. It is as if he is saying *"Man, I am here!"*[34] Hansberry does not equate

Stanley's survival and defiant swagger with the educational forces that prevent equal access and position him as a problem. She does, however, use his story to evidence an alternative understanding of humanity that lives in the daily actions of Black midcentury people. His physical carriage responds to his environment out of defiance and a need to redefine his surroundings.[35] Hansberry also questions, as she does in "Me Tink Me Hear Sounds in de Night," the impulse to position Black people as the cause of their oppression.

In a meta-reflexive moment, she makes room to understand her writing as a freedom practice. She compares Stanley's understanding of his world to descriptions he finds in editorials: "since the day he was born, presumably, there has been something wrong with *him.*" The editorials ascribe the failure to thrive to a lack of effort. Not to confuse Hansberry's depiction of individual becoming with unfettered agency, she makes clear the inequivalence of the "mere possession of" " 'imagination' and 'industriousness' " and "the possession of capital itself."[36] She explains that although filled with talent and aspiration, he remains constricted by economic structures infused with racism.

In a bold rhetorical move, Hansberry then situates her midcentury moment as a part of a waning history, unsustainable in its waste. Placing the modern era in a longer time frame, she describes the racist-social order as a "moment," and says, "A rather handsome fellow [Stanley]. American as the streets around him. . . . Yet, for one insane historical moment, a garment district cart pusher is the only place he has been able to find in his still racist and chaotic social order. The only place for one who wanted to 'build things.' It is a moment which must, before the waste is too enormous, be rapidly put to death."[37] Her essays elaborate the principles underpinning her dramatic work—the site for her crafting alternative possibilities for the present and enlivening histories that have not, in fact, past.

Hansberry's work as an artist enabled her to come to terms with her own desires as personal, political, and potential sources of possibility. Similar to her essays, Hansberry recovers the past in her poem "Ode to Edna St. Vincent Millay," in order to historicize her same-sex desire. The subject of Hansberry's praise poem and the inspiration for her short story "Renascence," Edna St. Vincent Millay, was well known among modern artists as a feminist poet who also helped to advance experimental drama. Millay lived in Greenwich Village and helped found the Cherry Lane Theatre. She was a popular figure as well as a Pulitzer Prize–winning poet, and the Harlem Renaissance poet Countee Cullen wrote a research paper about her work.[38] She also served as a fitting subject for Hansberry's poem about lesbian community in New York, because Millay was bisexual. In the poem, Hansberry describes young women, lit by the sign of a local theater, gathering "along the streets of the village," "Booted and trousered and barbered." Hansberry salutes Millay for her ability to transcend conventions of sexual orientation. She commends Millay for being a "Lover of long hair and the sweetpea blush." Hansberry finds her deserving of praise because she does not conform to the stereotype of a "dyke," cower from the violent regulation of sexual desire, or reconcile herself to loneliness.[39] Hansberry's poem reveals her efforts to situate her gender expression within midcentury conventions of sexuality. She turns to a fellow artist for a road map of how to use the tools of their craft to aid in presentation, self-exploration, and examination. Even when venturing into relatively unchartered waters, she did not presume the given expression of same-sex desire to be the totality of expression.

In a more reflective mood, around the same time that Hansberry wrote "Ode to Edna St. Vincent Millay," she penned an essay, "Queer Beer," that takes on some of the questions about self-fashioning that she alludes to in the poem. Hansberry understood the developing sense of her sexuality as not only a pursuit of personal freedom but also a historical project necessary for Black people becoming free. She opens the essay: "About five years ago I sat down to write an essay on homosexuality. Quite just like that. I was twenty-five years old about, married a few years, entirely uninvolved in—but utterly preoccupied with the subject. So I sat down and wrote about it. Tonight I cannot find those pages; they are somewhere among my papers and perhaps, as this little essay grows, I will come across them and quote from some of my more outlandish ideas of that time. Outlandish they were because I hadn't the foggiest notion in the world what the life of a simple practicing homosexual was like, not to mention what I subsequently discovered to be 'the gay life.' "[40] Hansberry admits that she had contemplated homosexuality since at least the age of twenty-five. It seems, however, that her success or maturation enabled her, five years later, to address a subject in her writing that she admits frightens her. Her writing as a freedom practice becomes a space to learn bravery. But as Hansberry suggests in her poem, her life in the Village also offered her a tutorial that allowed her to take up subjects in her writing and explore relationships in her life that would expand her political vision.

In "Queer Beer," Hansberry notes that like an anthropologist, she sits at her window in the Village and watches people coming and going from the gay restaurant across the street. Through observation she learned stereotypes that align sexuality with certain modes of presentation or appearance do not hold. She concludes gender is a performance and not constituted by sex or sexuality; a revelation that would not take hold in American popular culture until the late twentieth century. She notes her method of observation first: "At the time that I mention above [five or six years ago], I lived directly across the street from a fairly well-known Village restaurant. A gay one. My 'research' on the subject consisted of sitting at my window for hours, truly hours, at a time and watching who went and who came from that establishment; and, as a matter of fact, I did learn some things: [crossed out: Things which have been deepened from more reasonable experience—that is to say more immediate experience] . . . Right off . . . I observed that the stereotype, once again in life, failed as much as it succeeded in the way of truth. . . . To be specific: I quickly lost a prior assumption with regard to the male homosexual . . . that he was, in appearance, queer."[41] In Hansberry's reflection on her observation, she reveals visual presumptions fail her. Her expectations, set by the world around her, do not align with what she observes from her apartment window. The setting of her research not only helps to establish Hansberry's early theorization of gender, sexuality, and their troubles but also the ways she saw norms as a reflection of social and economic systems.

Hansberry's radicalism called for the shifting of bodies because she knew their shape reflected economic conditions. She also understood that the everyday instantiation of certain attributes, socioeconomic and physical, calcified historical positions. Within the theater, she shows the quotidian force of gender and heteronormativity regulated through social expectations; Beneatha and Iris, for example, cut their hair in *A Raisin in the Sun* and *The Sign in Sidney Brustein's Window*, respectively, to claim ownership of their bodies. The scenes also reposition each one within systems of desire that threaten their viability, according to their family members, as wives.

She challenges the idea of a biological impulse to reproduce and again, as in her review of *The Second Sex,* troubles gender as innate. Hansberry also likens the impulse to regulate queer desire to the drive toward self-regulation or mastery. She says, "It is probably true that all human creatures are aware of the homosexual impulse and that, consequently, are aware of its force in the face of society's quite clear and ever articulated present attitude. Therefore those who indulge have assumed a liberty and if they are not punished then why are the rest of us torturing ourselves from time to time? One must suppose that the socially adhering resent the lack of punishment for the non-adhering and that the detestation of the homosexual is really as simple as that."[42] The idea of disciplining oneself or others serves to forestall the threat of change that would adhere in a free society. Just as the characters in *The Drinking Gourd* are not ready to face a world disordered by freedom, Hansberry suggests the desire for mastery reflects the internalization of unfreedom.

Returning to an anthropologically inflected voice at the end of the essay, which exists along a spectrum with realism and draws similarly from the world-making force of the form, she begins to describe the lesbians that she knows, drafting character sketches. The document ends with a list of "ladies" and "gentlemen" that could potentially serve as sources for future writing. The lists also produce a community of men and women. Although Hansberry intimately felt the isolation of celebrity and of being a Black lesbian in the mid-twentieth century, she took active steps to forge intimacy in the absence of social contexts; her sketches serve a similar purpose to her efforts to work in community through her letters to *The Ladder*. She wrote to produce personal and political belonging.

The influence of the anthropological gaze reemerges in Hansberry's musical adaptation of Oliver La Farge's novel *Laughing Boy*. The novel depicts a couple of Native American star-crossed lovers who long to be together. The protagonist, Laughing Boy, first encounters the woman who will be his wife, Slim Girl, at a dance. The attraction is instantaneous and Laughing Boy runs away with Slim Girl despite the protestations of his uncle, Wounded Face, protests that other family members share over time. Soon Laughing Boy realizes that his family's reservations merit consideration. He finds that his wife, who has been educated in American schools and, until meeting Laughing Boy, lives alone in a modern house, affords her lifestyle because of a sexual relationship she sustains with a white man named George. Although the lovers reconcile, at the end of the novel, another one of Slim Girl's former love interests shoots her out of jealousy and she dies. The novel raises questions about integration and assimilation that resonate with *A Raisin in the Sun*. The structure of the novel, however, offers greater insight into why Hansberry would attempt to adapt this text into a musical.

La Farge used his training as an anthropologist to tell this story, spending significant portions of the novel focusing on the performance of rituals and the patterns of interaction that may seem foreign to a white readership. La Farge majored in anthropology and graduated from Harvard in 1924.[43] His approach attended to the specificity of the community he represented and allowed for the redemption of a woman who would be discarded in U.S. culture. Hansberry's use of observation as part of her evolving practice of freedom calls attention to how she sought to recalibrate looking as a mode of domination that permeated the regulation of Black and queer people.

Her engagement with La Farge's work reflects a writing practice that also emerges in her essay "Queer Beer" and her early work for *Freedom*. Through the work, focused on developing her skills of observation, she allowed herself to take stock of how she saw. These works often communicate the complexity of Hansberry's vision because they do not seek resolution or agency driven by a heroic protagonist. Hansberry's early engagement with ethnography and documentation as source material for her dramatic work demonstrates her understanding of how communal activities and the everyday action and coordination of bodies in motion shape reality.

In "Queer Beer," Hansberry extended a performative model of reflection that emerged in "Myself in Notes" and her adaptation of *Laughing Boy,* which she began in 1961. From Hansberry's time as a journalist to her staging of Black people in *A Raisin in the Sun* and *The Drinking Gourd,* she developed a way of looking that challenges the power of the normative gaze to put people in boxes. Theater became a fertile terrain for Hansberry because it served as a form in which the artist could explore double consciousness. Hansberry thought theater could serve an important function in justice work. As a performing art, it provided the opportunity to stage bodies in ways that limited the power of the white world to determine the value of the Black self. The operation of valuing and devaluing "one dark value" often occurs through visual transactions, as Hansberry described in her short story "The Budget" and theorized in "Queer Beer." She admitted the trepidation that writing about queer life in the 1950s caused her; fear and trepidation emerged repeatedly in Lorraine's personal writing. Although she had gained greater exposure by her early thirties, the social policing of gay life and culture, from the federal government to homophobia in the civil rights movement and the general conservatism regarding women's places in society, particularly middle-class women, rendered Hansberry isolated.

Hansberry's seat of analysis in the domestic sphere of her apartment sets up a central intervention of her essay, that her assumptions about lesbians did not follow her misapprehension of gay men because gay men circulated publicly in ways that lesbians could and did not. Moreover, she asserted: "The modern world has come to assume male homosexuality; almost everyone who writes of 'the homosexual' ultimately turns out to be writing about male homosexual. Society hardly regards the existence of women at all so long as women are not in some special way brought to society's attention."[44] Hansberry's observation expanded the domestic sphere to include lesbians, shifting the space that served as the basis of her fame and isolation.

Her writing also resists the impulse to center men as a necessary step to dismantle racial hierarchies set in motion through trans-Atlantic slavery. Undoing the damage of slavery requires undoing the economic, racial, and gender systems that emerge, as Hansberry demonstrates, in part through homophobia: "I imagine that the next great awareness of the liveliness of homosexuality in human experience will quite transcend national lines ('What? Not just the English?—But the Russians?') and a capitalist definition. It would appear that the 'freer' men become—the freer they become! Nowhere is this more acutely pointed to than in the question of female homosexuality."[45] Hansberry's keen attention to the relationship between gender hierarchies and the policing of sexuality helps to emphasize why lesbians pose a particular challenge to economic hierarchies.

As she suggested in her letters to *The Ladder,* economic insecurity functioned as a primary material prohibition for women in same-sex relationships in the 1950s. Hansberry detailed further in "Queer Beer" the necessity to reproduce, for the economic reason of providing a labor pool cultivated the taboo against homosexuality. She continued: "Man discerned early (and apparently universally) that the homosexual impulse was not anatural but natural and that, the problem of the perpetuation of the race being what it is, socially not personally regarded, something would have to be done. Thus it created a taboo that it needed then: the taboo against homosexuality."[46] Hansberry's description offers a theory of the relationship between the law and human behavior. Her understanding of how individual action functions in relation to the law and public policy informed her political theory and imagination as well as her activist work.

Just as Hansberry carefully depicted the instability of the institutions of slavery and family in *The Drinking Gourd,* she outlined here the historical contingencies of social and economic pressures that shape the family and cultivate gender roles. "All that must be considered at the moment is that the division of labor (the hunter and the sewer) is a barbaric idea truly—but that we are only now, apparently, rising ourselves out of the last stages of classical barbarism."[47] Hansberry makes the now familiar point about gender presentation being fluid and the economic implications of gendered divisions of labor and therefore material value. Equally important, she depicts the present as a horizon. Her installation of her period as a turning point summons new forms of communal and social organization that support the public visibility of same-sex desire. Her work calls for us to rethink bodies *and* embodiment as a necessary step to becoming free.

REFRAMING: *LAUGHING BOY* AND *TOUSSAINT*

Hansberry's self-exploration and studied consideration of identity required that she rethink the history of slavery and colonialism in the United States and in international contexts. Two unfinished works that she began writing in

1961, *Laughing Boy* and *Toussaint*, explore the impact of settler colonialism in the United States and slavery in Haiti, respectively, seemingly odd areas of exploration for a writer primarily known for representing Black American culture. Hansberry, however, had an expansive understanding of Black freedom struggles that linked independence movements in Africa, the Caribbean, and Latin America to the fight for civil rights in the United States and connected the struggle for women's liberation to that of Black people and those living in the global south.

From 1961 to 1963 Hansberry drafted an opera in three acts based on *Laughing Boy*, published in 1929. Similar to work by some of La Farge's Black contemporaries, most notably Zora Neale Hurston, *Laughing Boy* could be described as ethnographic literature. Focusing on modern Black writers' work, Daphne Lamothe wrote: "Ethnographic literature . . . shares many of the defining characteristics of ethnography, a genre that depends on method, namely fieldwork, to produce a narrative that simultaneously invents and documents a culture."[48] Hansberry had long been interested in the intersection between documentation and invention. Her fieldwork consisted of her participation in activist movements, which she recorded in writing and through sketches. For example, when she visited Montevideo, Uruguay, in March 1952 to serve as a delegate for the Inter-Continental Peace Congress Conference, she captured her experiences in notes and sketches. Hansberry used the drawings to document her perception of the speakers. She depicted men and women representing different parts of the world. Her drawings attempt to supplement the narrative with a trace of the physical presence. The body emerges in her documentation through the drawings, and her annotation of some of the images with the word "worker" helps to emphasize how her radicalism emerges at the intersection of materialism as a representational, embodied and economic position.

Hansberry also translated her notes into her own ethnographic literature. In an untitled and unpublished short story, she depicted Austin, a man traveling to a peace conference in Montevideo in place of his wife Edna. Reversing the gender roles in Hansberry's experience, in the story, Edna's passport, like Robeson's, has been revoked because of her peaceful demonstrations against the government. Edna explains, "Oh something perfectly ridiculous. The Government says I'm a 'security risk.'" Austin, driven by his desire to please his wife even though he feels ambivalent about going to Uruguay, also travels after she reminds him that "the reason our house is empty of the noise of grandchildren" is because their only son died fighting in Europe.[49] The story produces the connective tissue between the freedom fights during and after

Two women, pen drawing on paper by Lorraine Hansberry, 1952 (Permission to use images of artwork by Lorraine Hansberry granted by Joi Gresham)

Argentine worker, pen drawing on paper by Lorraine Hansberry (Permission to use images of artwork by Lorraine Hansberry granted by Joi Gresham)

Pan Am pilot, pencil drawing on paper by Lorraine Hansberry, 1952 (Permission to use images of artwork by Lorraine Hansberry granted by Joi Gresham)

Campesino de Uruguay, drawing by Lorraine Hansberry, 1952 (Permission to use images of artwork by Lorraine Hansberry granted by Joi Gresham)

Trinidad, is there work in the States? drawing by Lorraine Hansberry, 1952
(Permission to use images of artwork by Lorraine Hansberry granted by Joi
Gresham)

World War II, reestablishing the necessity of intra- and extra-state action to Hansberry's activism. It also draws attention to how Hansberry's process of documentation expounded on her political activities.

The work of crafting a narrative based on observation also translated into self-reflexive work. Throughout her life, Hansberry produced sketches that captured her perception of the world around her. Among them are self-portraits that draw attention to the difference between her public image and the one she sought to produce. In a sketch from 1959, Hansberry presented a handsome version of herself in profile. In a deep serious stare, her appearance does not bear the marks of her youth or the glamour that became associated with her image. In a simple and more abstract sketch from her hospital bed in 1964, she again foregrounded masculine physical characteristics. She did not emphasize the softness of her cheeks or jaw or the mirth sometimes captured in photographs of her smiling. The self Hansberry captured posed a challenge to singular understandings of gender, offering an invitation to herself and for those that meet her in the archive.

Hansberry's adaptation of *Laughing Boy* allowed her to experiment with the manipulation of the gaze as it functions in anthropological studies and theatrical production, what Richard Schechner calls "between theater and anthropology."[50] Using the well-worn story of the hooker with a heart of gold, *Laughing Boy* offered some specific insights into Navajo culture. The protagonist Laughing Boy tries to redeem Slim Girl, who has been corrupted through her exposure to U.S. culture. They are able to make a life together, but ultimately the sins of her past catch up with her, and she pays for her indiscretions with her life. On first analysis, given Hansberry's political investments, the choice to adapt an early-twentieth-century novel about Native Americans written by a white man who studied anthropology seems an odd choice. Coming from a wealthy family, La Farge assisted Tulane University professor Frans Blom on an expedition to Central America in 1925. La Farge also visited the southwestern United States in 1921, 1924, and 1926, which served as an inspiration for his writing.[51] His training equipped him to capture the customs and practices that make the novel specific.

Hansberry's choice to adapt the novel into an opera places emphasis on the storytelling through song and, in this case, choreography. Moreover, her engagement with ethnographic literature helped her clarify how bearing witness could forge political solidarities across geographical distances. Hansberry's work rehearses the rituals depicted in the novel, which in both texts serve to disrupt and specify the love story. Stage directions depict an early encounter between Laughing Boy and Slim Girl at a dance, where the young

Self-portrait, pen, ink, and watercolor drawing by Lorraine Hansberry, March 1959 (Permission to use images of artwork by Lorraine Hansberry granted by Joi Gresham)

Self-portrait, University Hospital, ink drawing by Lorraine Hansberry, May 1964
(Permission to use images of artwork by Lorraine Hansberry granted by
Joi Gresham)

women form a processional before the men. Slim Girl stands out "at the end of the line" because "she wears more jewelry and darker clothing than the others. And her dancing seems less sincerely shy." The dance continues and each young woman, flirting, pulls on a blanket covering a young man. The young man then must pay a small amount of money to be released from the woman's grasp. Laughing Boy notices Slim Girl watching him and initially rebukes her but she "breaks away suddenly from the line and races around behind him, in the direction he is not looking, and gives his blanket a violent sudden pull, almost toppling him."[52] She continues, causing laughter from the other young men, until she removes the blanket completely and Laughing Boy must follow her to retrieve it. All of the interaction between the two of them occurs without narrative. The playful courting scene requires Slim Girl to act in excess of gender norms exercised by the other young women in the line. At the same time, the stage directions suggest she performs for Laughing Boy and the community by participating in the ritual in the first place; "her dancing seems less sincerely shy" but not insincere. The subtle disruption through movement emphasizes how theatrical presentation actively participates in shifting the power of the white gaze to capture brown bodies. Inter- and intra-culturally, Slim Girl's performance situates meaning making as a negotiation that invents and documents culture.

As Schechner observes, the roles of the participant and the observer alter in the case of performance, which assumes an audience. Under other circumstances, an anthropologist may assert control over the community he or she studies, but in the observation of a performer "multiple selves coexist in an unresolved dialectical tension. Just as a puppet does not stop being, at some level, his ordinary self when he is possessed by a god or playing the role of Ophelia."[53] Hansberry's experimentation with choreography in *Laughing Boy* reemerged in *Les Blancs* through another transgressive woman character. Understanding Slim Girl as a precursor to the dancing figure called "the Woman" in *Les Blancs* offers important insight to Hansberry's conception of decolonization including settler colonialism in the United States. Hansberry's choreography in both works suggests women of color must make use of physical movement to challenge the alienation of the cultural order that attempts to freeze them in time and place or to reconcile them to certain spaces. Similar to *The Drinking Gourd,* Hansberry depicts women on the move; such movement amounts to a form of fugitivity, movement outside the law.

For Hansberry, working to reform the law and the state required the action of the outlaw. Her practice benefited from the statesperson *and* the outlaw working together to reconstruct American democracy. In 1961, she completed a draft of a scene from her play *Toussaint*. She never completed the play about the revolutionary figure, but she did present a finished version of the scene on May 21, 1961, for the educational television program "Playwright at Work." Margaret Wilkerson published the scene in *Nine Plays by Black Women*, a collection published in 1986. The production of the scene in 1961 followed several years of Hansberry contemplating Toussaint. In "a note to readers" dated December 1958, she wrote:

> I was obsessed with the idea of writing a play (or at least at that time even a novel) about the Haitian liberator Toussaint L'ouverture when I was still an adolescent and had first come across his adventure with freedom. I thought then, with that magical sense of perception that sometimes lights up our younger years, that this was surely one of the most extraordinary personalities to pass through history. I think so now . . .
>
> What the Haitian slaves accomplished under the leadership of the Steward of Breda is a testimony to purpose and struggle in life. They who were slaves made themselves free. That is not, to argue with current vogues, a tired cliché of romanticism. It is a marvelous recognition of the only possible manner of life on this planet. L'ouverture was not a God; he was a man. And by the will of one man in union with a multitude, Santo Domingo was transformed; aye—the French empire, the western hemisphere, the history of the United States—therefore: the world. Such then is the will and the power of man. Perhaps this is the secret of the greatness of humankind.[54]

The ability for a man with a multitude to change the course of history motivates Hansberry's beliefs, politics, and aesthetics. Hansberry aligns life, "the only possible manner of life," with the enslaved's pursuit of freedom; through the pursuit of freedom, Hansberry locates the purpose of life.

In 1958, the Nemiroffs received a postcard from Lonnie Bunch, who was visiting Haiti. The card noted an interest in the nation's history that Hansberry shared with other Black intellectuals and artists.[55] In March 1959, the violinist and composer Clarence Cameron White, considered one of the finest classically trained African American musicians of the early twentieth century, wrote to Hansberry to congratulate her on *A Raisin in the Sun* and inquire if she would send him a libretto for his work in progress.[56] Hansberry responded that she did not have a libretto ready and wondered if press reports of her interest in writing a contemporary opera had prompted his letter. She affirmed the reporting and explained that she planned to soon return to her work on L'Ouverture, which at the time she imagined as an opera. She also noted that he might have an interest in the work given his composition of an opera about Haiti, *Ouanga* (1932). She wrote: "It will not treat of the revolution as much as the personality who guided so much of it. I find in Toussaint L'ouverture a genuinely inspiring historical personality whom I should imagine will lend dramatic stature to the piece. I am quietly excited about this project, for which reason I try to discuss it as little as possible publicly. After a couple of years of looking around I have selected as my musical associate a young Negro composer of talent and imagination, Mr. Alonzo Levister. I hope by mid summer the two of us will be hard at work on our thus far untitled project."[57] In June 1959, the Black actor Davis Roberts sent Hansberry a letter offering her a list of readings that he found useful in his studies of L'Ouverture.

Although the scene performed in 1961 shifts from a libretto to realist drama, it reflects Hansberry's intention to focus on personality. Similar to *The Drinking Gourd*, however, the scene attends to the conditions that produce revolutionary personality rather than the heroism of the figure himself. The scene depicts the Great House of a sugar plantation in Santo Domingo in the 1780s, "immediately before the outbreak of the Haitian Revolution." In the house, the plantation manager, Bayon de Bergier, and his wife, Lucie, prepare for a party. Similar to *The Drinking Gourd* and Hansberry's adaptation of Charles Chesnutt's *The Marrow of Tradition*, the play takes place on the brink of historical change and also ponders the question who and what a 'master' might be. The setting of the play draws attention to how Hansberry offers a feminist version of material historicism through the focus on the domestic sphere and the attention to the negotiation of power dynamics in everyday interactions.

Similar to the characterization of Hiram in *The Drinking Gourd*, Bayon shows the limits of being a master of someone who does not and will not concede to being a slave. Toussaint does not speak in the scene, and only appears through reference. His presence, however, structures the interaction between Lucie and Bayon and demonstrates how race, gender, class, and ethnicity position individuals in a power structure that shapes perception and insight.

Bayon and Lucie's living quarters open to the world of the plantation through a sound: "There is the sudden crack of a whip off-stage and the piercing cry of a human being in terrible pain. The minuet halts for the merest fraction of a moment, and then resumes as a second and third cry are heard." A person howling in pain cuts through and rearranges the lush classical music that infuses the atmosphere. Lucie responds to the incursion, charging, "Toussaint is a brute." Defending his lieutenant of sorts, Bayon corrects, "He is a steward and an excellent one." Lucie wonders, given Bayon's reliance on Toussaint, "What would become of the plantation if he ever ran away, Bayon?" Showing his blind spot, Bayon explains, "He never will. He is content. He does his work and I give him plenty of leisure for his walks in the woods and his little mumble-jumble business. That is all that he requires for his personal contentment. Toussaint has his own sense of the order of things."[58] Bayon reveals more than he knows. Indeed, Toussaint does have his own sense of the order of things. It does not, however, include answering to a white master for the rest of his life or serving as his overseer.

Unsatisfied by Bayon's explanations, Lucie asks a critical question that helps to crystallize Hansberry's investment in exploring slavery as a trans-Atlantic phenomenon that shaped modern understanding of personhood, personality, and identity. In response to Bayon's assertion, "I have tried to explain to you again and again that [Toussaint] is not a slave," Lucie asks, "Well, is he free?" The conversation that follows helps to pinpoint how the system of slavery inscribes racism within capitalism and, at the same time, produces sexual economies.

BAYON No, he is not free either.

LUCIE Then he must be a slave. If you are not one then you must be the other.

BAYON It is a special situation. You are a woman, you cannot understand it.

LUCIE (*With deliberate wide-eyed innocence*) Oh, but explain it to me, Bayon. I will try very hard to understand it. And explain about yourself. Are you a free man, Bayon?

BAYON Of course I am a free man.

LUCIE Then why haven't you left Santo Domingo long ago? That is what you have wanted more than anything else for a long time—to be running about Paris. What is it that keeps a free man where he does not wish to be? Tell me, what is freedom, Bayon de Bergier?

BAYON As an abstraction that is something that no one can answer. Least of all, these days, a Frenchman. (*The cries intrude again; but the minuet continues and presently fades under.*)[59]

Lucie's inquiry draws its force from her early inquisition about Bayon visiting the grave of a formerly enslaved women with whom he had sex. The conversation emphasizes how the role of the master, in a pure capitalist sense, would be a tyrant primarily driven by extracting as much labor as possible from the enslaved. Lucie pinpoints, "Could it be possible, Bayon that if Toussaint knows how to command men, not merely slaves . . . that he may command even you?"[60] The figures in Hansberry's dramas about slavery, however, prioritize personal interests, sexual and otherwise, over economic ones. Similar to Hansberry's manipulation of looking in her short stories for *The Ladder* and *One,* she used theater and film to demonstrate how individuals usurp the power of the gaze, which is installed through social position, by leveraging the inefficiencies of desire. Hansberry understood that connection and the pursuit of intimacy motivated people to act in ways that often overwrote their economic interests. In accounting for how to motivate social change, she turned to art, in part, because it combined the "sighted eyes and feeling heart."[61]

In the scene from *Toussaint*, Lucie's social position as a creole woman, a mixed-race woman, enables her to understand the limitations of Bayon's reliance on his imagined contented slave. It serves Bayon's ego to think of Toussaint as satisfied because such a characterization does not require him to contend with his own ethical implication in a system of domination. It also allows him to look away from how that system makes men and women available to him for not only economic labor but sexual labor too. The latter produces the conflict between the couple. Throughout the scene, Lucie draws attention to the limitation of Bayon's point of view. She acknowledges that her position in Bayon's house exists on a spectrum with the enslaved, saying, "A creature purchased is a creature purchased! To dress one in laces and sit her at the head of your dining board is no true index of value! Nor is it an index of the daily, hourly humiliation of my awareness of the bastard legions roaming this plantation—opening and closing doors for me; waiting at my tables—playing minuets in my own home! My own daughters have more cousins and brothers than beaus in Santo Domingo."[62] The intertwining of familial relationships extends the implications of this domestic drama, because, as with the cries of pain that interrupt the curated conditions of the household, so too does the thin barrier that separates who lives within the frame of family and who does not. One could understand the battle for desegregation that raged in the United States as Hansberry wrote this play as a familiar sign of the ongoing legacy playing out on and lingering just offstage.

The dynamic of inside and outside, manufactured through sound and allusion, specifies Hansberry's domestic drama as a political commentary on the domestic and the inability of patriarchal capitalism to remain outside its doors. The scene ends with a tense interaction between Lucie and an enslaved woman, Destine, tasked with helping the mistress prepare for a dinner party. The stage directions read: "(She [Destine] goes on stolidly massaging the flesh with her face fixed like a mask, as the light converges on mistress and slave, and the minuet and the cries of human pain continue . . .)."[63] Destine's exercise of what Darlene Clark Hine calls dissemblance allows her to infiltrate the mistress's inner sanctum.[64] Similar to Rissa, Destine participates in the life world of the domestic sphere proper. Distinctively, the realist setting of the domestic sphere in the play spreads its tentacles into the world of the plantation and finds the brutality of slavery permeating the careful arrangement of the sitting room. In an episode of WNET's *Playwright at Work*, Hansberry discussed her work on the opera *Toussaint* and explained, "An oppressive society will dehumanize and degenerate everyone involved—and in certain very poetic and very true ways at the same time it will tend to make if anything the oppressed have more stature—because at least they are arbitrarily placed in the situation of overwhelming that which is degenerate—in this instance the slave society so that—it doesn't become an abstraction. It has to do with what really happens to all of us in a certain context."[65] Similar to her conception of death, Hansberry had an intimacy with domination that she channeled into the sitting rooms and private space of her characters.

"MYSELF IN NOTES"

In November 1961, Hansberry took stock of her thirty-one-year-old self in notes. Her list of likes included:

Dinah Washington as much as ever
Beethoven as much as ever
not having to get up and go out mornings to work
finishing something
. . .
coming out of the tailspin of profound emotionalism
African dance
Haitian culture
. . .
Dorothy
. . .
to sleep well
to have an appetite

Her likes far exceeded the things she was bored with or disliked. Her likes echoed things she appreciated in the past and drew attention to her ongoing struggle with the practice of freedom. Hansberry's work and meditation about her work demonstrate a deep investment in the feminist project of perpetual change and persistence as necessary and integral to producing moments of rupture. At the same time, she often grew frustrated with the pace of change and her own inability to arrive at a solution or a finished piece of writing. Hansberry's work, much of which remained in process at her death, caused her much consternation. It also functions as a challenge to activist-artists in the present to take up and engage with the horizon that she set. Instead of understanding her work's value in relation to its completeness, her political challenge requires us to understand the work left to be done as a central feminist mandate that repositions the autonomy of the author and considers work as a communal rather than individual process. Even in *A Raisin in the Sun,* the alternative endings leave room for producers, directors, actors, designers, and scholars to interact with her work. The collaborative process, after all, may be why Hansberry found her primary home in theater, because it requires revision, rehearsal, and return. The ongoing process of working through demonstrates the complexity of being free and not a contradiction.

Chapter 4 The Movement

As Lorraine made use of her fame to transition from playwright to screenwriter to public intellectual, a group of students in Greensboro, North Carolina, mobilized. In February 1960, four Black college freshmen from North Carolina A&T, who would later call themselves the Student Nonviolent Coordinating Committee (SNCC), sat down at a segregated Woolworth's lunch counter and requested service.[1] Their act of resistance transformed a publicly segregated space into a civil rights battleground. In taking up space, the students sought to transform their overall relationship to the nation and the nation itself. In many ways their occupation of Woolworth's reversed the logic of settler colonialism. Instead of asserting cultural or social superiority to claim space, they occupied a public space by exercising an unevenly enforced U.S. principle—equal protection under the law. Their act of civil disobedience also called attention to a larger question of who has the right to own and occupy space, given the U.S. history of Native American genocide and slavery. Their act of claiming space, similar to the occupation that Hansberry endured as a child and that she depicted in short stories and referenced in *A Raisin in the Sun,* made a foundation for Black people to repair the spatial dynamics established in response to the Great

Migration and the demands of segregation. If the students, like Hansberry, planned to embark on a project of reconstructing Black people's relationship to space (both public and private), they had to consider, to quote Bonita Lawrence and Enakshi Dua, "out of whose land would the '40 acres' be carved?"[2] The action surfaced a set of ethical dilemmas about the difficulty of collaboration, the dangers of political and personal intimacies, and the potential for betrayal.

Two months after the sit-in, activists formed an organization under the tutelage of long-time civil rights leader Ella Josephine Baker. She gathered the students from North Carolina A&T with other activists for a conference at Shaw University in Raleigh, and began to train them to be change agents. Having served as the executive secretary of the Southern Christian Leadership Conference and a field secretary for the NAACP, Baker brought a deep history of political organizing to the burgeoning organization of young activists. From experience, she knew how to structure an organization democratically. For these students, community superseded the individualism usually associated with the male-dominated leadership of older generations of the civil rights movement.[3] As such, they were ripe for Baker's tutelage.

Baker anticipated that these students had the potential to challenge some of the perceived wisdom about civil rights organizations. "SNCC members tried to live their politics by avoiding hierarchy and seeking unanimity in decision making. In their commitment to civil disobedience, grassroots organizing, decentralization, and consensus politics, and in their willingness to put their bodies on the line for their beliefs, this 'beloved community,' as SNCC members called themselves, took a moral philosophy and turned it into a political force."[4] The SNCC activists sought to build an organization that worked at the intersection of the secular and the sacred and that produced interracial community as a temporary response to civic estrangement and a source of social belonging.

Although Hansberry's formal relationship with SNCC would not coalesce until 1963, the political thought that laid the foundation for the collaboration began in 1960 with SNCC's formation and Hansberry's contemplation in essays of how interracial collaboration would inform the movement. Her commitment to working across difference also served as the ethical foundation for her understanding of how America could heal its ailing democracy. Hansberry's essay writing from 1960 to 1963 crystallized her investment in collaboration as a practice that could emerge through encounters and across difference. Collaboration necessitated foregrounding the good of the whole over individual achievement. It also required intimacy and vulnerability rather than competition. Collaboration, Hansberry's writing suggests, enables a rethinking of America and American democracy, making room for radical politics that reform how Black people appear in space and reconstruct the spatial dynamics that restrict the movement of Black people (from the plantation to the ghetto).

The principles that organized the SNCC coincided with Hansberry's political commitments in the early 1960s. She and the organization knew that Black people had to reclaim the South as a fundamental step in finishing the work of Reconstruction. That reclamation required a coordinated effort led by activists on the ground. It also demanded a rethinking of the idea of America. These two things—grassroots leadership and the making of a new American myth—must work together to redress the failures of Reconstruction and the ongoing injustices of segregation.

By 1963, Hansberry's political commitments never strayed far from material demands. In April 1963, she was diagnosed with cancer. A little over a month later, in the midst of the Birmingham campaign, she and a group of civil rights activists organized by James Baldwin, including Jerome Smith, Lena Horne, Harry Belafonte, Rip Torn, and Kenneth Clarke, met with the U.S. attorney general, Robert F. Kennedy, at the Kennedy family's apartment on Central Park South to discuss "the Civil Rights issue" in general and school desegregation in particular.[5] Kennedy wanted to understand "the new anger of the masses and the inability of Negro leaders to dampen it." The meeting called attention to the distinction between how the group of activists conceptualized the practice of democracy and the way the attorney general saw it. After several minutes of bureaucratic exchange, Smith, a member of the Congress of Racial Equality and a Freedom Rider, broke through the malaise to state the stakes of the meeting. Having suffered beatings for trying to integrate bus facilities in McComb, Mississippi, Smith spoke from experience. "The Negro masses knew who was on the line, said Smith, and the real trouble would come if those who had been willing to die became disgusted with nonviolence. 'When *I* pull the trigger,' he said, 'kiss it goodbye.' "[6] The friction between armed self-defense and nonviolent action reemerged as a threat to and of the movement.

Kennedy again registered genuine surprise when Smith said that he would not fight for the United States as a part of further Cold War military action.[7] In an article for *National Guardian*, "Miss Hansberry said the Attorney General was visibly shaken. 'He said something like, "I don't see how any American could refuse to fight for our country." ' At his response, Miss Hansberry said: 'Every Negro in the room said, "Oh you don't?" ' "[8] The incommensurability of perspective reflected Kennedy's understanding of citizens' primary allegiance being to the nation. He could not understand how actions taken in the name of the U.S. government served as an affront to many of its citizens.[9] For the Black people in the room, they could not understand why he would meet with them if he thought the nation had completed the project of reconstructing America in the wake of slavery. They felt that the paradoxes and contradictions at the heart of American society, epitomized by segregation, required redress in order to, to quote Baldwin, "achieve our country, and change the history of the world."[10]

Taking an ethical stand, Baldwin described how the group asked Kennedy to persuade his brother, the president, to escort a young Black girl to a segregated school in the Deep South. " 'That way,' we said, 'it will be clear that whoever spits on that child will be spitting on the nation.' He did not understand this either. 'It would be,' he said, 'a meaningless moral gesture.' 'We would like,' said Lorraine, 'from you, a moral commitment.' "[11] Hansberry foregrounded the intersection of ethical and political concerns that emerge when civil rights bleed into human rights. Terrence L. Johnson argues: "The problem . . . is one with a uniquely spiritual dimension. The crisis of anti-black racism remains a crisis because it is driven by *internalized* moral beliefs but executed within the primarily *external* world of politics."[12] Hansberry's request confirms how the attorney general's decision imparts an ethical compass for the country. Or, as Jackie Robinson described the outcome of the meeting, quoting a schoolteacher, John F. Kennedy "would like to be right. But he'd rather be President."[13] The activists could not convince Bobby Kennedy of the need to make a statement that would affirm the common humanity of all U.S. citizens and to halt the degradation that occurs when one person spits on another one.

Unmoved by the request or the accompanying explanation, Hansberry sought another line of argument to persuade the attorney general to intercede personally in desegregation efforts. She recalled in a speech given at a rally to support the Congress of Racial Equality (CORE) in June 1963 in Croton-on-Hudson that, although Robert Kennedy chose to meet with a select group of men and women, the movement extended beyond the so-called spokesmen and women. She said:

> It was when, during the genuine heat of the discussion—after Mr. Smith had indicated to Mr. Kennedy that the passion and the absence of patience of a sorely oppressed, native American people is beyond anything that we can sit around and be polite about anymore—the Attorney General exhibited impatience. And it was at that juncture—and feeling free that I was speaking for every single Negro

Flyer for the Congress of Racial Equality's Rally to Support the Southern Freedom Movement, June 16, 1963 (New York Public Library) and indeed white ally in that room—that I suggested that Mr. Kennedy re-examine his impatience, because while there might be in that room some of the celebrated figures of whom we all know . . . the qualitative change in the struggle for Negro freedom was that we are not, any of us, remotely interested in the all-insulting concept of the "exceptional Negro." We are not remotely interested in any tea at the White House. What we *are* interested in is making perfectly clear that between the Negro intelligentsia, the Negro middle class, and the Negro this-and-that, we are *one* people. And that as far as *we* are concerned, we are represented by the Negros in the streets of Birmingham![14]

In the conversation with Kennedy and elsewhere, Hansberry affirmed her commitment to mass and collective movement for change, which depended on understanding Black people as a collective and on hearing the voices of the student activists. She understood that carving out space for a few Black people to have access to social and economic privileges would not result in an egalitarian society. Black exceptionalism (the presentation of the success of a few talented Negroes as evidence that all should be able to transcend structural inequality), as history has shown, reinstalls the logic of American exceptionalism while masking the pervasive impact of racism. Although Hansberry's family joined a mass migration of Black people that left the south in pursuit of greater freedom in the north, her play *The Drinking Gourd*, showcases the nation's unfinished business there. The business entailed making greater space for Black radicalism. Hansberry's assertion does not erase the plurality of the people; rather, it establishes their commitments. The SNCC also sought in the early 1960s to carve out such a space predicated on mutual understanding and connecting across difference, and consequently emerged as the "confrontational arm of the Civil Rights Movement."[15] Through its occupation of space, the SNCC staged encounters that sought to transform the South.

When the two forces met—Hansberry and the SNCC—both had spent years in deep reflection on the impact of bearing witness to the movement through word and image. Together they formed a photo essay, *The Movement,* that grew out of Hansberry's larger aesthetic project to represent blackness with fidelity to the principles and histories that not only contextualized it in her present but also gave it vitality in the future. *The Movement* opens by taking the reader on a journey to the Mississippi Delta, where the story of America as a mass struggle for redemption begins. This is not the first or only site of America's formative violence in settler colonialism and slavery. The first few images capture instead the source of a movement for democratic possibility that fully acknowledges the myth of American exceptionalism. The images then chronicle the economic developments of the United States through

Rural road running into Yazoo, Mississippi, 1964, site of the Freedom Vote
(Photograph by Danny Lyon, courtesy of Magnum Photos)

industrialization and systems of oppression: prisons and segregation. This serves as the basis for the emergence of the SNCC. The remainder of the volume chronicles direct action on the part of activists through the arts, protests, and quotidian forms of resistance.

Hansberry and SNCC activists also believed that they had to package their protest for American audiences. Following Mamie Till-Mobley's decision to have an open casket for her son Emmett Till in 1955, SNCC and Hansberry thought that if they were able to show the nation what it did to its sons and daughters they could produce social change and ease civic exclusion. "The Emmett Till lynching, in 1955, received a different kind of press coverage, extensive coverage that was new in America."[16] Showing required documentation of events with evidence, compelling evidence.

Hansberry produced modes of realism that often centered the physical form. Her realism, however, did not take for granted, as is common in the European tradition, the verisimilitude of representation. She approached realist representation as a mode to reveal the truth of Black people to white audiences that often stubbornly strove to see blackness as an aberration. Hansberry's work on *The Movement*, and her artistic practice in general, advanced from "the desire to have the cultural product solve the very problem that it represents: *that seeing black is always a problem in a visual field that structures the troubling presence of blackness.*"[17] Given the need to reshape form and field, Hansberry's work took a dual approach to myth making. Her activism challenged the shape of the field in which her art emerged. Her curation of activist-art institutions and her relationships with fellow artists and producers attended to the delicate connection between structure and embodied modes of production.

After *A Raisin in the Sun*, Hansberry faced competing pressures that informed her public appearance and presentation. Although there were aspects of her life that she kept private, she remained committed to using her platform to elevate the voices of people working on the front lines of freedom movements. She saw her commitments to mass movements for justice as corollary to her aesthetic choices. According to Rebeccah Welch, "In a letter to Hoyt Fuller, the editor of *Negro Digest*, for instance, she outlined her inclinations toward popular venues: 'As far as I am concerned there is no audience worth writing for (or otherwise producing for) other than the popular one.' Hansberry continued, 'I regard myself, and ever will do so, as a "popular" writer. I am aware that the artists in the world hold that as an epithet: to me it is the supreme tribute, as I know of no achievement or development in the history of world literature, drama, painting, film that was not evolved out of the process of communication with the broadest base of "the people."'"[18] In claiming the moniker "popular writer," Hansberry ushered forth "those forms and activities which have their roots in the social and material conditions of particular classes; which have been embodied in popular traditions and practices," in the words of Stuart Hall.[19] Popular culture stands in tension with dominant culture, drawing attention to how power relationships produce domination. This push and pull of popular—"forms and activities which have their roots in the social and material conditions of particular classes"—and dominant culture specifies the nature of Hansberry's artistic practice and how it served a political purpose. Attentive to the need to focus on process, product, and means of production, the idea of creating one's own media informed Hansberry's commitment to popular writing. This investment emerged in her work as a journalist at *Freedom* and resonated with SNCC activists.

Diane Nash, a student at Fisk University who helped organize sit-ins in Nashville, Tennessee, in 1960, served as one of the founding members of SNCC. Her penchant for self-determined forms of representation characterized how the group's political commitments coincided with a cultural agenda. She said, "If we object to the way the media is covering something, then we know that the media is controlled by the powers that be. It has very limited use to let the media or the government or whomever know that we don't like it. They know that we don't like it already. The idea is, decide what you need and do it yourself. Take matters into your own hands and do it yourself." The ability of civil rights activists to claim power through news coverage of Black freedom struggles intensified in the 1960s, with independently run outlets framing themselves and their experiences. Nash recalled, "And if you remember when television came, black families had begun to see leaders from Africa. They had heard about the Algerian War, which was still raging at the time of the sit-ins—one million Algerians had been killed in a struggle with the French for control of their own country."[20] Nash's comments suggest the circulation of media not only framed the efforts of activists for wider American audiences, but also provided a blueprint of possibilities inspired by struggles for independence abroad. Although some viewed the sit-ins "as an outgrowth of racial assimilation and as an expression of the desire for further assimilation," the direct action of college students served to prepare them for other acts of militant resistance.[21] It also demonstrated the power of bearing witness, through the documentation of their activities, as an act of solidarity and a scene of instruction.

According to scholar Rebeccah Welch, Hansberry cut her teeth integrating art into activism during her work with the Civil Rights Congress. Welch explains that William Patterson, the executive secretary of the CRC and office-mate during Hansberry's days at *Freedom,*

> believed that most people were "visually minded," and he considered it generally difficult to present a full and clear appreciation of the issues to a wider public "through lecture and discussions alone." As a result, he actively encouraged cultural performances of CRC initiatives. Experienced in theater, many young writers were asked specifically to contribute dramatic work to the campaigns. Writer and theatre historian Loften Mitchell remembered attending rallies "first as an usher, then as a script-writer," a pattern of apprenticeship that matched Lorraine Hansberry's experience. In numerous meetings to agitate or raise money, Hansberry was asked to compose or direct a short piece, or was called upon to give a reading.[22]

In the 1950s, Hansberry's involvement with the CRC corresponded to her work for *Freedom* and served as a training ground for her as an artist and activist. This earlier period also prepared Hansberry to take center stage as a public intellectual—a role that, of all her roles, would prove most difficult to fit. The public wanted the beautiful middle-class housewife, while her publics, those she sought to serve, needed a leftist Black radical.[23] In an often circulated image from the *New Yorker* in May 1959, Hansberry sits next to her desk, her arms cradling herself.[24] She appears youthful, nonthreatening, and erudite, with papers strewn about her typewriter and taking up much of the frame in the foreground. Her platform, unfortunately, depended on appearing as a housewife and not a radical.

THIS IS AMERICA

The photographs in *The Movement* and the narrative arc of the photo essay show how to build a multiracial collaboration steeped in trust. Hansberry sought collaboration rather that coalition. Coalition forms when two different and distinct preformed groups come together to work toward a common goal while maintaining their distinctiveness. Collaboration requires risk and intimacy because it entails coming together to make something new. Coalition meets collaboration in the rehearsal room that is for but is not the revolution. Hansberry learned how to collaborate in the offices of *Freedom,* at Camp Unity, and through the production of *A Raisin in the Sun.* Her work as an activist shaped the collaborative dimensions of her art. The documentary mode of *The Movement* returns to skills of observation she nurtured as a reporter in the early 1950s, as a queer cultural witness from her windowsill in her Village apartment, and through her adaptation of *Laughing Boy.* For over a

Photograph by David Attie for *Vogue Magazine*, April 1959, at 337 Bleecker Street

decade, Hansberry laid the foundation for her vision of a democracy steeped in mutuality. A radical idea in the context of American individualism, Hansberry's idea of what American democracy could be is revolutionary if we think of radical change as women's work that happens in the interval between the fires this time. If we think of revolution as shifts in consciousness of people that prepare for the next time the world cracks in two, the perpetual infrastructural work of women qualifies.

Photography, similar to realist drama, uses devices to frame subjects in order to encourage a particular way of looking. "For a grassroots organization like SNCC, photography proved especially important as a means to position the group," according to Leigh Raiford.[25] SNCC photographers sought to frame the organization politically, physically, and spatially in order to democratize the South. The photographs offered insight about how to intervene in hostile territory and transform the individual's relationship to that space and, therefore, the social order. Positioning shapes the body and its relationship to space. Nicole Fleetwood argued, "A dialectical concept of visual culture cannot rest content with a definition of its object as the social construction of the visual field, but must insist on exploring the chiastic reversal of this proposition, *the visual construction of the social field.*"[26] As a collaborative photo essay, *The Movement* gives form to and highlights the body as form. It also frames spaces (roads, trains, cars, and pulpits) to establish how activists intervened in the regulations that produce the built and organic environment.

SNCC knew that the battle for freedom required gaining material as well as philosophical ground. The organization not only fought for local inclusion in the public sphere through voter registration drives, for example, it also sought to challenge the history of American exceptionalism. Danny Lyon, a white student who attended the University of Chicago and joined the organization as a photographer, explained, "I think for the record it should be clear that SNCC had its own media. I was the media of SNCC. I was what would become a profession: a photojournalist, a film maker, an author, but I was SNCC staff. In other words, they were telling me what to do, I was fighting them off trying to do it the best I could, but the result was SNCC was turning out its own propaganda and SNCC was trying to control the media and create its own mythology and it did it. Now the word 'myth' here was completely intentional. There was a legend of SNCC. These are legendary people."[27] Lyon's comment explains the radical philosophical work of SNCC to produce its own myths but also, through its work, transform the idea of America.

A fundamental U.S. myth, American exceptionalism advances the possibility of an individual being able to move from rags to riches within a single generation through hard work and the exercise of democratic possibility. American exceptionalism does not account for structural barriers to ascension, such as racially restrictive lending practices or housing covenants. Offering a different model of uplift, SNCC sought communal modes of advancement that did not focus on individual achievement. By the time Lyon left the organization in 1964, he was one of twelve photographers. Having multiple people in the role increased the scope of their work and addressed the singularity at the heart of Lyon's claim that he "was the media." For SNCC having any "one" undermined their political goals.

Lyon joined the organization after traveling to Cairo, Illinois, as Raiford described, "to photograph another civil war."[28] Activists at the time hoped the student movement could complete the work of realizing an American democracy that acknowledges but does not depend on recapitulating its ties to slavery.

A student of history and photography, Lyon saw the SNCC's activities as a justice movement in his time reflecting a historical juncture similar to the one photographer Mathew Brady covered in the Civil War. Through the intertwining of word and image, *The Movement* offered a mode of reconstruction predicated on reshaping the south and the bodies that occupy the territory.

Hansberry, also seeking to rethink how America thought of itself, crafted origin stories that exposed the distortion at the core of American democracy and called for a more egalitarian system. Her work, in all its manifestations, sought to reframe Black people, and, as a result, rethink their worlds. Such work required capturing Black people within the filmic frame and deploying the skills of Black women's fugitivity to practice freedom in the trap. Lyon began taking the photographs that appear in *The Movement* in 1962. In that time, from 1961 to 1963, Hansberry too began to amass a set of materials that sharpened her insight and clarified her aesthetic and political vision. When the two came together, Hansberry and SNCC, they produced a photo essay drawing from civil rights organizations' deft use of media as a means of advancing their political vision and Hansberry's refined understanding of how she could function as a spokeswoman of, not for, Black people.

The Movement opens with a reverse migration similar to the one that Hansberry describes in her journals and appears in the introduction to *The Drinking Gourd.* It begins with an image of a long road taken from the base of a steep hill shrouded by trees. The opening shot suggests movement but not necessarily movement backward. Although the image is of the rural environment that northern migrants left, it also depicts elevation, going higher, ascension. The next few images depict now quintessential markers of the old south: a pastoral plantation with a "big house," a monument, and the racial violence of lynching with white people old and young, happy and stern, looking straight at the camera. The photographs begin the story of the movement in the south with racial violence. They call to mind a long history of Black freedom struggles that reached a significant turning point during the Civil War.

The progression of the narrative in *The Movement* suggests Black Americans must reclaim and redeem the south in order to move forward as a more democratic union. "Although the civil rights movement of the 1960s, particularly in the South, was often fought over Jim Crow laws requiring segregation in schools, parks, buses, and other public accommodations, these battles were fought within the context of racially divided cities whose social geography had been shaped, at least in part, by city planning," Charles E. Connerly argued. Zoning laws and racial covenants become the expression of settler colonialism to determine the use and value of land based on racial histories. As Connerly explained in *The Most Segregated City in America,* "At its roots, city planning is about controlling the land—most directly about what uses land is put to—but also, at least indirectly, about who gets to live on the land and where. From its earliest days, city planning and its primary regulatory tool, zoning, have been used not only to determine land use but also to protect property values and keep out or restrict groups of people whose presence was not desired by those in power." Zoning laws helped to install the conceptual framework of settler colonialism via segregation. As with the history of settler colonialism, vigilante justice supplemented the law. In the 1950s and 1960s, when Black residents attempted to integrate white neighborhoods in Birmingham due to the low inventory of housing in Black neighborhoods, violence followed, resulting in the city's designation Bombingham.[29] Birmingham was not alone in its double-pronged approach to maintaining segregation after the Supreme Court's second ruling in *Brown v. Board of Education* that explored how to implement school desegregation.

SNCC and Hansberry sought to change the conceptual framework that shaped spatial arrangements in the South. In *The Movement,* Raiford explained: "The photographs gave form to the multiracial, integrated, and just society SNCC participants were risking their lives to create. In this sense then, SNCC photographs served as both performances of liberator possibility and as documents of democracy in action."[30] The lens shapes the figures as their work gives shape to a movement.

Similar to SNCC, Hansberry's clarity about the interlocking relationship between economic structures and political ones informed her choice to work in representational modes, in particular making use of the body. She knew that acts of imagination, forms of myth making, enabled America to pretend that its greatest conflict had nothing to do with racial domination. She also knew that myth making required labor, an ongoing practice that emerged through the body. In January 1961, Hansberry discussed with James Baldwin, Langston Hughes, Nat Hentoff, Alfred Kazin, and Emile Capouya the ongoing significance of the Civil War, in a radio symposium called "Integration into a Burning House."[31] The title calls into question how the Union army sought to maintain the U.S. house that race built.

At the symposium, Hansberry marveled at the ongoing litigation of the Civil War. She made the case, as in *The Drinking Gourd,* that the inability to come to terms with America's past informs perceptions of "the Negro." Echoing Du Bois, she described how the Negro creates a problem for American democracy. To reclaim the south means to draw forth the formative violence of America as a nation founded in settler colonialism and racial domination.

Drawing together the relationship between settler colonialism and slavery in a reflection dated July 4, 1954, and titled "Yankee Doodle," Hansberry established Native American music as the first American anthems.[32] She located the fundamental Americanness in songs of the colonized and enslaved. Hansberry's comments at the symposium suggest that becoming free in a U.S. context requires claiming the insurgency that the nation demands for its survival. She said, "the Negro question, does tend to go to the heart of various and assorted American agonies beginning with slavery itself. And I am so profoundly interested to realize that in these hundred years since the Civil War that very few of our country men have really believed that their federal union and the defeat of the slaveocracy and the negation of slavery as an institution is an admiral fact of American life."[33] If the Union's victory were to act as a repudiation of slavery, Lincoln's reconstruction would have also required a renunciation of racial hierarchies and therefore segregation. The ongoing legislation of the Civil War through the civil rights movement evidences an unwillingness to see the negation of slavery as a laudable fact of American life.

In the symposium, Hansberry offered two other insights that describe how slavery participates in advancing capitalism *and* how America functions as an act of imagination. Turning to the liberal mood that enables national amnesia of the nation's founding in racial violence, she says, "We've been trying very hard, this is what Jimmy and I mean when we speak of guilt, we've been trying very hard in America to pretend that this greatest conflict didn't even have at its base the only thing it had at its base. Where person after person will write a book today and insist that slavery was not the issue. You know they tell you that it was the economy, as if that economy were not based on slavery, but it's become a great semantic game to try and get this particular blot out of our minds."[34] To fully face capitalism as a racial manifestation that interlocks with American democracy shakes the very foundation of Americanness. The redemption of the nation relies on capitalism and democracy being at odds. One may hear in Hansberry's statement echoes of W.E.B. Du Bois. In *Black Reconstruction*, Du Bois wrote: "It was thus the black worker, as founding stone of a new economic system in the nineteenth century and for the modern world, who brought civil war in America. He was its underlying cause, in spite of every effort to base the strife upon union and national power."[35] Following Du Bois, Hansberry insisted that democracy as enacted in the United States supports and perpetuates racial capitalism, which in the words of Cedric Robinson, "expropriated the labor of African workers as primitive accumulation. American slavery was a subsystem of world capitalism" furthered through its representative democracy.[36]

The extension of the American myth of democratic possibility emerged through the morphing of slavery into racial capitalism under the guise of liberalism. At the symposium Hansberry noted, "Now, when all those millions of Americans went out only a month or two ago and voted for a federal president presumably in a culture which does not respect the fact that if the North had not won, the union forces had not triumphed over slavery that this country that we're talking about would be a lot of imagination and Americans today are ashamed and frightened to take a position even on this."[37] In winning the Civil War, the Union incorporated the racial domination within as a defeated and yet thriving component of its constitution. Segregated spaces in the south, from schools to lunch counters to neighborhoods, demonstrated the unfinished business of the Civil War. As Hansberry well knew growing up in Chicago and living in New York City, race predetermined space from north to south. Hansberry's collaboration with SNCC on *The Movement* sought to address the particular ways the racial violence associated with the South determined Black people's economic, spatial, and symbolic positions.

Continuing the narrative of American economic ascension as a function of rather than in spite of structural racism, the images that open the pages of *The Movement* chronicle the economic developments of the United States through industrialization and systems of oppression: prisons and segregation. The photographs show the bleak conditions written all over the faces of children. A close-up of a young white boy sits above a portrait of a group of Black children standing on the porch of and playing beside a rural home. Taking up the majority of the layout, an image of industrialization spans a page and a half, and features a young child in the bottom right corner. Children skirt the edges of the scene, humanizing and calling attention to the future impact of economic choices. Hansberry captions, "The New South Slams up against the Old, but the coming of industry into the Southland has not changed the problems of many of its people—white or black—for the better."[38] In her view, a violent juxtaposition that functions as a continuation of the past is not a new day, not reconstruction.

SEPARATISM

Although today it is difficult to imagine an alternative economic system to capitalism, in 1960, the world weighed its options. In 1959, the Cuban revolution, led by Fidel Castro, resulted in a socialist Cuba. Additionally, much to the dismay of the British and American empires, 1960 marked the year of African independence. Mary L. Dudziak writes: "Between January and

November of that year, seventeen African nations achieved independence. A total of twenty-five former colonies on the continent had now been liberated. Eighty more would follow while Kennedy was in office."[39] The fierce winds of the Cold War spurred on desires and freedom dreams of Black people. Days before John F. Kennedy took office in January 1961, Hansberry remarked, "What are we faced with. We are faced with the fact that due to these three hundred years of the experience of black people in the Western Hemisphere, not only the United States, that a possible difference of ultimate cultural attitude now exists as a reality. So that there are the tones now of Negro nationalism articulated in a far more sophisticated and pointed way than perhaps years ago. Where the question is openly being raised today among all Negro intellectuals and among all politically conscious Negros . . . is it necessary to integrate oneself into a burning house?"[40] Hansberry describes a widespread consideration among Negroes of political systems that do not depend on Black people to resuscitate America or the idea of democracy. She understood this questioning as a part of an international conversation that puts pressure on American exceptionalism, which underpins the operation of U.S. democracy. Her comment underpins the debates about integration or segregation that drove James Baldwin's *The Fire Next Time.* Hansberry, similar to Baldwin, opted to continue with the American experiment, believing that the mass movements of Black people around the world had the potential to redeem America too.

Situating herself squarely within the fight for Black liberation through self-determination, Hansberry's participation in the radio symposium on January 20 was one appearance among many that she advocated for Black people becoming free by any means necessary. Her assertion of these ideas, ones that she expressed in her writing for *Freedom,* made it more difficult to reconcile the public self she crafted through her speech acts with her media image. Hansberry evidenced the national and international scope of what she called "the movement" in the next sentence of her comments, saying, "There are real and true things existing in the consciousness of Negroes today that have to do with why on two different occasions the Negro delegate of the United Nations will disassociate herself from her government when we refuse to vote for Algeria, an Algerian Algeria, when we refuse to vote for the end of colonialism, that the most compromised element from which these people are drawn, otherwise they wouldn't be allowed to represent us, when they are moved to disassociate themselves in an international hall."[41] The United Nations not only functioned as the site of international governance—it was the same body that denied the CRC redress when it petitioned for oversight of the United

States in 1951 with its document "We Charge Genocide." And even within that body, a body presumably motivated to maintain the status quo, the case for African independence resonates. Hansberry's comments weave domestic struggles into global Black movements for spatial justice. The Algerian war for independence from France began in 1954 and ended in 1962. In the symposium she acts as a witness, documenting the case for Black freedom as a necessary step to impede mundane violence of white supremacy passed off as routine governmentality.

Just a few months before Kennedy's election and Hansberry's radio symposium, in September 1960, the U.N. General Assembly hosted Fidel Castro and the Cuban delegation. Castro's speech noted the U.S. government's interference with his travel, which resulted in him moving from the Shelburne Hotel in midtown Manhattan to Hotel Theresa in Harlem.[42] While in Harlem, Castro met with "foreign leaders—like Soviet Premier Nikita Khrushchev, Egyptian President Gamal Abdel Nasser, and Indian Prime Minister Jawaharlal Nehru—as well as American civil rights figures, such as Malcolm X, New York NAACP President Joseph Overton, and, according to some reports, Jackie Robinson," journalist Steven Cohen notes.[43] In recalling Castro's visit, Hansberry offered a glimpse into Black Americans' attraction to independence as an essential part of reconstruction—a nation stripped clean of its reliance on racial domination to support its economic system. She explained, "And when 10,000 Negroes will come out to greet Fidel Castro in Harlem and wave at him and cheer him every time he shows his head, this is an indication to our country this dichotomy is going to become more articulate and we are going to see it more and more in Negro literature."[44] White and Black Americans had different perceptions of international affairs. Hansberry's final prediction, "we are going to see it more and more in Negro literature," connects a conversation about integration versus separatism to the arts, her central space for working through politics. Hansberry, like Baldwin in *The Fire Next Time*, contemplates the allure of Black separatism. Her own positioning, however, inside and outside several communities, likely limited her ability to totally embrace it. Her comments do, however, demonstrate the necessity of imagination to radical freedom projects. Activists claimed space and with artists imagined ways to transform it.

Although Hansberry deeply understood the motivation behind separatism, her political work and friendships included interracial and class collaborations. In January 1960, around the same time that SNCC formed into an organization, Hansberry considered collaborating with Daisy Bates. Returning from a recent visit with the Nemiroffs in their Waverly Place apartment, Daisy wrote to Bob and Lorraine to thank them for the hospitality they showed her and her husband, L.C., during a recent visit to New York. In 1957, as the leader of the NAACP branch in Arkansas, Bates prepared nine students, later known as the Little Rock Nine, to desegregate Little Rock Central High School. Three years later, Bates continued to field interest from reporters about her involvement in civil rights struggles. Her participation in desegregation efforts also brought her to the attention of the State Department, which enlisted her as an official host to Mr. Abubaker Mayanja, from the Nationalist Party of Uganda.[45] After catching her friend up to speed on the last forty-eight hours' whirlwind of activity, Daisy focused on the matter at hand, Lorraine's help with Bates's memoir.

The collaboration began as a piece focused on Little Rock that Lorraine volunteered to do for free. Daisy insisted that Lorraine reap half of the royalties and encouraged her to visit Little Rock "to get a feel of the story. Tell Bob that he is also invited and that I will double the guards." She also named the bureaucratic dangers, noting that the publisher would be responsible for defending "libel suits." By February, Hansberry's chronic self-doubt and overwhelming aspirations dampened her interest in co-writing the memoir. Bates wrote Hansberry a letter urging her not to give up on the project. Daisy appealed to Lorraine's Marxist investments by mentioning how the book would answer the criticisms of uneducated and intellectual Blacks alike.[46]

Hansberry ultimately did not collaborate with Bates on *The Long Shadow of Little Rock: A Memoir,* but the correspondence evidences a friendship rooted in the shared investment of intraclass collaboration that deeply understood the legal, physical, and material risks of participating in the movement. In a letter from February 1960, Bates reported that the home of the youngest member of the Little Rock nine, Carlotta Walls, was bombed. Materializing the danger of spatial justice efforts, the students faced the battle for integration in the public schools and the privacy of their homes. The danger evidences the necessity of reclaiming space as a fundamental part of the civil rights movement. It also calls attention to the central role women played in such efforts.

Hansberry cultivated political friendships that served as the basis for her practice of freedom. Through her political relationships, which often also held the intimacy of friendship, she explored the possibility of challenging racial violence within intimacy. For Hansberry, the act of being in relation (physically, historically, politically) held the potential for change. In an essay titled "1961 Dialogue with an Uncolored Egghead Containing Wholesome Intentions and Some Sass," Hansberry staged a debate between a Black and a white intellectual. She had participated in such debates since the production of *A*

Raisin in the Sun and, although she often left such events feeling depleted, she understood the latent possibility such encounters hold. The essay called attention to one of the political processes that theater helped her to ascertain, the encounter. A mode of relation, the encounter enables peers to meet on equal footing in open and honest dialogue with the hope of greater clarity and, not necessarily, resolution. The debates she staged in her writing use encounter to produce intimacy and, hopefully, mutuality. The interracial and intraracial encounters in the essay emphasize the idea of relating across difference to challenge the appeal of separatism.

Following World War II, artists and activists debated the virtues of assimilationism versus Black nationalism, and these debates only intensified as African nations gained independence. "Dialogue with an Uncolored Egghead" stages a conversation between a "colored" woman and a first-generation white German male intellectual. The essay begins with the Uncolored Egghead criticizing the Black intellectual's propensity to forge interclass coalition by "affecting the speech and inflections of the Negro masses." In response, the Colored Egghead retorts, "Let me inform you, *liebchen,* that we colored intellectuals use the idiom and inflection of our people for precisely the same reason. We happen to adore and find literary strength and vitality, sauciness and, sometimes, sheer poetry in its forms."[47] Making use of folk history informs Black cultural production from the nineteenth century to the twentieth and has particular implications for how blackness functions as a political and aesthetic category in the mid-twentieth century. Hansberry saw neither the United States nor blackness as stable uniform categories that should serve as the basis for political striving. She understood that just as America functioned as an idea, so too did Black nationalism. Hansberry's investment in Black independence movements reflected her abiding call for a reorganization of power relations that enabled individuals to have greater freedom from constraint. She did not, however, understand blackness as a uniform characteristic and, rather, understood Black people as having a shared history that informed contemporary political organizing and cultural production. Therefore, Hansberry willingly collaborated across class and racial lines because she understood the permeability of these categories and pinned her freedom dreams on their proliferation.

Hansberry saw the possibility for collaboration among Africans, Asians, and American Negroes through a shared commitment to anti-imperialism. In the essay and in her drama, she suggested that the fulfillment of such reorganization requires robust political debate that demands a sober understanding of domination as a key feature of empire and its manifestation in American democracy. Although the conversation draws to mind arguments about Black cultural production and politics from the early twentieth century, the Colored Egghead makes a striking assertion that situates the conversation in national feeling after World War II. Lawrence P. Jackson adds, "Hansberry basically rubbed against high modernists whose intellectual brush with the world seemed to have left them convinced mainly of the permanence of despair."[48] She asserts:

> What has induced the melancholy other than the collapse of empire? Despite his occasional obtuseness on other questions, Camus was remarkably explicit in asserting that the only obligation of the million Frenchmen in Algeria is to grant the eight million Arabs "justice"—not national independence. . . . When Camus writes of man he means subjectively, Western man, as you do. That is the worst provincialism abroad in the world today; it is the most intense parochialism. I am grateful that my evolution in America permits me alienation from its seduction, for at best it is disastrous. . . . Perhaps that helps you to understand why the gloom and doom of so much of Western art and thought which so captivates you leaves me cold. Africa and Asia and American Negroes . . . are in anything but states of collapse or decay. On the contrary, they are in the most insurgent mood in modern history.[49]

The midcentury debates over race and how it informs coalition emerged in the context of states reforming themselves and enriching sets of insurgent international political relationships. For Hansberry, the fight for Algeria was part of a global fight for Black independence that challenged models of empire predicated on the spatial logics of the plantation and the ghetto. The battles over space, whether private, local, or national interrelate to produce a unique set of possibilities in the mid-twentieth century for freedom from interference.

Hansberry's essay stages a dialogue between a Black woman and a white intellectual who shares views with Hansberry's Black counterparts, including E. Franklin Frazier and Fanon. The imagery prioritizes the debates to emphasize how the exchange among Black artists holds the potential for the highest form of democratic possibility because it produces a new mode of meaning making. Conceding to the Uncolored Egghead's point about the lure of middle-class ascension, the Colored Egghead situates the participation in middle-class accumulation as a brief and insignificant moment in a progression of history toward a time when the folk figure "Bilbo would be on one mountain shouting 'You ain't!' and Charlie Parker would be on another, blowing his saxophone, answering in a million notes, 'I am!'?" The call and response typifies the form of Hansberry's essay. It also offers a vernacular mode of creation, situating jazz as the instantiating articulation of world formation. The Colored Egghead says of the exchange between Bilbo and Parker, "There is great lyrical imagery in that ... But do you know, we are going to go beyond even that eventually; reach on up where our assertions or identity don't require Bilbo's negations. Oh yes! It's going to come gently, and beautiful like the sweetness of our old folkways; going to spill out and over the world from our art, like the mighty waves of a great spiritual ... "[50] Hansberry suggests that encounter provides the possibility to move beyond the negation at the heart of Black identity formation in Fanon's configuration. The insurgent mood enables revolutionary politics and modes of thought that do not abandon or find history constraining.

By the end of Hansberry's essay the sound of the song "No Ways Tired" drowns out the voice of the Uncolored Egghead. The end does not suggest he has no place in the world renewed with insurgency but rather his renderings of blackness appear illegible in such contexts. His place then requires a rethinking of the relationship between blackness and freedom in the context of the end of World War II and the mounting challenge to empire. By the end of the essay, Hansberry shifts focus from mourning man's inhumanity to man, rendering it, as a consuming preoccupation, a cop-out from confronting the melancholy associated with loss of imperial power.

Hansberry staged interracial and interclass encounters in her drama as a way to work through the negation that Fanon placed at the heart of blackness. Similar to the staging of interracial encounter in James Baldwin's 1962 novel *Another Country*, Hansberry's fictional accounting sought to arrive at a truth too dangerous to emerge in public conversation. In order to bring to public view what remained hidden in private, Hansberry had to use her imagination. She found in the theater a space to challenge the alienation often associated with Black identity from Du Bois's theories of double consciousness to Fanon's depictions in *Black Skin, White Masks* by placing unfamiliar people or ideas in familiar settings. Similar to her own seeming misplacement on Broadway, she knew setting activated appearance. The way into the interior required an integration of her experience as an American insider—Broadway darling—and perpetual outsider—Black lesbian woman. In the public space of embodied exchange that is theater, Hansberry could say what public debate left unsaid in order to get at the truths that prevented any true communion across race or class lines. Hansberry's art functioned as a space of communion and encounter in which characters work through moments of misrecognition in order to develop freedom practices.

Encounter served as a crucial device to examine the distrust that would ultimately doom SNCC's interracial collaboration, that threatened the integration efforts of the civil rights movement as early as 1960, and that enabled the misapprehension of Hansberry's activism as fundamentally about integration. Drawing from the long history of theatrical enactment of the democratic through the staging and elaboration of public debate, Hansberry not only depicted encounter as an opportunity to work through political quagmires that served as stumbling blocks during the civil rights movement, she also produced criticism that furthered public debate about the shortcomings of American democracy.

Hansberry distinctively tapped into the theoretical ideal of democracy without overlooking its corruption in America. Her writing captures the specific U.S. operation of intertwining democracy with capitalism and, therefore, slavery. Nevertheless, Hansberry's investment in the democratic seeks to draw forth the fundamental investment in free and open debate that includes the voices of women and people of color. In this context, encounter becomes a site of possibility for communion rather than an opportunity to shut down discussion.

In *The Movement*, encounter takes on much higher stakes because the images capture the state violence meted out for nonviolent protests. Civil rights activists seeking to integrate schools, public pools, and housing faced angry mobs and police. The photo essay captures the close historical proximity of the March on Washington and the Sixteenth Street Church bombing in Birmingham in 1963. The day after the bombing, Hansberry wrote in a journal entry, "My own heart is filled with a passion for sheer vengeance. I imagine that the solution is Negro counter terror."[51] Hansberry's response resonates profoundly with the more well known reaction of her friend and partner in struggle, Nina Simone. After hearing the shooting, as Salamishah Tillet writes, Simone went in search of her gun. After failing to manufacture a weapon from scrap materials she gathered, she wrote the protest anthem "Mississippi Goddam." The rage Hansberry called counterterror helps situate the experience of Black people living in the United States for hundreds of years. The threat of death looms large for Black people and takes on a particular sting when exercised on children. Hansberry's diary entry shows a less popular but certainly circulating part of Black radical thinkers and activists' response to encountering physical violence—retribution. This line of thought emerges in Malcolm X's writing and the Seven Days, the organization that Toni Morrison imagined in *Song of Solomon* (1977).

(RE-)VISIONING AMERICA

The violent response to nonviolent protests, from the early days of the movement to the mid-twentieth century, made activists explore the merits of self-defense. In *The Movement*, to illustrate the long history of Black assertion,

Hansberry quoted Reverend Theodore Parker, a Boston abolitionist, writing in 1850, "I have in my church black men, fugitive slaves. They are the crown of my apostleship, the seal of my ministry. It becomes me to look after their bodies in order to save their souls. I have had to arm myself. I have written sermons with a pistol on my desk, loaded. . . . You know I do not like fighting. . . . But what could I do?"[52] Parker's church became an underground space that participated in reforming the coordinates of freedom and unfreedom. He communicated the necessity of self-defense as his vocational responsibility. Holding out hope for nonviolent solutions, the end of *The Movement* depicts the necessity of all modes of resistance.

Hansberry suggests that the remedy to America's racial nightmare is a true reckoning with what the nation would have to change about itself to live up to its creed. She suggests that change will come in two forms: a more active populace, and a plural democracy. In a fourth-wall-breaking gesture, she commanded her readers, "The next time you pass a demonstration, hum a little or clap your hands, pick up the words. Perhaps the time after that you will join in and sing—for my freedom and for yours. You, I mean you, my countryman, reading this." Through direct address, Hansberry stages an encounter with her readership that seeks to activate practices of freedom. The impoverishment of American democracy through racial violence, procedural or physical, limited all Americans. Drawing the reader into the movement, the volume then demonstrates what "the American vision can be."[53] Collective action, according to Hansberry, requires collaboration across difference.

The vision of America depicted in SNCC photographs includes a diversity of age, race, class, gender, religion, and sexuality. It shows individuals protesting, playing, and organizing. She ends, "They stand in the hose fire at Birmingham; they stand in the rain at Hattiesburg. They are young, they are beautiful, they are determined. It is for us to create, now, an America that deserves them."[54] Hansberry's collaboration culminated in a series of artistic works that sought to redefine America as a set of possibilities not in spite of but in full acknowledgment of its violent organization.

The framing of the movement distinguishes it from the media function of SNCC photographers in its early years. The volume represents a culmination and collaboration between an organization and artist, coming to clarity on the necessities of the movement. While individual photographs circulated widely as fund- and consciousness-raising tools, the volume as a whole helped to share the work of activists from southern rural communities with northerners. Hansberry knew from her experiences in Chicago and New York that reclaiming the south also meant transforming the north. The volume captures the work from 1960 to 1964 of an organization that shifted drastically from individual direct actions to coordinated local and federal efforts. The shift in action coincided with one in mindset. They came to realize, according to Clayborne Carson, the "need to challenge both the segregationist social order and the more moderate civil rights organizations." They embraced the term "revolutionary" to indicate the fundamental social reordering that democratic justice required.[55]

The ability to reconstruct the social order required coordinated collaborative efforts and, therefore, informed the nature of SNCC's protests and the way Hansberry positioned herself in the movement. Her dramatic writing became more explicitly radical after *Raisin*. Following the 1960 SNCC conference, organization members advocated that if they were arrested participating in nonviolent protest, they would not pay for bail. The jail-no-bail policy served to challenge the validity of a legal system that did not fully protect and acknowledge their rights. According to James Lawson, a leader in the Nashville movement, "the student protests were the start of a 'nonviolent revolution' to destroy 'segregation, slavery, serfdom, paternalism,' and 'industrialization which preserves cheap labor and racial discrimination.'"[56] The intimate relationship between prisons as a form of punishment *and* a mode of economic exploitation came starkly into view when Lawson exposed the criminal justice system as a front for the continuance of capitalist exploitation. The moral dilemma of the jail-no-bail stance could only be resolved by no jail and no bail, elimination of the system that ostensibly kept civil order but actually addressed economic demands.

The protesters learned, however, that their moral stance quickly lost momentum once they were locked behind bars and out of the public eye. As a result, Lyon traveled to Leesburg, Georgia, to document the protests. Fleetwood explains that in documentary photography, "(1) the photography is the historical document; (2) it stands in for the historical moment; (3) it provides evidence of a historical event; and (4) it frames the possibility of understanding a specific historical time period."[57] The image of the young women protesters cramped together in a dirty cell echoes an earlier image of a prison camp in Ruleville, Mississippi. In an image of a work camp, a guard occupies a large portion of the foreground and faces away from the camera. The men, hard at work shoveling and faces turned toward the ground, are difficult to recognize as individuals. The young women face the camera, eyes clear with open stances. Working together, the images produce a visual reckoning with abusive power that undermines democracy and challenges the American myth.

The Movement sequences a set of historical events to evidence an ongoing resistance to America's anti-blackness in the form of physical (lynching and

Young women being held in Leesburg Stockade after being arrested for demonstrating in Americus, Georgia, August 1963. Left to right, Melinda Jones Williams (13), Laura Ruff Saunders (13), Matie Crittenden Reese, Pearl Brown, Carol Barner Seay (12), Annie Ragin Laster (14), Willie Smith Davis (15), Shirley Green (14), and Billie Jo Thorton Allen (13). Sitting on the floor: Verna Hollis (15). (Photograph by Danny Lyon, courtesy of Magnum Photos)

fire hosing, and assaulting protesters) and structural (jail, segregation, and economic exploitation) violence. Hansberry links these acts of insurrection to the abolitionist movement. She writes, "The Movement is very old. It began in the seventeenth century when Africans being transported to the New World Mutinied on the high seas. Under slavery, it took the form of sabotage, escape and insurrection. It came to a climax in the Civil War, when thousands of black men and women fought for freedom . . . there has been virtually no institution of Negro life, from the churches to the blues, which has not had a fundamental preoccupation with freedom."[58] The grand historical narrative that Hansberry provides does not diminish her shared deep investment with SNCC activists in local, incremental change as the source to propel the movement forward.[59] It also references the sustaining aspect of artistic traditions that SNCC activists learned motivate community members. From 1961 to 1962, SNCC activists coordinated a series of protests in Albany, Georgia, for desegregation. The protests were ultimately unsuccessful, but as a result of the organizing, activists, Carson says, "became more aware of the cultural dimension of the Black struggle. SNCC workers in Albany, for example, quickly recognized the value of freedom songs, often based on Black spirituals, to convey the ideas of the southern movement and to sustain morale. Bernice Reagon, an Albany student leader who joined SNCC's staff, described the Albany Movement as 'a singing movement.' "[60] The use of song, image, and word sought to reshape the myth of America, as an idea and ideal as they informed material conditions.

Hansberry demonstrated her commitment to social change through grassroots activism and artistic innovation. Often this commitment produced a tension with her public image and the idea of a movement driven by celebrity. After showing the faces of well-known figures in the movement (A. Philip Randolph, Roy Wilkins, Bayard Rustin, Ossie Davis, Robert Moses, Dick Gregory, Dorie Ladner, Fannie Lou Hamer, James Forman, John Lewis, Gloria Richardson, James Farmer, and Malcolm X), the sequence of images closes with a woman and a girl. As with the volume as a whole, the photographs work together to demonstrate the diversity of recognizable leadership—gay, straight, male, female, Christian and Muslim, young and old—and to clarify that, according to Hansberry, "people don't always need poets and playwrights to state their case."[61] Although Hansberry felt comfortable serving as a spokeswoman, she consistently emphasized the importance of grassroots leaders making the case for justice.[62] In the first photograph, the unnamed woman holds her hands up in surrender. This stance has become a familiar gesture among twenty-first-century protesters in response to law enforcement's categorization of unarmed Black bodies as lethal weapons. The image captures an encounter and a moment of recognition that the desire and pursuit of freedom emerges through the everyday actions of citizens. Lyon writes in the description of the second photo that the girl participated in a protest in which a pickup truck hit her. The young girl with a slight frame and determination in her eyes functions as foot soldier in a movement that will only succeed if it sees her.

Hansberry shared with Baldwin a notion of radical movement work emerging out of communion. The risky intimate coming together of distinctive parts to make a new whole would serve to rupture if not explode existing forms of identity and social configuration. Hansberry's realism reflected her investment in a Black feminist radical tradition that drew from but did not remain beholden to the past. Her realism honors the young people who served as the foot soldiers of the movement, past and present. She wrote, "They stand in the hose fire at Birmingham; they stand in the rain at Hattiesburg.

Girl from a protest in Greenwood, Mississippi (Photograph by Marion Palfi, courtesy of Center for Creative Photography)

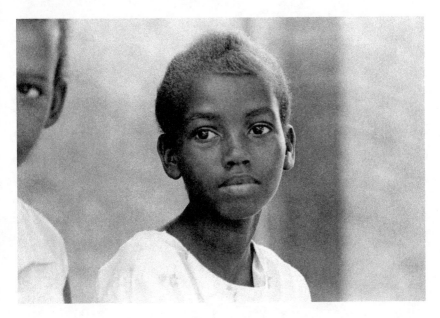

Civil rights demonstrator, Cairo, Illinois, 1962 (Photograph by Danny Lyon, courtesy of Magnum Photos)

They are young, they are beautiful, they are determined. It is for us to create, now, an America that deserves them."[63]

The period documented in *The Movement* traces political concerns that Hansberry and SNCC shared. It also captures the interracial collaboration that Hansberry benefited from and found herself wrestling with at the end of her life. Just as SNCC recognized the myopia of liberalism by the end of the organization's first phase in 1964, so too did Hansberry. She addressed that limitation in national and international contexts in *The Sign in Sidney Brustein's Window* and *Les Blancs*, respectively. *Sign in Sidney Brustein's Window* also provided Hansberry the opportunity to examine the impact of the Village culture that served as one of Baldwin's sites of inquiry in *Another Country*, a space for Amiri Baraka's political growth, a location for Ella Baker and others to gain education at the New School, and, ultimately, a neighborhood that perpetuated racial hierarchies and their violence.[64] The Village served as another site to consider reconstructing spatial dynamics as a fundamental part of becoming free.

Chapter 5   From Liberals to Radicals

The problem is we have to find some way with these dialogues to show and to encourage the white liberals to stop being a liberal and become an American radical.
—Lorraine Hansberry

Hansberry's collaboration with SNCC on *The Movement* builds on her signature style of realism, which allows powerful women to appear, open debate to unfold, and revolutionary action to transpire. Hansberry's investment in realism coincided with her desire to tell the truth about how domination distorts political, personal, and intimate relationships. In her essay "Genet, Mailer, and the New Paternalism," she critiqued the impulse to reduce Black movements for self-determination to imperialism in blackface. She wrote the essay in response to Norman Mailer's review in the *Village Voice* of Jean Genet's play, *The Blacks: A Clown Show.*

Mailer offered a critique of what he deemed the corrosive force of middle-class aspiration. Although beginning from a different starting point than E. Franklin Frazier's criticism of Black striving, Mailer's umbrage similarly reflected the inability to parse having access to resources and exploiting them.

Hansberry's political and artistic model of collaboration, however, sought to disrupt the domination at the heart of accumulation through a culture of sharing. Mailer lamented: "Let us leave the mediocre at this: the real horror worked on the Jews and the Negroes since the Second War is the mass-communication of nothingness into their personality. They were two of the greatest peoples in America, and half of their populations sold themselves to the suburb, the center, the secure; that diarrhea of the spirit which is embodied in the fleshless query: 'Is this good for the Jews?' So went the Jew. So went the Negro. The mediocre among them rushed for the disease."[1] Mailer questioned the assimilation of Black and Jewish people into an American culture of complacency but did not account for how Black people, in particular, disrupt the status quo. Even as Mailer called into question the impulse for Black people to aspire toward American articulations of the good life, he did not challenge the notion of American exceptionalism itself, but rather the desire for it of certain groups. Hansberry did not oppose Black people having access to "the good life." She questioned the apportioning of that life to a few elites through the exploitation of masses of others.

From the mid-twentieth century to the early twenty-first century, Mailer, an American best-selling novelist, journalist, playwright, and filmmaker, penned provocative essays that challenged general assumptions about political organization. He called himself a "left conservative," for example, because he found the work of Marx and his views on historical change and Edmund Burke's investment in cultural heritage compelling.[2] Mailer understood innovation as intimately tied to possibility in America.[3] He saw U.S. culture as uniquely positioned to move past the coffin-like confines of World War II and the Cold War. Co-founder of the *Village Voice* in 1955 as a cultural critic, he penned a career-defining essay, "The White Negro," that describes the experience of the "the American existentialist—the hipster." Reflecting on existentialism as a whole, Mailer's essay focuses on white Americans' orientation to life after the concentration camps.

> If the fate of twentieth century man is to live with death from adolescence to premature senescence, why then the only life-giving answer is to accept the terms of death, to live with death as immediate danger, to divorce oneself from society, to exist without roots, to set out on that uncharted journey into the rebellious imperatives of the self. In short, whether the life is criminal or not, the decision is to . . . explore that domain of experience where security is boredom and therefore sickness, and one exists in the present, in that enormous present which is without past or future. . . . The unstated essence of Hip . . . quivers with the knowledge that new kinds of victories increase one's power for new kinds of perception; and

defeats, the wrong kind of defeats, attack the body and imprison one's energy until one is jailed in the prison air of other people's habits, other people's defeats, boredom, quiet desperation, and muted icy self-destroying rage. One is Hip or one is Square (the alternative which each new generation coming into American life is beginning to feel) one is a rebel or one conforms, one is a frontiersman in the Wild West of American night life, or else a Square cell, trapped in the totalitarian tissues of American society, doomed willy-nilly to conform if one is to succeed.[4]

Conformity poses the greatest danger to life in Mailer's estimation. Drawing from a history of westward expansion, in Mailer's formulation, individuals must resist mandates from the past and cultivate new experiences in the present. The Hipster or "White Negro" extracts from Black experience, "living on the margin between totalitarianism and democracy for two centuries."[5] This precarity functions as the Negro's source of possibility, but Mailer's essay does not focus on Negroes. He attends to how Hipsters can draw from Negroes to pursue their journeys of the self. Although Mailer and Hansberry shared some overlapping concerns about the impact of the Cold War on artists' ability to create, they departed drastically in conceptions of how exceptionalism should inform life pursuits. Hansberry's art and activism challenged investments in exceptionalism. She did not consider Black people's striving for civil rights as a pursuit of Black exceptionalism but rather revolutionary change. Mailer, for his part, equated Black people's pursuit of self-determination as an investment in the conformity of American middle-class malaise that would threaten the history and ongoing potential of their culture contributions.

After *A Raisin in the Sun*, Hansberry participated in several public debates that shaped her as an intellectual. These encounters, whether in writing or in person, advanced the possibility of coming to a new understanding across difference. Hansberry's public engagement with Mailer drew attention to her larger critique of liberalism dependent on maintaining white privilege and the presumptions of egalitarian effort and access that underpin it. The very idea of modeling new victories on westward expansion or settler-colonialism seeks to reinscribe the imperialism that mass Black freedom movements challenge. Radicalism for Hansberry required that white liberals give up their idea of America as a space of equal opportunity born through rugged individualism and personal responsibility and form a new understanding of political struggle that accounts for a long history of exploitation. Hansberry's engagement with life in the Village and figures, including Mailer, at the center of the Village arts scene disrupted the feeling down that had overtaken downtown with the transformative vision of the civil rights movement. In 1959, examining the relationship between social and cultural movements, Hansberry asserted, "there's an affirmative political mood and social mood in our country. . . . I'd also like to see a parallel to it in terms of the culture of our country. I can see no reason in the world why the American theatre should be lined up on about six blocks on Broadway in New York City. I'd like to see a little agitation to get national theatre and other art programs in this country. So that the kids all over the United States can go see Shakespeare without thinking it's a bore, you know, or Lorraine Hansberry or Eugene O'Neill."[6]

Although Hansberry's statement may be seen as anticipating the regional theater movement that developed in the United States in the 1960s, it may also be read as a call to extend the federal theater traditions traced in Kate Dossett's *Radical Black Theatre in the New Deal.* Based on Hansberry's relations with artists and activists of the Cultural Front (W.E.B. Du Bois, Alice Childress, Paul Robeson), her statement functioned as an ushering forth of underground possibilities, waiting to be reanimated. In addition, she knew culture was not just a product of artistic work but the foundation for social understanding. So she engaged in debates at the center of U.S. cultural critique, in this case the New York downtown arts scene, in order to shift the grounds for movement.

In *The Blacks* (a play examined in more detail in chapter 6), Genet suggests that if Black people won independence, then self-rule, free from interference, would amount to imperialism but just with Black people in power. As the history of the CIA demonstrates, even successful independence movements in Africa were plagued by Western interference. In a capitalist democracy, access to the basic benefits of citizenship often emerges in proportion to one's intergenerational class status. While Genet's play focuses on independence movements abroad, the implications of it for Black people in America were not lost on Mailer or Hansberry.

Mailer's review essay of Genet's *The Blacks,* similar to "The White Negro," offered a conscious oversight, reducing the desire to leave the ghetto plagued by overcrowding to an ethical failure. He suggests that Black people's aspiration to become middle class amounts to a desire to enjoy the mythical status of self-willed autonomy. He explained of the production, "Rehearsals inevitably must commence in a state. For the actors are not Africans. They are American Negroes, they belong some of them to the Black Bourgeoisie which any proud Negro is quick to tell you is a parody of the white bourgeoisie— the party's-getting-out-of-line kind of cramp on the jazz." Mailer critiqued the actor's purported lack of authenticity in terms of nationality and class. The "proud Negro" lives in a state of disruption but one that is not revolutionary. In Mailer's lament: "Now contemplate the problem of a director. He is to deal with 13 actors, all Negro, in the truest and most explosive play anyone has yet written at all about the turn in the tide, and the guilt and horror in the white man's heart as he turns to face his judge. For after all where do nightmares go when they are gone? Who is to say the gates of heaven are not manned by cannibals mumbling: Lumumba?"[7]

Mailer's understanding of *The Blacks* as the "truth" taps into a feeling of guilt that he may only assuage by reducing justice seekers to "cannibals mumbling: Lumumba." His review refuses to consider the laws and policies that preclude Black people from enjoyment of the American myth of equality. Hansberry, in a response published in the *Village Voice,* argued: "That is why, blues or no blues, life roots or no life roots, Negroes of *all* classes have made it clear that they want the hell out of the ghetto just as fast as the ascendency of Africa, the courts, insurance money, job-upgrading, the threat of 'our image overseas,' or anything else can thrust them. . . . Misery may be theatrical to the onlooker but it hurts him who is miserable. *That* is what the blues are about." Her challenge to Mailer's depiction of race called for a rethinking of whiteness as the expression of democratic possibility and blackness as bodies driven by carnal impulses and feelings (mumbling cannibals). Mailer's value and evaluation of the blues reflected a reconciliation of blackness with subservience. Hansberry said, "they shall be disappointed if the blacks really do give more attention to building steel mills and hydroelectric plants throughout Africa than to slitting a few hundred criminal throats."[8] The focus of Mailer's review essay and "The White Negro" limited Black imagination to replication when historical evidence demonstrates Black people's propensity to innovation and transformation.

The effort to reduce Black people's desire for access to the basic benefits of citizenship to greed, vengeance, blood thirst, or mediocrity obscures the threat independent blackness poses to the very operation of whiteness as the appearance of ascension through individual excellence while all the time depending on structural inequality sustained through violence. Hansberry wrote: "For 'The Blacks' is, as Mailer partially observed, more than anything else a conversation between white men about *themselves.* This seemed to me the final trick, not upon reality which tends to hold its own, but upon illusion." Hansberry's art intervened in the production of illusions in order to shift political and historical realities. If Genet's play wanted to speak a true word concerning geopolitics in the mid-twentieth century, it would feature a CIA agent orchestrating "the blacks' " rule. "Even the most profound white men find it incomprehensible that a black man may behold the moon and stars without agonies of concern for how those images may have seemed to—the Whites."[9]

Hansberry's engagement with Genet and Mailer established her in the white theater world as a critic, although she began writing criticism in the 1950s. As an insider, she sought to transform the culture of the art world and therefore political possibility by destabilizing whiteness.

Mailer and Genet misrepresented Black people and their political movements because they did not have the courage to confront the violent history of white supremacy. For both Mailer and Genet, self-determination functions in a historical vacuum that sucks out Black people's lived experience of systematic Western domination. Hansberry quips, "Well, there is certainly nothing fresh in the spectacle of white people insisting on telling all sorts of colored peoples how they should behave to satisfy them. It is, to say the least, the most characteristic aspect of the nation's foreign policy."[10] The framing of their work leaves no room for Hansberry's style of realism because it forecloses any possibility of blackness appearing outside of white expectations and desires.

As Hansberry's diplomatic and activist work had taught her, reasonable articulations of the limits of capitalism would not convince masses of people to demand fairer labor conditions or self-determination. She knew people did not care about fairness. As James Baldwin wrote, "People are not, for example, terribly anxious to be equal, but they love the idea of being superior."[11] Hansberry understood the power of ideology and narrative, which fueled how people feel and how the world around them makes them feel. As a public intellectual and artist, she offered new myths that drew from freedom practices old and new. She also made use of realism to engage with people's understandings of truth and offer them new ideas about blackness and freedom, not only what is but also what is possible. Her direct engagement in public debate served as an extension of her artistic work, allowing her to serve as a witness. Hansberry sought to remedy the misapprehension that marked her own public perception and that of Black culture and its producers more broadly. Her art offered new visions; her criticism bore witness.

MOOD

On April 21, 1962, Lorraine sat at her typewriter and took stock of her relationships. She wrote in her journal on the eve of Easter, "it really is better to be alone; it is horrible but better." "Would like to be with a company of friends laughing and clowning and drinking. Most of all: with those among whom I might find one whom I wanted to please. I would give my soul to be with someone whom I really and truly longed to please. That would be la paradise. But there are no such." Alone with her dog and her drink of choice, scotch, by 1962, both of Hansberry's long-term relationships were on the rocks. The diary entry shows Hansberry's deep desire for a loving mutual connection, but not solely a sexual one. Although in the entry she evaluates her dating prospects, by the end of it she returns to friendship. She writes, "I should like—I should like a company of friends. Brilliant ones! Laughters [*sic*] and dancers. We might do the twist and then African and then Russian and laugh. But dance well!! Not so much liquor and sparkling living conversation and flirtations. Ah, how I should like it."[12]

Hansberry's fame, personality, and mood impacted her ability to build community and connect with other people. In 1962, with the proceeds from the film adaptation of *A Raisin in the Sun,* she bought a house in Croton-on-Hudson, a small town in Westchester County about forty miles from New York City. She named the house Chitterling Heights, paying homage to how the house would disrupt Victorian ideals of womanhood with its specific blackness. Chitterling Heights named a sociality and called forth a surreal Black estate. It specified how Black radicalism could reconcile with Black domesticity, centering intimate spaces in transformative political work.

Lorraine's Hudson River home would serve as the site where she composed her last plays: *The Sign in Sidney Brustein's Window, What Use Are Flowers?* and *Les Blancs.* Ultimately, her relationships with Bobby and Dorothy would sustain her. But her journey to understanding how her personal desire related to her intellectual and political interests mirrored a larger social and political landscape.

The feelings that structured Lorraine's personal and political engagements reflect an international mood, one that took hold in the Western world after the war and the devastation caused by Nazis and nuclear warfare alike. The national mood ebbs, flows, and shifts as the winds of the civil rights movement began to blow the country toward change. The shift, however, never fully accounts for the Black insurgency that produced another feeling all along.

The long history of this mood emanating from the underground emerged in April 1961 when Baldwin addressed a group of activists at Judiciary Square for a disarmament peace rally. In his speech, he drew attention to how racial histories of domination intertwined with seemingly new debates about warfare in the nuclear age. As reported in the *Washington Post,* he explained: " 'What am I doing here?' . . . 'Only those who would fail to see the relationship between the fight for civil rights and the struggle for world peace would be surprised to see me.' 'Both fights are the same' . . . White society will point to what affluent gains Negroes have made, Baldwin said, and label that progress.

'But nothing has happened in the social sphere.' "[13] His comment linked the struggle for racial equality to the movement for peace. The destruction of life in Hiroshima and Nagasaki presented a disposability of non-white life that informed the unfolding of the Cold War in Africa. According to Vincent Intondi, "In the summer of 1959, France announced plans to test a nuclear weapon in the Sahara. Frightened and angered, many Africans saw the French test as another form of European colonialism." Placing African nationals into Cold War battles, particularly Ghana, which under the leadership of Kwame Nkrumah "had avoided taking sides in the Cold War," interwove the history of nuclear war with the ongoing pursuit of decolonization in Africa, the Americas, and Asia.[14]

The emergence of nuclear war, however, shifted the scale of devastation the United States would willingly deploy against Asia and threaten to use against European adversaries. The Western world had, however, participated in acts of genocide against native populations, and slavery, for hundreds of years. As a result, Black thinkers had a specific perspective on the meaning of life and how it matters in the midst and aftermath of the war. The United States' use of nuclear warfare produced a cultural crisis reflected in the writing and art associated with existentialism—a strand of philosophy that emerged in relationship to the war. Existentialism expresses, in part, a response to loss and a sense of being lost, disempowered, and unable to effect any meaningful collective change. Hansberry's work bears the mark of existentialist thought, particularly that of Simone de Beauvoir, but it also accounts for a longer history of devastation and systematic violence in United States and elsewhere than that inaugurated by the war. In *The Sign in Sidney Brustein's Window,* she also established through the character Wally that the root of existentialism's depressive mood stems from "the loss of an empire."[15] Although writing from a seat of empire, Hansberry's work accounts for the interlocking implications of nuclear warfare and decolonization. She recognizes the coincidence of Black and brown nations moving toward self-determination and mass destruction becoming a tenable resolution to international conflict.

Publicly Hansberry adamantly opposed the pessimism of her time, which found artistic expression through the theater of the absurd. Before the theater of the absurd emerged as a genre, philosophers, perhaps most forcefully Jean-Paul Sartre in *Being and Nothingness* (1943), established some of the central tenets of existentialism, including that individuals act freely and in so doing define who they are in the world. Through action, taking stock of that action, and reflection, individuals come to be. Sartre's collaborator and companion Beauvoir writes, "Sartre, in *Being and Nothingness,* fundamentally defined man . . . that subjectivity which realizes itself only as a presence in the world, that engaged freedom, that surging of the for-oneself which is immediately given for others." Exploring the implications of understanding subjectivity as governed by choices rather than structures, belief systems, or histories encodes life with arbitrariness. Beauvoir explains with reservation, "it is also claimed that existentialism is a philosophy of the absurd and of despair. It encloses man in a sterile anguish, in an empty subjectivity. It is incapable of furnishing him with any principle for making choices. Let him do as he pleases. In any case, the game is lost."[16] In *Existentialism Is a Humanism,* Sartre clarifies:

> As for "despair" the meaning of this expression is extremely simple. It merely
> means that we limit ourselves to a reliance upon that which is within our wills,
> or within the sum of the probabilities which render our action feasible. . . . I
> remain in the realm of possibilities; but one does not rely upon any possibilities
> beyond those that are strictly concerned in one's actions. . . . When Descartes
> said, "Conquer yourself rather than the world," what he meant was, at bottom,
> the same—that we should act without hope.[17]

Hansberry differed with Sartre in her understanding of action as the enact-ment of individual essence tied to singularity. She understood action as not necessarily toward the advancement of hope but in terms of freedom that emerged through encounter. For Hansberry encounter served as a mechanism to meet across difference and produce witnesses. In Sartre's distillation, exis-tentialism assumes that individuals may act divorced of history and that their actions have no ongoing impact. Meaning, each action exists within the time of its elaboration and then ends. The idea of self-willed autonomy boldly asserts the power of individual will and constrains it at the same time. This notion of being does not account for the circulation and impact of feelings that structure political histories and movements.[18]

More influenced by de Beauvoir than Sartre, Hansberry's direct engagement with existentialism in the last play produced while she was alive, *The Sign in Sidney Brustein's Window,* reflects the freedom in what de Beauvoir describes as ambiguity rather than arbitrariness. Although some of Hansberry's contempo-raries, including Albert Camus, understood the universe as governed by chance that leaves the individual completely disempowered and subject to the random absurdity and violence of life, de Beauvoir, a friend in Hansberry's head, challenged that rendering of existentialism in *The Ethics of Ambiguity* (1948). Her volume offers a preemptive response to the interlocking of existen-tialism, absurdity, and suicide as explored in Camus's *The Myth of Sisyphus and Other Essays* (1955). Her writing also challenges the isolation that emerges from the racial profiling described in contemporary Frantz Fanon's *Black Skin, White Masks*. Taking seriously the writing of feminists in the mid-twentieth century challenges many of the fundamental assumptions about how Black lives matter then and now.

Existentialism asserts that individuals are in charge of making meaning in their lives and that meaning for Hansberry and de Beauvoir was tied to connecting with others through the pursuit of freedom. For both women, meaning extended beyond the individual and did have a historical component. Hansberry's interest in finding a meaning for living emerged alongside her personal struggles with depression and contemplation of suicide and her political commitment to Black freedom struggles. These questions preceded and continued after *A Raisin in the Sun*.

Writing *Sign* reinvigorated a set of concerns that had preoccupied Hansberry at least since her time writing for *Freedom*. In a review of Richard Wright's *The Outsider* in 1953 she questioned his allegiances, using a spatial metaphor: "Richard Wright has been away from home a long time." She attributes his homelessness to crafting a character, Cross Damon, that "is someone you will never meet on the Southside of Chicago or in Harlem. For if he is anything at all, he is the symbol of Wright's new philosophy—the glorification of—nothingness." The despair at the core of Wright's characterization offers an insight into the eventual impact of the glorification of nothingness: "Richard Wright is correct in one thing: he is an outsider, he is outcast from his own people. He exalts brutality and nothingness; he negates the reality of our struggle for freedom and yet works energetically on behalf of our oppressors; he has lost his own dignity and destroyed his talent. He has lost the bright and morning star—but the Negro people have not."[19] Hansberry never confused racial similarity for solidarity. She understood that allies could work at cross-purposes and that part of her activism required meeting across difference. She also understood that sometimes people cast themselves out of the struggle, so they must do the work to find their way home.

Hansberry's public derision of Wright and her calling Mailer to task in print take on even more force when one accounts for her personal struggle for meaning. The instability of the postwar era took up residence in Chitterling Heights. Hansberry's position as a Black celebrity, political activist, and heterosexually married lesbian produced isolation. In addition, her vocation required seclusion. Hansberry found rigorous debate and collaboration enlivening, but her professional goals and social positions often prevented both. In a journal entry from December 1962, she wrote, "Eventually it comes to you: the thing that makes you exceptional if you are, at all, is inevitably that which must also make you lonely." In the journal kept from 1962 until her death, she often expressed loneliness. The severity of it shifted from an expression of a desire for companionship to yearning for intimacy to expressions of isolation coupled with despair. On the same day in April that she concluded it is better to be alone, she also wrote: "I am thirty-two now. I do not long for fame—except in a vindictive way, because some have said such unkind things. I feel I must prove a thing or two now. But mainly a company of friends for money and fame I would make the exchange. But that has always been so; only now I could pay the devil his wage. Tomorrow is Easter."[20] Hansberry did not believe in God. Nevertheless, the cultural importance of major Christian holidays placed her in a reflective mood. She believed in her growing ability to negotiate with powerful external forces that structured her life, and she knew that same power limited her ability to build intimacy. Nevertheless, her work suggests intimacy became a fundamental part of her artistic, political, and personal practice.

While Hansberry is uniquely positioned in the postwar world, her sense of isolation coincides with a collective longing for connection, expressed in the philosophical writing and art of the period. The feeling Hansberry specifies has different historical antecedents depending on one's historical relationship to empire. Hansberry's personal and public writing then gives insight into an international mood specified by her unrelenting attention to her position as a Black lesbian woman.

Hansberry had to confront how to be a public figure, not in a commodifiable way, but a woman for masses of people, and forge meaningful personal connections in that context. In the public context, she often tried to forge relationships by producing witnesses or acting as a witness.

Although Hansberry invested deeply in the political power of the encounter because it disrupted the seamless unfolding of dominant culture, she did not take such modes of engagement lightly. In July 1961, LeRoi Jones (later named Amiri Baraka) wrote Hansberry a letter inviting her to have a public " 'exchange' with Norman Mailer" "along with Jimmy Baldwin." He explained that the exchange would benefit an organization he had developed for young Black youth in the arts: "I had the idea that perhaps we could get You, Jimmy, and Norman, along with W.E.B. Du Bois and either Max Lerner or Roy Wilkins, to go at it at some kind of forum."[21] Hansberry apparently declined Jones's offer, because a week later he wrote back: "Thank you for the prompt reply. Although, I must admit, I am extremely disappointed that you don't think your differences with Norman Mailer are 'significant.' This I find difficult to understand, i.e., that you could and would expend energies,

&c., and seem to arrive at certain conclusions (even build your work on them) and yet think they are not 'significant.' Or, more baldly, how you can think that the differences which make for you such antithetical conclusions to Mr. Mailer's socially as well as aesthetically, can be of such little import to yourself as you say. I suppose it is as they say, i.e., talk is cheap."[22] Jones understood the performance of confrontation as an important political and cultural act.

Hansberry, however, understood the significance of her work having impact not only for those involved in the encounter but those witnessing as well. In Hansberry's staging of encounters, individuals meet across difference to produce understanding. Even if the conversation results in an impasse, the moment of interaction provides a possibility for those who bear witness to gain greater clarity. Hansberry said her piece and did not opt to return again to that conversation. Jones found her choice particularly disappointing because "Your writing comes out of and speaks for the American middleclass. Of course it is more informed by a peculiar group within that class, but it represents the entire class nevertheless. . . . And as an articulate voice of an entire class you certainly do become a 'leader,' like it or not."[23] Hansberry most certainly would not have liked the designation because it obscured great portions of her work and her fundamental commitment to mass movements for freedom. Jones's categorization reinforced a misapprehension at the heart of his request, that her public debates served a primarily theatrical rather than political purpose.

Drawing from her engagement with *The Second Sex* in the 1950s, Hansberry's practice of freedom insisted that, through direct engagement with others in the world, freedom emerges. In the 1957 essay on de Beauvoir's book, Hansberry expressed the personal intellectual influence of the French philosopher's tome, accounting for ideas de Beauvoir had previously elaborated. In 1948, de Beauvoir published *The Ethics of Ambiguity*, which outlined her understanding of existentialism and how it builds on and departs from Sartre. She explained the necessity of rooting existentialism in the pressing issues of the time. Rather than debate the meaning of man's existence, she asserted: "Man exists. For him it is not a question of wondering whether his presence in the world is useful, whether life is worth the trouble of being lived. These questions make no sense. It is a matter of knowing whether he wants to live and under what conditions." Her volume tries to makes sense of a world reordered by the possibility of large-scale devastation in the West. Turning her attention to the problem of freedom, she explained: "One of the chief objections leveled against existentialism is that the precept 'to will freedom' is only a hollow formula and offers no concrete content for action. But that is because one has begun by emptying the word freedom of its concrete meaning; we have already seen that freedom realizes itself only by engaging itself in the world: to such an extent that man's project toward freedom is embodied for him in definite acts of behavior."[24] The notion of embodiment clarifies how theater becomes a central cultural site of debate over making meaning of life and exercising freedom.

Although de Beauvoir shared with other existentialists the investment in human action as the primary locus of freedom and meaning making, her writing goes a step further, requiring interaction. Freedom required collaboration and exchange, which installed the usefulness of its pursuit beyond the span of any one individual's life. She wrote: "Thus, just as life is identified with the will-to-live, freedom always appears as a movement of liberation. It is only by prolonging itself through the freedom of others that it manages to surpass death itself and to realize itself as an indefinite unity."[25] For de Beauvoir, the pursuit of freedom is the reason an individual would struggle in a world teeming with death and destruction; a world where there are concentration camps and fire hoses that are routinely turned on citizens for peaceful protests.

For de Beauvoir the idea of transcendence requires understanding how individual human action relates to interdependence: "It is only when the moments of his life begin to be organized into behaviour that he can decide and choose. The value of the chosen end is confirmed and, reciprocally, the genuineness of the choice is manifested concretely through patience, courage, and fidelity. If I leave behind an act which I have accomplished, it becomes a thing by falling into the past. It is no longer anything but a stupid and opaque fact. In order to prevent this metamorphosis, I must ceaselessly return to it and justify it in the unity of the project in which I am engaged. Setting up the movement of my transcendence requires that I never let it uselessly fall back upon itself, that I prolong it indefinitely."[26] This explanation of revolutionary action resonates with Asagai's speech to Beneatha in *A Raisin in the Sun,* particularly when he says that in the movement of his country toward self-rule even his "own death will be an advance. They who might kill me even . . . actually replenish all that I was."[27] The idea of action requiring confirmation through repetition demonstrates how practices build and sustain movements. It also shows how actors connect across time. Through the act of return, which Hansberry does through recurring artistic and political actions (for example, revising stories in her plays that she told versions of in *Freedom*) she shifts the fact of her action to a movement.

LIBERAL MYOPIA

In *Sign* Hansberry revisits some of the ideas she expressed in *A Raisin in the Sun* about freedom and freedom movements being rooted in quotidian interactions. She locates the foundation for social change in the repair of a romantic relationship. The play depicts a set of characters coming to political maturity through experiences of loss and betrayal. The first two acts of the play depict failed collaborations and relationships. The central character, Sidney Brustein, no longer has a meaningful connection with his wife Iris and struggles to achieve professional fulfillment. Similarly, his neighbors and friends have met personal or professional plateaus that force them to question their ethical and political commitments. The first act features a man, similar to Walter Lee, who must face all of the dreams that he has deferred. Unlike Walter Lee, however, his primary concern is philosophical rather than material. One may understand the distinction between the two characters in racial terms, but it could also reflect the shifting terrain in Hansberry's life, from struggling artist to financially secure playwright.

The characters in the play express dissatisfaction with their current state and lack the motivation to make any meaningful change. Hansberry depicts their inertia as stemming from a misunderstanding of history. The play opens with Sidney returning home with the last remains of his latest failed business venture, glasses from the Silver Dagger. Although his friend Alton and wife Iris refer to the "Silver Dagger" as a nightclub, Sidney insists, "It wasn't *supposed* to be a night club." "I thought it was something people wanted. A place to listen to good folk music. Without hoked-up come-ons." The not-nightclub nightclub represents Sidney's identity as a Hipster through his general discomfort with given definitions and categories. He is unwilling to conform to expectations and lacks the will to sustain something new. Frustrated with her husband's perpetual works in progress, Iris responds to the set of glasses in their small apartment saying, "We are not going to have the residue of all your failures in the living room."[28] Also in the process of finding herself, Iris works as a waitress but wants to be an actress and has sought out psychotherapy to help her make better sense of her life.

In the play, Sidney confronts the social, emotional, and historical attachments that prevent liberals from becoming radicals. Sidney believes that he cannot be fulfilled, that his efforts do not make a meaningful difference, and that he does not and perhaps never had the capacity to connect with his wife. He confesses, "I do admit that I no longer have the energy, the purity or the comprehension to—'save the world.' . . . I no longer even believe that spring must necessarily come. . . . Or, that if it does, that it will bring forth anything more poetic or insurgent than . . . the winter's dormant ulcers." In the last years of Hansberry's life, she suffered from intense stomach pain. She died of cancer of the small intestine, but she did not know that she had cancer as she lay dying. During her long sickness, she associated her physical pain and illness with ulcers. Sidney's comment suggests he sees life as consisting of stubborn and persistent unpleasant states of being that Hansberry knew too well. Moreover, his state lacked the possibility of revolutionary change. He explained, "I am afraid that I have experienced the *death* of the exclamation point. It has died in me. I no longer want to exhort anybody about anything. It's the final end of boyhood."[29]

In presenting a world ill-suited for Sidney's flourishing, Hansberry questions how long he will hold on to a dying empire, characterized by a liberal and yet still sexist, racist, and homophobic society. Sidney associates his mood with maturity and finds that mood dissatisfying. In a conversation with his neighbor, a playwright named David who represents Western theater's engagement with theories of existentialism in the mid-twentieth century from Camus to Samuel Beckett to Jean Genet, Sidney confesses, "Well, I admit it: I *care!* I care about it all. It takes too much energy *not* to care. Yesterday I counted twenty-six gray hairs in the top of my head—all from trying *not* to care. And you, David, you have now written fourteen plays about not caring, about the isolation of the soul of man, the alienation of the human spirit, the desolation of all love, all possible communication. When what you really want to say is that you are ravaged by a society that will not sanctify your particular sexuality!"[30] Sidney's comment brushes up against his ongoing suggestion throughout the first act that the categories and structures that govern modern life do not fit, yet he and his neighbors lack the conviction to challenge them.

The lack of will prevents the characters from having to choose, which de Beauvoir describes as the first step toward the ongoing process of pursuing freedom. Once again echoing *Raisin,* which ends the first act with an argument between Walter Lee and Ruth, the first act of *Sign* ends with a conversation between Iris and Sidney about the status of their marriage.

> IRIS. It's getting different, Sidney, our fighting. Something's either gone out of it or come into it. I don't know which. But it's something that keeps me from wanting to make up with you a few hours later. That's bad, isn't it?
> SIDNEY. Yeah, that's bad.
> IRIS. Then let's put up a fight for it, Sidney! I mean it—let's fight like hell for it.[31]

The outward-facing pursuit of freedom, the pursuit of freedom for others, requires making meaningful connections through collaboration that may be painful. Hansberry incisively foregrounds the romantic relationship to illustrate that both Sidney and Iris must work to create something new that extends beyond each one of them individually. Their relationship cannot adhere to the traditional mandates of marriage presented through Iris's middle-class sister who is a housewife and mother. Iris's sister Mavis serves as a foil to Iris, highlighting the bohemian lifestyle of the interfaith Brusteins in comparison to her sister's WASPish values of profit over ethics and public perception over personal satisfaction.

Although Sidney resists the racism, anti-Semitism, and classism that characterizes Mavis, he welcomes gender hierarchies and sexual fantasies of domination. The opening scene of Act 2 features Sidney lounging on the staircase landing outside his building. He fantasizes about life in the mountains with "the Iris-of-his-Mind"; she "appears, barefooted, with flowing hair and mountain dress, and mounts the steps. She embraces him and then, as by the lore of hill people, is possessed . . . and dances in the shadows before him." Sidney finds the scene deeply satisfying because it affirms Iris's regional and ethnic difference, "Greco-Gaelic-Indian hillbilly," and, more important, her primary role being to serve him.[32] The appearance of a dancing woman in this play functions differently from the dancing woman who guides Hansberry's protagonist in *Les Blancs,* because here she functions as a suture, holding together Sidney's version of domestic tranquility, while in *Les Blancs* she acts as an incursion, urging the protagonist to disrupt the status quo. The shift in the use of the device also reveals a different side of Hansberry—the revolutionary.

The desire for human connection and intimacy also underpins Sidney's fantasy, but only on his terms. Sidney's myopia costs him. At the same time, even as individuals strive to forge relationships to each other, social positions change and produce alienation. Sidney has an exchange with David in the second act that demonstrates how both men have become maladjusted to their new positions, David as a successful playwright and Sidney as the new owner of an independent newspaper. In a conversation similar to the one Hansberry recalled with Baldwin after *A Raisin in the Sun* catapulted her to fame, when "her phone kept ringing," David laments to Sidney, "*I'm famous. (A grin)* I have to go outside and find out what it's like to wear it in the streets. (*Sobering*) As if I can't guess. Everybody will just be more self-conscious, phonier than they would have been yesterday. Just because my picture was in the papers. It's crazy. The phone keeps on ringing. For years I made fun of people who had unlisted numbers. First thing Monday—I'll have to get one."[33] Fame produces hyper-visibility that renders the individual seeming more accessible even though he is actually distanced from his newfound public. As he becomes more recognizable, he also becomes hyper-aware of his visibility, making him question the establishment of new connections. Fame serves to inhibit making connections and helps to facilitate the loneliness that plagued Hansberry and permeated the downtown New York arts scene.

The conversation devolves from there as David realizes Sidney too has changed his expectations for their relationship based on his newfound success. In an effort to mend his relationship with Iris, Sidney asks David to put her in his play. He pleads, "she *needs* something to happen for her, don't you understand." David, yet to be seduced by fame, questions Sidney's ethics, charging, "Such a tiny little corruption. Not three people in the whole world would ever really care whether or not my little insignificant play did or did not have its unities stretched to just happen to include a part for your wife in trade for a patch of glowing praise in your paper. Not three people in the whole world. That's the magic of the tiny corruptions, isn't it, Sidney? Their insignificance makes them so appealing."[34] His use of the word "corruption" points to the ethical and political stakes of what Sidney proposes. The willingness to sacrifice the integrity of David's art in order to provide Iris with an opportunity that would placate her serves to maintain Sidney's control of her *and* defer the hard work of connecting with her as an equal. The connection that Iris wants requires Sidney to participate in redefining their relationship, something he does not want to do. As a result, he attempts to take a shortcut that threatens his relationship with David. In the play, the political, communal, familial, and artistic collaborations hold equal weight. Therefore, although David and Iris's relationship may seem more important in a social context organized around heterosexual coupling, this scene sets in motion Sidney's ultimate fall at the end of the act and, in so doing, establishes the central role his friendship plays in the ethical ecosystem of the play. Sidney's willingness to sacrifice his relationship with David to purportedly assist his relationship with Iris serves to undermine all of his connections. The tiny corruptions that personify Sidney prevent him from making ethical choices and establishing intimacy.

More at ease in condemning other people's behavior than in examining his own actions, Sidney's perceptions and comments about Iris produce contention through the first two acts of the play. His decision to buy a newspaper and support his friend Wally O'Hara's political campaign provides some hope. Sidney sees Wally's candidacy as a chance for city reform and a response to political corruption. Sidney celebrates Wally's victory by exclaiming, "We dead have in fact awakened . . . do you know the main trouble with us believers in this world? *We don't believe!* . . . Twenty years of political history overturned." Similar to his relationship with Iris, Sidney sees in the campaign only what he wants to see. Reminiscent of Beneatha's haircut in *A Raisin in the Sun*, Iris returns home with much shorter blonde hair. Her haircut, like Beneatha's, makes an assertion of her bodily autonomy. It also disrupts the fantasy that Sidney has of her. Instead of being his doting housewife, she wants to be an actress. She has booked her first job in a commercial, which for Sidney amounts to selling false promises. Exhausted with her husband's sanctimony, Iris tells Sidney that the establishment owns Wally.[35] She exits, leaving Sidney devastated. The first two acts establish how the social (shifting understandings of race, gender, sexuality, and family) and political contexts (communism/Old Left, budding progressivism) of the United States in general and life in the Village in particular distinguish ways of being and the pursuit of freedom.

INTIMACY WITH DESPAIR

The remainder of the play engages with some of the central concerns of existentialism. Hansberry knew well the depressive state associated with the philosophical movement, particularly in the writing of Camus, but she clarified in her creative work and personal writing that the context for her feeling reflected a different geopolitical order than the one expressed from the metropoles. In 1963, Hansberry wrote in her journal repeatedly about her declining physical health and her depression. She contemplated suicide on September 19, and again on December 13, writing: "Will I ever have the courage to kill myself? Well, I wouldn't be able to look back and read about how I felt while it was happening—and this—alone, I think, gives me pause." She found some physical comfort from the narcotic prescription pain reliever Darvon, but she feared becoming addicted to it. She needed quiet to write, but she also found isolation disabling. Her physical and mental health took a toll on her productivity, which then fed her depression. On July 17, 1964, she wrote, "Am now sitting thinking about many things. All the narrowness and selfishness of this last year of my life seems to crowd in on me. In two years, nothing. I have just finished reading an article on Harlem in the current 'Look' and hardly feel that my existence is justified, let alone the 'style' of life I lead."[36]

Hansberry's conclusion, "let alone the 'style' of life I lead," specifies her isolation as a function of her social, communal, and political positions. Although she made every effort to mitigate the gap between herself and the student activists she admired, her work positioned her differently in the movement. Given Hansberry's fame, race, gender, sexuality, and class, she keenly understood the barriers to and complex necessity of collaboration rooted in intimacy and a clear-sighted understanding of another. Although she cared deeply for Dorothy, in December 1963 she wrote, "I trust no one but Bob."[37] Hansberry found the holiday season difficult and particularly isolating. She also often expressed decisive action on one day, declaring the end of a relationship, for example, and then reconciliation the next. Her actions, however corroborate her expression of trust in Bob, making him the trustee of her papers even though they were divorced by the time she passed away, and depending on his feedback to finish *Sign* and *Les Blancs*.

By 1964, Hansberry had forged family bonds that the designation husband or wife could not hold. Her divorce from Nemiroff marked a turning point in her personal becoming that had long been on the horizon. Through her friendship with Jimmy, her sometime muse and repeated interlocutor, she found a deep sense of understanding that also sustained her. Imani Perry writes that they swam "in each other's imaginations. Neither one imitating the other, but after bathing in the other's words they return back to the shore, to work, shaped by the beloved's waters." Outlining the conversation between Lorraine and Jimmy in their letters and published work, the contending force of interracial relationships in *Les Blancs* and *Blues for Mister Charlie* and the exploration of the Village in *Sign* and *Another Country*, mark just two conversations among many deep meditations together. Perry writes, "Lorraine and Jimmy met again when *A Raisin in the Sun* was in tryouts in New Haven and he came to see it. That was when their friendship really began. About a month before their reencounter he'd had a dream 'in which he was joined by a beautiful, very young black woman who, after performing a song and a cakewalk with him, seemed to merge with him "her breasts digging against my shoulder-blades." ' Jimmy prophesied Lorraine."[38]

Baldwin also appeared as a figure in Lorraine's writing, calling forth a different form of sociality than the familiar heteronormative one of her youth. In her unpublished essay "Queer Beer," Hansberry appended a note of portraits: thirty-six "ladies," "uncertain—borderline type," and the gentleman, of which "Jim Baldwin" was the first. The portraits never took shape, but Jimmy also appeared in a reference Hansberry made to Studs Terkel during an interview in 1959. In considering what Black writers inspire her, she said that Baldwin "from what [she's] read of his essays and some of his fiction that he's undoubtedly one of the most talented American writers walking around and if he can wed his particular gifts, which are just way beyond most of us trying to write on many levels—to material of substance, then we have the potential of a great American writer."[39] Much like their relationship, Hansberry lauded and affirmed Jimmy's genius and challenged him too. "She and James Baldwin were great friends, although at times a passerby might believe that they were about to slug it out at a party or at his place or hers. They yelled at each other, ranted and raved, drank. They also laughed."[40] The dynamism of their friendship emerges in a draft of *Sign,* when the central character refers to an American negro expatriate living in Paris who agonizes over his rootlessness. Her less than flattering reference to Baldwin urges him on as *Sign* sought to urge on the white liberals of the Village, including Bob, to become radicals. Hansberry's connection to Baldwin, expressed in her published and unpublished work, places him in the political future she sought. Her writing always reflected what was and what could be. Even in challenge, Hansberry saw the figures of her work and their inspirations as sources that fed her radical imagination, "the imposition of a point of view."[41]

Hansberry's commitment to life accounts for the disillusionment fundamental to and conditioned by her era. She understood the devastating impact of the war on how her contemporaries saw the world. At the same time, she knew destruction characterized the West and did not function, in this instance, as an exception. As a result, she saw living as the only response to an unjust world. Hansberry took on the question of despair directly in *Sign.* In a conversation among Sidney, Mavis, David, and Sidney's African American friend, Alton, the characters discuss the political implications of reconciling oneself to the corruption of the social sphere or striving for revolutionary change. Mavis claims, "Well, sure. When you come right down to it, one politician *is* just like another." Sidney responds, "And a new religion is upon the West and it has only one hymn: 'We are all guilty . . . Father Camus, we are all guilty . . . *Ipso facto,* all guilt is equal . . . Therefore we shall in clear conscience abstain from the social act . . . and even the social thought . . .' "[42] The inability or lack of desire to distinguish the ethical implications of acts reflects a general sense in Camus's work that individual action has no import. It also enables the easy slippage of understanding acts outside of their historical contexts, once again serving to depoliticize them. The same act has different implications depending on the historical actor and the contexts for the action. Hansberry specifies "social" act in her play to call attention to how individual affirmations produced society. Sidney's inability to make such distinctions, in part, leads to his downfall.

In a world in which mass destruction looms as a possibility, and "all guilt is equal" how does one feel at home? In *The Myth of Sisyphus* (1955), Camus explores the "one truly serious philosophical problem, and that is suicide. Judging whether life is or is not worth living amounts to answering the fundamental question of philosophy." His inquiry stems from a reckoning with the alienation caused by the modern world, "in a universe suddenly divested of illusion and lights, man feels an alien, a stranger. His exile is without remedy since he is deprived of the memory of a lost home or the hope of a promised land." How does man not look back historically and see the past as nothing more than a ruse? Camus suggested that, given these circumstances, the only choice an individual can make that actually matters is suicide. Although Camus finally argued that he did not choose suicide, his conclusion maintained the reconciliation to "the dull resonance that vibrates throughout these days."[43] Hansberry shared with the Hipsters the urgency to challenge the feeling of ineffectualness in the mid-twentieth century. She differed, however, in her understanding of its source. She challenged conformity through a reframing of racial and sexual capital as a fundamental way to realize America.

But in that time, and perhaps our own, Hansberry suggested that we take another look at the history Camus dismissed, not as the source material for giving our lives meaning but as a context for our pursuits. Certainly, the aspect of existentialism that appealed to Hansberry most profoundly included the idea of making the world anew. But she knew, as did Sartre and de Beauvoir, that the impact and import of individual choices emerges through relationships across time, difference, and space.

Hansberry's career and its impact on how others understood her and how she understood herself challenged her firm commitment to collaboration as the basis for movement work. She set her play in the Village, which served as a site for new forms of communal organization in the mid-twentieth century, often guided by a shared investment in the transformative power of art. Artists migrated to Washington Square and surrounding areas "as avant-gardists dedicated to overturning traditions, in making their communal art they had to reinvent community," according to Sally Banes.[44] Since her letters to the *Ladder* in 1957 and 1958, Hansberry had wondered what forms of community would enable political flourishing. She differed from many of the avant-gardists in that she still identified strongly with the Old Left's class critiques and questioned "the consensus" that "life in the United States was good—and getting better." She thought the United States had the potential to become a better version of itself and, like many of her peer avant-gardists, critiqued bourgeois values centering on capitalist accumulation. Hansberry, however, was one of the rare few who focused on the persistent link between sexual and racial economies. Her contemporaries felt emboldened to loosen the hold of "the sexual codes of the bourgeois family" without addressing America's miscegenated family tree.[45]

In *Sign,* Hansberry depicted a conversation that draws on the interwoven sexual and racial economies that Baldwin and LeRoi Jones charted in their autobiographical and creative work. On the heels of learning that Wally won the election, Alton asks Sidney about Gloria, if it's "true she's a hooker." Sidney tries to convince Alton of how his political commitments should determine his intimate life, reminding him, "You were a revolutionary! Doesn't that stand for anything anymore?" In the intervening years between the breakdown of the Old Left and the coalescence of a New Left, Sidney searches for ethical footing by challenging his friends' actions. Although Alton's interracial relationship has the potential to pose a challenge to the mainstream coupling conventions of the early 1960s, he, like his peers, does not want to take responsibility for the histories they seek to disrupt. Alton asserts men have "used her like . . . an . . . inanimate object . . . a thing, an instrument . . . a commodity . . ." He continues, "Don't you understand, Sidney? (*Rubbing his head*) . . . I am spawned from commodities . . . and their purchasers. Don't you *know* this? I am running from being a commodity. How do you think I got the color I am, Sidney? Haven't you ever thought about it? I got this color from my grandmother being used as a commodity, man. The buying and the selling in this country began with *me*. Jesus, help me."[46] Although Alton understands the interlocking of racial and sexual economies as the basis of American history, he runs from it. His refusal to share in a collective heritage forecloses his ability to reclaim his identity as a revolutionary, not through his relationship with Gloria but in his relationship to himself.

Sidney's liberalism blinds him to understanding the core of his interactions with Mavis and David too. After Wally's election win, Mavis comes to Sidney and Iris's apartment to celebrate. Grateful that Sidney has finally matured enough to participate in the system, she gives him a donation for the newspaper. The misunderstanding (Sidney thinks Wally's win is a blow to the system and Mavis understands it's a win for the system) produces false intimacy. As a result, Mavis reveals to Sidney that her husband Fred has a mistress. Sidney is shocked. Mavis explains with nonchalance, "In this world there are two kinds of loneliness and it is given to each of us to pick. I picked. And, let's face it, *I* cannot type."[47] Sidney is surprised because he invests in women playing supportive roles. Although he purports to respect women, his affirmations do not inform how he behaves or the decisions that he makes. Theater scholar Mark Hodin noted, women's "material experience" does not " 'chang[e] anything.' "[48] And the distinction that Sidney seeks to make between the three sisters' roles does not account for their similarity within patriarchy. Hansberry's depiction of the sister living along a patriarchal spectrum, beholden to the sexual politics of a male-dominated society, speaks to Genet's depiction of a brothel in *The Balcony*, which places the conditions of the prostitute outside of the city; Hansberry draws the activities of the middle-class home and the brothel together to challenge the structures they share.

Sidney's blind spot with Alton, Mavis, and David results from his willingness to be tolerant but not to fundamentally change his perspective by way of his interactions with them. After Sidney's conversation with David about including Iris in one of his plays, he returns and has a conversation with Gloria. Initially, he lauds the freedom of prostitution as an expression of "anti-bourgeois decadence he identifies with."[49] Gloria, finding David offensive, spurns him. Rebuffed but undeterred, he leaves and returns later to request that Gloria assist him in fulfilling a sexual fantasy. David's lover desires a woman's presence during their sexual encounter. She agrees but commits suicide before venturing up to David's apartment.

Critics have charged, as Margaret B. Wilkerson outlines, that Hansberry's depiction of David produces a "contradiction between her own personal preferences and her treatment of the subject in her produced plays."[50] Mark Hodin suggests, "Hansberry seems to link David's sexual identity with the bohemian and avant-garde postures that she wants to criticize."[51] Hansberry does intertwine her critique of bohemian and avant-garde culture, which she associates with the mood of despair, with David's sexual identity. The move may be troubling, but so was the racism and sexism of the early homophile movement. The characterization reflects Hansberry's own alienation and isolation in the gay and lesbian communities as a Black woman. She expresses her position in her letters to *The Ladder* and her public cries for liberals to become radicals. Hansberry also understood that Black people must also become radicals. As Martha Biondi explains, "The Cold War and domestic anticommunist crusade caused a split between African American liberals and leftists in their attitudes toward the federal government and their stance toward U.S. foreign policy."[52] The emergence of the civil rights movement coincided with some activists turning away from the leftist calls for a reorganization of racial capitalism. Moments of encounter serve as the basis for political possibility. The moments of misunderstanding call attention to lost opportunities for intimacy and collectivity.

The missed opportunity reveals a shared sense among Black writers in the Village about the racism inherent to the scene. Hansberry's depiction echoes that of friend Baldwin and, at that time, foe Jones.[53] Similar to Hansberry, Baldwin's experience living in the Village informed his creative work. Recalling Baldwin's time in New York City in 1959, David Leeming's biography describes Baldwin's friend Engin Cezzar, another white friend, and Engin's girlfriend going out for a drink at a small bar, the Village Paddock, near

Baldwin's Horatio Street apartment. The group enjoyed the time at the bar, laughing and singing. "At one point Engin's girlfriend, who was white, put her head on Jimmy's shoulder in the course of laughing at something he had said." Strangers at the bar commented on the interaction between Jimmy and his friends and then they attacked them. "Chairs were broken over heads, Engin was badly beaten up, Jimmy received a gash across his nose and was hit over the head. The police arrived, did little about the offenders, but did send Cezzar to the hospital, where he had to remain for several days."[54] Soon after, Baldwin left for Paris, another cosmopolitan city that would prove to be less progressive than advertised. His novel *Another Country*, set partially in the Village, features several scenes of violence fueled by racial animus and sexual desire.

Understanding the potential violence that interracial relationships could cause amid the bohemianism of the Village, Jones armed himself after he began dating Hettie Cohen, a Jewish woman from Queens. Jones would have two children with Hettie, and they later married. He claimed "he sexually pursued white women because it was a sign of black bohemian identity. In describing his first sexual encounter with a white Soho woman, he wrote . . . 'It seemed to me part of the adventure of my life in the Village. The black man with the white woman, I thought. Some kind of classic bohemian accoutrement.' "[55] Like other mixed couples in the Village, the neighbors of Jones and Cohen "gave them cold stares, catcalls, and jeers" when they walked through the neighborhood. Jones "carried a length of pipe with him whenever he walked through the South Village," realizing racial boundaries may have been permeable but still remained squarely in place.[56] Hansberry's play suggests she observed similar racial dynamics during her time in the Village.

Sign questions how to build a movement within such hypocrisy, how to transform a liberal into a radical. In the third act of the play, Sidney's sister-in-law Gloria comes to visit. Sidney gives Gloria the letter Alton left to end their relationship. Sidney and Gloria joined by David begin a wild night of debauchery to ease their collective but not shared disappointment. In the scene, they assert the pervasiveness of guilt and, echoing the title of Edward Albee's absurdist play *Who's Afraid of Virginia Woolf?* they sing "Oh, who's afraid of Absurdity! Absurdity! Absurdity! Who's afraid of Absurdity! Not we, not we not we!"[57] The song, similar to the title of Albee's play, according to the playwright, "means who's afraid of the big *bad* wolf . . . who's afraid of living life without false illusions."[58] In many ways, the invocation of the song calls attention to the need for the characters to cling to an idea of community and nation that impedes their thriving. The illusion enables the characters to not have to confront their failures and take responsibility for their actions.

Sign evokes Albee's play to challenge the perception of the futility of human action and effort. Following existentialist thought, human beings are born without a preordained purpose. They must, through their stubborn effort, make meaning in a chaotic world. According to Camus, who differs from de Beauvoir, even with humans' best efforts one must recognize the limits of individual humans' ability to make meaning in the world. Camus did not see human effort as connected, hence the allusion to Sisyphus rolling a boulder up a hill for eternity. Hansberry, on the other hand, saw the possibility of human collaboration. In "The Negro Writer and His Roots," she asserted, "when hope begins to die, reason is often swift to follow. . . . Having discovered that the world is incoherent, they have, some of them, come to the conclusion that it is also unreal. Having determined that life is in fact an absurdity, they have not yet decided that the task of the thoughtful is to try to help impose purposefulness on the absurdity. In these same circles display of emotion is considered the mark of the unspeakably unsophisticated, while a sense of fraternity with the human race is but of course, the accoutrement of the most outlandish, utter 'square.' "[59] For Hansberry form (realism, the absurd) was tied to a political feeling (despair or hope). Form had everything to do with life and death for her because her organizing of the world weaved through political and artistic collaborations held together by affective ties, not necessarily biological ones.[60]

Hansberry's art, like that of her peers, engaged the philosophical debates emerging after the war. She questioned the willingness of her contemporary playwrights, mostly men and mostly white, to indulge in the reprieve from moral and political responsibility that absurdism offered. At the same time, Hansberry was aware that her American contemporaries were as much lamenting the implications of the war as they were contemplating the implications of the civil rights movement. The shift in time from the European writing of the 1940s to the early 1950s to the artistic production and modern civil rights movement from 1955 to the 1960s follows a shift in Cold War anxiety as a function of independence movements in Latin America and Africa to an independence movement in America. For Hansberry, the theater provided a space to investigate how illusions inform humans' ability to make material changes. She understood that material change did not function as the highest interest of most Americans, yet the movement required it.

As a student of history, Hansberry knew that her fellow activists were as concerned with representational inclusion (being able to use public facilities and receive service in private establishments) as they were with structural transformation (voting rights, the reform of federal housing policies, and city planning). In an American context built on the illusion of inherent racial hierarchies, Hansberry's art confronted the real impact and circulation of false illusions. Hansberry never completely adopted the beliefs of either existentialism or Marxism, neither of which fully accounted for racial alienation. She did, however, borrow from both, noting how theater served to traffic in illusions and make material, through bodies on stage, sets, and props, ideas about bodies that had material impact.

Although Sidney tries to find solace in his individual ineffectualness, he quickly learns that he is unable to shake the responsibility he feels for the death of his sister-in-law. In *Sign*, Act 3, scene 1 ends with Sidney passed out on the couch and Gloria in the bathroom overdosing from the bottle of pills she takes. The play suggests not that Sidney is responsible for Gloria's action but rather that his relinquishing his investment to care set the stage for his personal loss. Gloria suffers because of the isolation imposed by social alienation. In Hansberry's personal writing and art, barriers to intimacy, collaboration, and communion become the fodder for despair.

Although it was a play with seemingly insurmountable problems, Hansberry found solace in getting back to work on it; her writing practice built the foundation for her ideas and taught her how to live. Hansberry's routine diary entries demonstrate her persistent accounting for how to survive in a hostile world. Although Hansberry's journal entries often expressed sadness, depression, and in moments despair, she found refuge in her writing. In December 1963, she wrote, "Am grappling with what seems the eternal problem with *Sidney Brustein*. If anything is ever this much trouble to me again I shall scrap it long before these agonies." She continues, "I honestly believe I am learning something about myself and how to survive. Worked hard and well yesterday. Today much, much thinking about it (3 p.m.) But not the evasive kind. The real kind of work—thought."[61]

Sign has an ambiguous ending much like *Raisin* and *Les Blancs*. The play ends with Sidney and Iris making a commitment to try. The ending of the third act differs from that of the first, however, because it accounts for how their experiences shape their ability to try to move toward greater freedom. Before Sidney and Iris make their renewed commitments, Sidney has one final standoff with Wally. Wally comes to bid his condolences for Gloria. His presence reminds Sidney of how he gave himself over to despair.

> SIDNEY. (*With wonder—genuine wonder*) Wally, don't you know what kind of house you've walked into? Didn't it hit you in the face? Didn't death breathe on you as you came through the door . . . While I lay stoned on that couch, a girl who tried to accept everything that you stand for died in that bathroom today.

Do you think I haven't learned anything in the last few hours? The slogans of capitulation can *kill!* Every time we say 'live and let live'—death triumphs!

WALLY. Sidney, what is it that you're trying to say?

SIDNEY. That I am going to fight you, Wally. That you have forced me to take a position. Finally—the one thing I never wanted to do. Just not being *for* you is not enough. Since that girl died—(*To* Iris) I'm sorry, honey, but I have to—since that girl died—I have been forced to learn I have to be *against* you. And, Wally, I'm against you—I swear it to you—and your machine. And what you have to worry about is the fact that some of us will be back out in those streets today. Only this time—thanks to you—we shall be more seasoned, more cynical, tougher, harder to fool—and therefore, less likely to quit.[62]

Since her early days writing for *Freedom,* Hansberry knew the dangers of political compromise. While she also understood the necessity of incremental change, she challenged understanding that change as *the* change. In terms of the mission, the slogan for a movement, Hansberry insisted that only revolutionary change could set the groundwork for the freedom she envisioned. She did not, however, understand revolution as a singular unexpected event that happens suddenly. The beginning of revolutionary change begins with taking a position. Just as Walter Lee takes a stand and resists selling the Youngers' house in Clybourne Park, although the economic gains are clear, so too does Sidney take a stand even against Wally's threat that showing opposition will result in the failure of Sidney's newspaper.

The clarity wrought by despair also distinguishes the political neutrality of collaboration. Sidney responds to Wally's accusation that he reeks "of innocence" by charging that Wally "reeks of accommodation. He reeks of collusion. He reeks of collaboration—with Power and the tools of Power . . . *This world*—this swirling, seething madness—which you ask us to accept, to help maintain—has done this . . . maimed my friends . . . emptied these rooms and my very bed. And now it has taken my sister. *This* world! Therefore, to live, to breathe—I shall *have* to fight it!"[63] Although Hansberry saw the necessity of collaboration, she also understood the dangers of accommodating systems built to produce your destruction. *Sign,* similar to *Raisin,* ends with ambiguity, but in this case the ambiguity permeates the family unit and colors the last produced play as Hansberry's divorce play. Sidney and Iris's marriage may not survive, but their political future has reached a turning point based in a shared understanding.

Hansberry struggled with despair and reflected regret in her personal writing, but she also found hope in the possibility for renewal brought by each day. On January 1, 1964, Hansberry set her resolutions. She wrote, "The work goes superbly. Yes: Sidney Brustein! His character for the first time—beckons feeling from us! I am please [*sic*]. And certain of his speeches now—they transcend themselves and become good language of the theatre. I am anxious to get on to 'Toussaint' soon—Only death or infirmity can stop me now. The writing urge is on . . . 1964—will be work. Glorious work. I will finish Sidney, then Les Blancs—then Toussaint and then Laughing Boy—All this winter. And this spring I shall—what? Maybe go to see the California Coast—maybe go to Scotland. and 1965? I will be 35 then—greyer—but alive? I have set no goals in my life and accomplished none."[64] Hansberry made of her pain the fodder for her work. She spent the next year of her life battling cancer and finishing her play. Sidney's assertion that he "believes that death is waste and love is sweet and that the earth turns and men change every day . . . and that I hurt terribly today, and that hurt is desperation and desperation is—energy and energy can *move* things" expressed Hansberry's commitments.[65] The renewal of faithfulness to her craft served as an alternative practice of freedom that Hansberry cultivated through her writing and in her political work.

COMMUNITY BUILDING

The Broadway production of *The Sign in Sidney Brustein's Window* in 1964 produced a war between Hansberry and her audiences. On one side were the critics that Hansberry often debated publicly and critiqued in her private writing; on the other were her fellow artists, producers, activists, and community members. In this rare case, community staved off the ferocious pressure of the Great White Way establishment, at least temporarily. The production showed the power of Hansberry's artistic and political investment in collaboration based in intimacy. Theater is an inherently collaborative art form. In order for Lorraine to do her work, she relied on Bob as a trusted friend and advocate for her work. He helped forge the relationships that would enable the production of *Sign* and had been central to the production of *Raisin*. In an essay, "The 101 'Final' Performances of Sidney Brustein," Bob outlined the public support that enabled production to continue beyond all projections.

Focusing on the reception from critics, fans, and collaborators alike helps to emphasize how Hansberry's ideas became embodied. *Sign* premiered at the Longacre Theatre on October 15, 1964, to mixed reviews. In an introduction to the Vintage book edition of the play, Nemiroff offered a detailed accounting of the production history and how the reception, economics, and Hansberry's health informed the initial run of the play. He quoted lines from *Sign* that respond to what Hansberry understood as the mood of despair: "The *why* of why we are here is an intrigue for adolescents; the *how* is what must command the living. Which is why I have lately become an insurgent again."[66] Moving from theory to practice, from why to how, advances Hansberry's work and becomes manifest in the responses to the 1964 production, which focus on how to keep the play alive rather than why it should not survive on Broadway.

The critics could not see past Hansberry to her plays, and that lack of vision became the metanarrative of *Sign,* a play precisely about the ability, or lack thereof, to connect across difference through moments of recognition. In a scathing review for *Newsweek,* Richard Gilman wrote: "There is a sort of inverted miracle in the way Miss Hansberry manages to distort so many things. . . . A further miracle is her union of bitchiness with sentimentality. But it is borrowed bitchery, for in her incredibly awkward drama . . . Miss Hansberry plunders from every playwright around, most thoroughly, Edward Albee."[67] Putting to one side Gilman's critique of Hansberry's use of intertextuality and his oversight of the ways *Sign* cites *Raisin,* the sexism of his critique, common practice at the time, sounds familiar from Mike Wallace's dismissive description of Hansberry as a "girl" in his 1959 interview. Moments of misrecognition clarified for Hansberry the necessary steps to move toward a radical politics and becoming free.

Other reviews had a more measured approach but still found the play challenging. In a review for the *New York Times,* Howard Taubman reported: "There are, in brief, many good things scattered through 'The Sign in Sidney Brustein's Window.' But the truth must be faced that Miss Hansberry's play lacks concision and cohesion." He concluded: "Although 'The Sign in Sidney Brustein's Window' is uneven and would benefit from tightening in script and performance, it has commendable virtues."[68] Less equivocal, in the *Wall Street Journal,* Richard Cooke reported: "If Broadway has needed a play by someone who can reach into the turbulence of contemporary New York life and come up with a true report which also is a work of dramatic art, Lorraine Hansberry has accomplished it. . . . 'The Sign in Sidney Brustein's Window' is by far the most interesting play of the new season, even though it seems packed too full with ideas and situations."[69] Critics, in the main, were unwilling to take up Hansberry's challenge. Although the reviews offered praise and critique, Nemiroff explained: "In the light of such reviews the lay theatre-goer might logically assume modest success—and indeed, many of our friends called to offer congratulations. But to anyone who understands the stringent economics of Broadway the contrary was clear . . . the drama that is not a 'hit' is dead . . . [*Sidney Brustein*] *would have to close.*"[70]

Although critics had difficulty deciphering Hansberry's latest offering, her community did not. In response to the seeming imminent closing of the play, her friends extended the production. Publicly lauding the play and working behind the scenes, producers, fellow artists, activists, and fans organized. In a meeting in October, Jerome Smith, the CORE field secretary who had joined the meeting with Bobby Kennedy just a month earlier, recalled his first meeting with Hansberry at the fund-raiser she organized to help purchase a station wagon for James Chaney, Michael Schwerner, and Andrew Goodman to use in their investigation of the burning of Mt. Zion Methodist Church in Philadelphia, Mississippi, the site of a CORE Freedom School. During their investigation, the three men were abducted and murdered. Smith reflected on Hansberry's " 'commitment beyond race . . . the need to reach out and touch each other . . . without which civil rights in themselves don't mean a thing.' " Hansberry knew well the barriers to her own visibility. She did not, therefore, fall into the trap of racial solidarity as cure-all. Her writing showed that connecting across difference required great and necessary risk. Smith's comments inspired the group to place an ad in the *New York Times* that read, in part: "*The Sign in Sidney Brustein's Window* is concerned with the turbulent life of our times. It is, in turn, powerful, tender, moving and hilarious. Whether it survives or closes will be determined this week. . . . We the undersigned, who believe in it enough to pay for this ad, urge you to see it *now*."[71] The signatories of the ad were James Baldwin, Paddy Chayefsky, Sammy Davis, Ossie Davis, Ruby Dee, William Gibson, E. Y. Harburg, Julie Harris, Lillian Hellman, Sidney Kingsley, Viveca Lindfors, Frank and Eleanor Perry, Arthur Penn, and Shelley Winters.

In addition to the ad campaign, the production invested in robust community engagement. Following the November 4 matinee, which contained groups of clergy people, the actors invited the audience to participate in conversation about the play. Sidney Kingsley, Herman Shumlin, Shelley Winters, Viveca Lindfors, and James Baldwin joined the actors on stage. Baldwin expressed his own difficulties with the play and his "troubling ambivalence" after seeing it—

> until, that is, I realized just what about it was making me so uncomfortable . . . It was the particular quality of commitment in this play. Sidney Brustein believes things that I, that most of us, believed a long time ago . . . in the thirties . . . only Sidney still believes them. And now the poor bastard is a set-up to have his head busted in for it—in the third act he would *have* to . . . I was *shocked*—and believe me . . . I am *one* individual I really thought was almost *beyond* shocking—at my own discomfiture . . . at the degree we have, all of us, permitted ourselves to

retreat from what we once were ... at the distance one decade, the era McCarthy, has driven between us and our own ability to commit ourselves as Sidney is committed ... that caused me to examine more deeply into myself and my own motives than any other in a long, long time. If it cannot, survive, then we are in trouble ... because it is about nothing less than our responsibility to ourselves and to each other.[72]

Hansberry's play means to produce a reckoning, seeing oneself again in "that engaged freedom, that surging of the for-oneself which is immediately given for others." The reception would continue until the play closed following Hansberry's death in January 1965. It included public letters and reporting of the efforts to keep the play alive. *Sign* ended up being one of the longest running shows on Broadway that year. The collective effort of individual theater-goers and well-known patrons kept the show alive in the midst of a war of reception.

WAIT NO MORE

Hansberry's most explicit battles with the despair that took hold of the theater world following the war emerge in her tragedy *What Use Are Flowers?* and the unpublished comedy *The Arrival of Mr. Todog.* Both plays engage Samuel Beckett's *Waiting for Godot,* the second explicitly in the title's inversion of the key figure's name. The first productions in English of Beckett's now classic drama brought confusion. Written in French, the play opened at the Théâtre de Babylone in Paris in 1953. The play left audiences baffled and intrigued by the concept of watching a play about nothing. After the controversy sparked by the Paris run, which had been scheduled only for a month but was extended to nine months based on audience interest, Beckett translated the play into English, and it premiered in London at the Arts Theatre Club in August 1955, and in September moved to the Criterion Theatre. Although the play proved more perplexing to audiences than anything else, London theater critics, particularly Kenneth Tynan, convinced audiences the play merited attention.[73] The London production won the *Evening Standard* Drama Award for most controversial play of the year.

The accounts of the *New York Times* theater critic, Brooks Atkinson, to the New York production at the John Golden Theatre in 1956 establish how it intersects with some of the chief philosophical concerns that preoccupied Hansberry in the 1950s, as she wrestled with *The Second Sex,* and informed her writing until her death. Atkinson's coverage of Beckett's play in 1956, 1957, and 1958 contributed to its transformation from a curiosity to a canonical work.

He wrote: "Since 'Waiting for Godot' has no simple meaning, one seizes on Mr. Beckett's experience of two worlds to account for his style and point of view. The point of view suggests Sartre—bleak, dark, disgusted. The style suggests Joyce—pungent and fabulous. Put the two together and you have some notion of Mr. Beckett's acrid cartoon of the story of mankind." The play tapped into a feeling of futility, using an appealing style. Why not meet doom with humor? Atkinson concluded: "Mr. Beckett is no charlatan. He has strong feelings about the degradation of mankind, and he has given vent to them copiously. 'Waiting for Godot' is all feeling. Perhaps that is why it is puzzling and convincing at the same time. Theatregoers can rail at it, but they cannot ignore it. For Mr. Becket is a valid writer."[74] The allure of Beckett's work, a play that, in Atkinson's review, is "all feeling," produces a shared emotion divorced from material concerns. Hansberry preferred to produce work that used feeling to structure political engagement.

Beckett's play seduces audiences to embrace the feeling of despair and, in so doing, engages in a political and philosophical project. Theater in the mid-twentieth century became a site to work through political and philosophical questions, and criticism became a place to parse, debate, and extend the conversation artists began. Hansberry's writing, dramatic and polemical, established her character as a public intellectual and linked the debates of the civil rights movement to those animating leftists. In both arenas Hansberry urged liberals to become radicals. In a subsequent review for the *New York Times* in April 1956, nine days after the first review, Atkinson responded to the perception in Paris, London, and New York that *Waiting for Godot* was a hoax. The play is a "serious comment on the degraded state of man in the Christian civilization of today," he wrote.[75] Man suffers, waiting for, in Atkinson's reading of the play, God that never comes. He concluded that the play's bleakness intones man's doomed fate.

The history of *Waiting for Godot* took an interesting turn when the producer Michael Myerberg decided to revive the play at the Ethel Barrymore theater in 1957 with an all-Black cast. Although Atkinson found some merit in revisiting the play, he lamented: " 'Waiting for Godot' is not so much of a minstrel show as it has become in Herbert Berghof's new style of direction." Atkinson analyzed the acting of Mantan Moreland, Earle Hyman, Rex Ingram, Geoffrey Holder, and Bert Chamberlain. Moreland's acting in vaudeville and low-budget films borrowed from troupes of minstrelsy, particularly his way of making his eyes bulge for comedic effect. In the 1957 production, the Negro cast's deployment of humor, according to Atkinson, threatened the central concern of the play, "the suffering of mankind."[76] Curiously, these Black actors more easily produced laughter and had more difficulty evoking sympathy. The dynamic that Atkinson observed in the production established a more universal concern that Hansberry had about how despair as a feeling that structures political engagement operates for Black people. The question is not whether or not despair is a valid response to unceasing suffering, but rather what use that feeling serves as a context for political action. Although Hansberry agreed that supernatural forces would not intervene to save humans from the destruction they cultivate and deploy, she did not conclude that abandoning the wait for God reconciled them to death.

In *Sign,* Hansberry took up communal concerns over the Holocaust. Although native and Black people had long lived with the terror of mass annihilation and extinction, the thought of camps in Europe brought a new sense of dread to the Western art world. In *What Use Are Flowers?* and *The Arrival of Mr. Todog,* she returned to the overwhelming sense of despair that characterized American theater and pockets of American culture while attending to the willingness to use nuclear force against Japan. Does the American theater despair for Japan too? According to Nemiroff's introduction of the play, "*Godot* was only one of the more striking expressions of the prevailing attitudes of a generation that had come to maturity under the shadow of the Bomb, to which the young black playwright brought a quite different point of view. In her first public address as a writer, to a conference of black artists and intellectuals, she affirmed the need for black writers to devote themselves to *all* aspects of the freedom struggle, including that which opposed the forces of despair, destruction and war in the world."[77]

Certainly, to Hansberry's chagrin, *Godot* continued to speak to audiences that well knew the violence of the state before the unleashing of nuclear warfare on Japan. In November 1957 the San Francisco Actor's Workshop produced the play for the inmates of San Quentin penitentiary. The workshop also took the production to the Brussels World's Fair, in 1958, at the invitation of the State Department.[78] And just days after Hansberry's death, the Free Southern Theatre (FST) performed *Godot* at the Mt. Zion Baptist Church in rural Mississippi. John O'Neal, a former member of SNCC, with Gilbert Moses formed FST as a part of "the cultural side of the civil rights movement."[79] The Cold War necessitated understanding civil rights struggles as material and ideological. For Hansberry, Black people's understandable romance with despair posed an imminent danger and required activists' resistance.

In one response to Beckett's work, Hansberry took a note from the political theater of German playwright Bertolt Brecht. Known for crafting drama that disrupts the alienation that adheres through the gaze, Brecht served as a key figure in thinking about how to restructure appearance and illusion. Hansberry drew the epigraph to *What Use Are Flowers?* from the penultimate song in Brecht's *Mother Courage and Her Children.* The epigraph reads, "Lullaby baby / What's rustling there? / Neighbor's child in Poland / Mine's who knows where." The song that Mother Courage sings after the death of her third child reads in full:

> Lullaby, baby, what's that in the hay?
> The neighbor's kids cry but mine are gay.
> The neighbor's kids are dressed in dirt:
> Your silks are cut from an angel's skirt.
> They are all starving: you have a pie.
> If it's too stale, you need only cry.
> Lullaby, baby, what's rustling there?
> One lad fell in Poland. The other is—where?[80]

Throughout Brecht's epic drama, Mother Courage, the titular character, loses all three of her children in the midst of her capitulation to war. Mother Courage makes the most of the havoc that sets the world of the play, the seventeenth century during the Thirty Years' War. She continues to sell merchandise out of her cart and sacrifices her children along the way. Instead of mourning the death of her final child, Kattrin, Mother Courage sings a lullaby, suggesting that her daughter has taken a nap rather than died. The song also presents Mother Courage's children as thriving in the midst of scarce resources, wearing silk and eating pie. The final lines, however, introduce some ambiguity, at the very least, about the whereabouts of the children, acknowledging that one died in Poland and the other is missing. Based on the play, the audience knows that the "missing" child Eilif died at the hands of soldiers. Throughout the play, Mother Courage must make decisions that put her children in harm's way. While the choices may offer momentary gratification, the capitulation to war ultimately consumes everyone, and particularly those that try to profit from it.

The ideological struggle at the heart of *Mother Courage and Her Children,* whether to die with principle or live with injustice that may temporarily benefit you but will ultimately destroy you, surely resonated profoundly with Hansberry after losing her father and seeing the effects of Cold War persecution on her mentors (Robeson, Du Bois, and Childress). Brecht's play also emphasizes that profit helps to ease discomfort with ethical ambiguity. The specific investigation of materialism informs the shape of *What Use Are Flowers?* and certainly speaks to Hansberry's larger investments in Marxism.

What Use Are Flowers? contemplates the aftermath of mass destruction and wonders about the importance of art in a world that does not value human life and achievement. Hansberry wrote a precursor to the play in the short story "Gedachtnis."[81] Similar to the story, the play depicts a Hermit that retreats from the world to escape "the dominion of time in the lives of men and the things that they did with it and to it and, indeed, that they let it do to them."[82] The Hermit's retreat from modernity may be understood as a resistance to commodification. His refusal of the clock, however, does not result in his ability to escape the impact of time. He continues to age and returns from his sojourn in the woods looking for the civilization he left behind and knowing he draws near to death.

He quickly learns that in retreat he furthered the destruction. Upon return, he finds instead a world devastated and only peopled by "wild" children.[83] The Hermit comes out of the woods, after living alone for twenty years, and meets a band of several boys and one girl. At first, he asks them to direct him to the nearest town. After attempting to communicate in a different language and asking several questions, he realizes that they are prelingual. The rest of the one-act play consists of the Hermit trying to reestablish civilization. His efforts to teach the students the meaning of the word "use" propels a set of questions that return to the issue of capitalism and its excesses.

Hansberry presents a world both post- and pre-modern. She knew the impact of the industrial revolution and the hyper-commodification of goods and people, reducing human life to exchange value. Fred Moten's *In the Break* explains, "The words Marx puts into the commodity's mouth are these: 'our use value . . . does not belong to us as objects. What does belong to us as objects, however, is our value,' where value equals exchange value. Marx has the commodity go on to assert that commodities only relate to one another as exchange-values, that this is proven by the necessarily social intercourse in which commodities might be said to discover themselves. Therefore, the commodity discovers herself, comes to know herself, only as a function of having been exchanged, having been embedded in a mode of sociality that is shaped by exchange."[84] Hansberry's play returns to a prior juncture in terms of economic development in the West in order to evaluate the potential of disrupting the growing penchant for mass destruction as a final devaluation of life.

The political power of art comes to attention when the Hermit realizes everything cannot be reduced to use value. Some things (such as art), experiences (community), and feelings (desire) exceed use *and* serve as primary motivations for behavior. The Hermit first teaches the students about "use" when he tries to explain the function of a clay pot. His instructor centers on how making objects work for the children demonstrates their use value; a pot carries, a knife whittles. The idea of "use" comes into sharp relief when William asks the Hermit what use are flowers? The Hermit answers by describing their aesthetic value—how they smell, feel, or inspire poetry. The Hermit becomes distracted in his examples and encourages the children to sing a verse. Before long several children join in the singing, but Lily returns to the original question, asking, what use is music? The Hermit, exasperated, instructs the children to just sing. His effort to civilize the children reaches a critical breaking point when he fails to distinguish different types of value.

Hansberry's investment in art as a mechanism for social change reflected her larger ideological resistance to accumulation of private property as a practice of freedom. By the end of the play, according to Hansberry, "we are left . . ., hopefully, with some appreciation of the fact of the cumulative processes which created modern man and his greatness and how we ought not go around blowing it up."[85] Hansberry saw the reduction of humans to their use value as a degradation of humanity, familiar to descendants of slaves and becoming increasingly present to many in the Western world following the Holocaust. In a short piece of speculative fiction, "Accident of the Cosmos," Hansberry portrayed a world after the complete annihilation of Europe and North America.[86] The story sees history after empire as a means to delink the possible from the present state of things.

Hansberry also explored the philosophical implications of mass destruction in her unpublished play "Arrival of Mr. Todog: A Bit of Whimsy or 'A Little Camp on a Great Camp.'" The one-act play, more than any of Hansberry's published works, demonstrates her sense of humor and incisive wit. At every turn, the play pokes fun at the despair nothingness produces in *Waiting for Godot*, but by the conclusion of the play, instead of supernatural intercession, the characters realize they are the ones they have been waiting for. The opening stage directions read, "Two indigents appear. They are dressed to show this, as it were. They also carry the traditional bundles which we associated with tramps in the comic strips and in modern drama. The first tramp, whose name, of course, is MARY, does not know the second tramp, POOPOO. Mary appears from left and POOPOO from right. MARY puts down his bundle and sits on it and takes off his shoe and smells it and puts it back on again and then takes it off again and then puts it on and then takes it off and then puts it on and then takes it off. This goes on until the action is, as it were, established. POOPOO raises his hand as if to sight in the distance and does so, as it were."[87] Hansberry's language in the stage directions, the repetition of "as it were," and the reference to modern drama implicitly and explicitly parody Beckett's play. The names of the characters also call into question the assumptions of his play. While critics understand *Waiting for Godot* as a play about anyone, hence the easy, or perhaps not so easy per Atkinson, transposition of the characters from white to Black actors, Hansberry presses the issue by naming one of the figures Mary, traditionally a woman's name, and referring to the same character with male pronouns. How easy is it for Beckett's world to accommodate gender that does not conform to modern expectations?

Hansberry then returns to a concern central to *Sign* that had emerged in her short stories for *The Ladder*, the idea of human connection as a treatment for alienation and isolation. In the opening moments after hearing Poopoo say, "well," Mary realizes, "I'm not alone in this world, after all. Why can't we learn that? That even though we think we are alone in this lonely, world, which is Life, we are not alone. That is my brother—if only I could break through the wall and talk to him. If only. Then this wasteland could be endured. But—I cannot bear to speak to him. What if I should be rejected?"[88] Hansberry's art and artistic practice suggest making the work provides opportunities for collaboration that result in breaking through the walls that divide individuals from experiencing intimacy. Discriminatory laws on same-sex and interracial coupling reinforced those walls in Hansberry's time.

The desire Mary expresses turns the interaction between the two characters from inconsequential farce to a recognizable comment on perceptions or assumptions about proper forms of community in the mid-twentieth century. Poopoo explains that when he began his journey, an unnamed person told him he would meet another one. Poopoo questions if Mary is the "one." Mary, unclear, responds, "Oh, you came to meet someone else?" Shaping up more like a bad first date than an existential crisis, Mary laments, "I knew you would be here to meet someone else! The cute ones never like me! I knew it, I knew it!"[89] The opening conversation counters the growing belief in individuals' grave difficulty to connect, particularly across difference—for example, Baldwin's meditation on the difficulty for individuals to come together in *The Fire Next Time*. Hansberry, following de Beauvoir, offers a campy challenge to the assumption that the human condition inherently produces insurmountable alienation. Instead, she questions if the way modern artists and philosophers theorize the human may be the source of despair, subsequently perpetuated through social structures, namely, in terms of the arts' reviewers and producers as gatekeepers.

Realizing a mutual attraction, the flirtation between Mary and Poopoo persists as a traveler enters with a large food basket. Mary wonders if he is the one they are waiting for and reasons that even if he is not, they should partake of his feast. After another series of miscommunications, the three return to the central question of the play, where is the man they seek. Less reconciled to the waiting that preoccupies the characters in *Godot,* the characters learn they share a surname, Todog, and that they don't know, or don't think they know, the name of their potential savior. The Traveler questions Poopoo and Mary's ability to identify the man if they don't know his name: "How will you know if you don't know which name is the right one? My word, suppose another Todog should show up. I mean almost anything seems possible in this play."[90] The traveler's metacommentary about the world of the play, calling attention to the narrative as a constructed one with purposefully crafted boundaries, helps to establish why Hansberry sees the theater as a useful space to intervene in philosophical debates. The world of a play, particularly a realist drama, imagines the contexts of human interaction and its constraints. Audiences measure realist drama's success based on the believability of human interaction. Of course, in the world of Beckett's absurdism, the interaction of characters draws attention to a seeming misapprehension of constraints on interactions based on a common belief in the value of human life challenged by the negligent disregard of Europeans' lives during World War II.

Hansberry's comedy suggests that anything can happen in her play because it exceeds the expectations for who qualifies as human and thus what structures interactions. But before the characters continue down the existential rabbit hole, Poopoo reveals, "I have his name" written on a piece of paper. Before Poopoo reads the name, he notes the similarity between this moment and the birth of knowledge in the Bible, once again pointing to this play's role in Hansberry's larger philosophical project. He tells, "the name . . . is Todog! It—it is our name . . . Oh, my word, this is desperate! . . . It means—it means—that there is no he. We are he. All of us. All of us—on this barren landscape. WE ARE TODOG!" Although Poopoo at first expresses grave concern, the characters quickly realize that they now have the power to set the rules and govern how they feel. Mary muses, "we are really and truly completely and in all ways free—and that, moreover, (*gesturing*) ALL of this belongs to us—not him?"[91] Mary connects the sense of belonging to the land as a reorientation of collectivity producing shared property rights. The play ends with the characters celebrating and singing to the tune of "Auld Lang Syne." Marking a new day (perhaps in the same spirit as the Luther Vandross song "A Brand New Day," from the 1975 musical *The Wiz*), the play ends with a feeling of hope in making the world anew.

Hansberry channeled her growing frustration with the pace of the civil rights movement, the escapism of the New York theater scene, and the cowardice of liberals into her art. *Sign, What Use Are Flowers?* and "Arrival of Mr. Todog" demonstrate the necessary work of art as a mechanism to structure feeling. In order to convince liberals to become radicals, Hansberry knew she had to reclaim America as an object of desire.

Chapter 6 With Her Mind Stayed on Freedom

...attention must be paid in equal and careful measure to the required triumph of man, if not nature, over the absurd. Perhaps it is here that certain of the modern existentialists have erred. They have seemed to me to be overwhelmed by the mere fact of the absurd and become incapable of imagining its frailty. The balance which is struck between the recognition of both may be the final secret of Shakespeare.
—Lorraine Hansberry

I can't be a pessimist because I'm alive. To be a pessimist means that you have agreed that human life is an academic matter, so I'm forced to be optimistic; I'm forced to believe that we can survive whatever we must survive. But the future of the Negro in this country is precisely as bright or as dark as the future of the country. It is entirely up to the American people and our representatives, it is entirely up to the American people whether or not they are going to face and deal with and embrace the stranger whom they maligned so long. What white people have to do is try to find out in their own hearts why it was necessary to have a nigger in the first place. Because I'm not a nigger, I am a man, but if you think I'm a nigger, it means you need it ... If I'm not a nigger here and if you invented him—you, the white people, invented him, then you've got to find out why. And the future of the country depends on that.
—James Baldwin

As Lorraine Hansberry lay in a hospital bed dying of cancer, she edited her last plays. The personal medical crisis Hansberry faced as she finished *Les Blancs* evoked in her an uncharacteristic expression of despair. On July 17, 1964, she wrote:

> Have the feeling I should throw myself back into the movement. Become a human being again. / But that very impulse is immediately flushed with a thousand vacillations and forbidding images. I see myself lying in a pool of perspiration in a dark tenement room recalling Croton and the trees and longing for death—/ *Comfort* has come to be its own corruption. I think of lying without a painkiller in pain. In all the young years no such image ever occurred to me. I rather *looked forward* to going to jail once. Now I can hardly imagine surviving it at all. Comfort. Apparently I have sold my soul for it. / I think when I get my health back I shall go into the South to find out what kind of revolutionary I am.[1]

Her meditation is found in a diary entry included in *To Be Young, Gifted, and Black*, an "informal autobiography" that Nemiroff compiled after her death. The meditation begins with longing for purpose. Her tone suggests the all-consuming nature of what she calls *the movement* and the way it fed her understanding of what it means to be human. Hansberry understood *being human* as an act of will, a choice undertaken in resistance to violence and chaos. This daily choice acknowledges chaos as an alternative that furtively lays in wait for the battered, bruised, and exhausted. Ravaged by disease and encumbered by her fear of hospitals, Hansberry depicts political action as a persistent personal struggle that serves a meaningful purpose only when understood as a part of a long history of struggle for freedom. For Hansberry, active participation in freedom movements, domestic and international, served as the antidote to despair.

In her meditation, she longs for rest and the ability to welcome death, but in her weary state she can imagine only giving herself fully over to the pain. Her inability to rest even in her darkest hours powerfully signifies the nature of her artistic vision. Because even as she laments the loss of her fearlessness and decries the seduction of comfort, she emphatically concludes, "I think when I get my health back I shall go into the South to find out what kind of revolutionary I am." Her diary entry provides insight into the abiding power of her artistic vision and the ways it offers a roadmap for actions that can maintain and further Black freedom movements. At the same time, her expression of pain calls attention to the tragic circumstances of her death and the vacancy left in her unfinished work. *Les Blancs* is a powerful expression of audacious dreaming in the midst of despair, of great possibility in "a season of sorrow."[2]

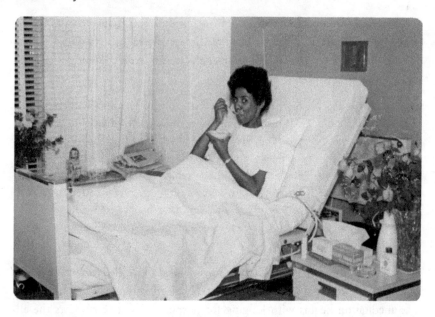

Lorraine in hospital bed (Photograph courtesy of Joi Gresham)

By 1964 Hansberry's involvement with the civil rights movement, which she understood as a part of a global movement for freedom, reinforced her understanding that freedom would require more than diplomatic and legal measures. Her meeting with Robert Kennedy in 1963 only reinforced lessons from her childhood that reverberated as she followed the fights for independence in Ghana, Algeria, and Kenya, and considered the assassination of Patrice Lumumba, the first prime minister of the independent Democratic Republic of the Congo. In *Les Blancs,* a play that responds directly to Jean Genet's *Les Nègres* (The Blacks), Hansberry stages a debate over the utility and political expediency of diplomacy. Set in the fictional African country Zatembe, the play depicts three brothers—Abioseh, Jr., Tshembe, and Eric—struggling to come to terms with the revolutionary legacy that their father, Abioseh, Sr., left them. Although the play reveals their father's role in the struggle for the native population to take control of the government from the settlers, as children the sons see Abioseh, Sr., as a communal leader working with the settlers and in their early adult lives as a defeated man. His status gives the two older sons, Abioseh and Tshembe, access to the privileges the missionary provides, including formal education. At the beginning of the play, Abioseh and Tshembe return from Europe for their father's funeral. Similar to William Shakespeare's *Hamlet,* the father's death produces a ghost but not the father's ghost. Rather, Abioseh, Sr., leaves behind a ghost of the revolutionary spirit he embodied as the leader of his village and one of the first advocates for self-rule. Conflicted about the status of the government upon his return, Tshembe spends most of the play talking about the insurgency that threatens to topple the government while the revolutionary spirit haunts him and causes him to question his longing "to be in a dim little flat off Langley Square, watching the telly with [his] family."[3] After pages of talking, the futility of diplomacy confronts Tshembe, and he must make the difficult decision of fleeing to Europe or taking up arms. After an anguished cry, Tshembe chooses; he decides to fight, enacting his first blow for independence on his brother Abioseh, Jr.

Tshembe's *choice* to stay and fight for independence reflects the crossroads Hansberry faced at the end of her life and of the U.S. civil rights movement, which was being influenced by international movements for independence in the mid and late twentieth century. Specifically, *Les Blancs* registers the struggle for independence in Kenya from Jomo Freedom Kenyatta's imprisonment (he was arrested in October 1952) to self-rule (December 12, 1963). Hansberry began writing about the fight for independence in Kenya in 1952, publishing an article in *Freedom* advocating for self-rule. Her depiction of diplomacy and direct action in *Les Blancs* accounts for the decade-long international struggle. She channels the conflict through a character, Tshembe, that exhibits a historically conscious resolve. Her play considers the mutuality of anti-Black violence and political victories that mark the civil rights movement in the United States from 1963 to 1964. The death of NAACP field secretary Medgar Evers occurred two months before the historic March on Washington in 1963, followed just weeks later by the bombing of the Sixteenth Street Baptist Church. In November, President Kennedy was assassinated, forging the way for Congress to pass the Civil Rights Act, banning discrimination in employment and public places, in July 1964. Even with the passage of this historic act, by 1964 the patience of many civil rights activists in the U.S. was wearing thin.

Hansberry's play participated in an unresolved conversation among civil rights activists over the merits of nonviolence as *the* protest strategy that best aided diplomacy. Although Martin Luther King, Jr., the figure most readily associated with the civil rights movement and the first president of the Southern Christian Leadership Conference (SCLC), saw nonviolence as an ethical imperative, Ella Baker, a prominent grassroots activist and director of the SCLC from 1957 to 1960, articulated the merits of diverse protest practices. On June 5, 1959, in Birmingham, Alabama, Baker asked, " 'What is the basic right of the individual to defend himself'?" She charged in response, " 'Guideposts to first-class citizenship call for utilization of all resources at the group's command.' "[4] Five years and many deaths later, Martin Luther King's Nobel Prize acceptance speech in 1964 chronicled the violence that activists faced even as he maintained the moral necessity of nonviolence: "I am mindful that only yesterday in Birmingham, Alabama, our children, crying out for brotherhood, were answered with hoses, snarling dogs and even death. I am mindful that only yesterday in Philadelphia, Mississippi, young people seeking to secure the right to vote were brutalized and murdered. And only yesterday more than 40 houses of worship in the State of Mississippi alone were bombed or burned because they offered a sanctuary to those who would not accept segregation." Nevertheless, he concluded, "nonviolence is the answer to the crucial political and moral question of our time—the need for man to overcome oppression and violence without resorting to violence and oppression. Civilization and violence are antithetical concepts."[5] King's depiction of the reciprocal function of violence explains why he places an ethical purchase on nonviolence.

Similar to Baker, Hansberry did not share King's singular commitment to nonviolence because the arc of what she called "the movement" had many endpoints reaching back to slave insurrection and perpetually into the future. Hansberry was personally and intimately aware of historic and ongoing violence and anticipated future occurrences; the Watts riots began in August 1965, seven months after Hansberry's death.[6] In "The Black Revolution and the White Backlash," a Town Hall debate Hansberry joined in June 1964, she offered biographical evidence to explain her resistance to setting diplomacy and nonviolent direct action in opposition to self-defense because she associated such opposition with despair. Recalling her father's famous struggle against restrictive housing covenants in Chicago, Hansberry noted his unwavering commitment to social justice, fighting "the case in the courts all the way to the Supreme Court of the United States." Yet Chicago remained a segregated city, and her "father died a disillusioned exile in another country." With the complicated legacy of her father as a backdrop, Hansberry asserted: "That is the reality that I'm faced with when I get up and I read that some Negroes my own age and younger say that we must now lie down in the streets, tie up traffic, stop ambulances, do whatever we can, take to the hills if necessary with some guns and fight back, you see. This is the difference."[7] Though the distinction between self-defense and nonviolent civil disobedience began to mark the end of the civil rights movement in the summer of 1964, Hansberry's practice (artistic and political) required the coexistence of multiple forms of activism, drawing from the example her mother and father set for her as a child. Given her introduction to freedom movements, her vision to "*impose* the reason for life on life" functioned as a practice that drew from distinct strategies and brought together several people and organizations in its implementation.

Hansberry's consideration of how political practices mitigate the disabling power of despair assumes individual actions are meaningful and historical. Although the political landscape that framed Hansberry's activism required a correlation between political practice and historical outcomes, the artistic contexts for her work did not operate under the same assumptions. Early in *Les Blancs,* Tshembe suggests that choice unhinges the actor from history. In describing his decision to move to Europe and marry a white woman with gray eyes, he concludes that he chose freely and once he chose "it was all over with me and history."[8] Referencing Albert Camus and the absurdist tradition that *Les Blancs* questions, Tshembe establishes his individualism as a " 'free man' " in that "*I chose*" and, in so doing, loosened the perceived force of the past. In Hansberry's annual inventory of herself, what she called "Myself in Notes" for the year 1960, she wrote, "I hate Jean Genet's plays and Jean Paul Sartre's writing."[9] The play, however, complicates Hansberry's personal disdain through its contemplation of the relationship among choice, history, and individualism by offering characters with seemingly incongruent aspects of their subjectivity. Although Tshembe is African, the influence of the mission and his Western education challenge him to negotiate the competing desires of colonial rule and the independence movement. The characterization of Tshembe emphasizes how all acts have histories that constitute the subject, even though the central character has bought into the promise of liberal individualism. Tshembe's crisis of identity, his existential crisis, reflects how "for Hansberry, existentialism encoded, politicized, and dramatized racial and sexual identities . . . but it denied the historical material conditions that gave rise to both oppression and social change. . . . Hansberry found Simone de Beauvoir's existentialist feminism integral to rearticulating the meanings and relationships between sexual, racial, and national liberation," according to Cheryl Higashida.[10] The play suggests that all choices exist within a historical context that influences the individual, enhancing the transformative nature of choice while still challenging the absurdist tradition, which renders decisions arbitrary and ineffectual because it is emptied of impacting anyone but the individual actor.

The position Hansberry faced at the end of her life, confronting the failures of the civil rights movement (a movement that made her life worth living), the shortcomings of independence movements, and her impending death, mirrors Tshembe's impossible position, teetering between violent and nonviolent action or some combination therein. Like her character, Hansberry was born with relative privilege and a legacy of familial activism. Hansberry's father and uncle, Africanist scholar Leo Hansberry, provided examples of how the courts and the written word serve as weapons in the fight for social justice. Though one might easily predict Hansberry's activism based on her upbringing, the form it takes, an unyielding resistance to nihilism and an unwavering commitment to human life, specifies the power of her artistic vision to imagine a political future in the waning years of the classical phase of the civil rights movement.

Hansberry's life served as one of the sources of her drama, but her choice to have Tshembe stay and fight reflects a decision to defy the power of death and to command the force of history. Instead of conceding to the random absurdity of life, Hansberry's play depicts how Tshembe's political consciousness emerges through his choice to further the independence movement of his father. Although Tshembe acknowledges that he would rather enjoy the escapism that his colonial and Western education provides him access to as an expatriate that lives in Europe, by the play's end, he chooses to participate in the struggle for independence. Tshembe's actions disrupt the life in Europe that his missionary education provides and harness the historically disruptive ghostly force of revolution.

TRAGIC TIMES, BLACK INTERNATIONALISM DURING THE COLD WAR

The promise of civil rights in the United States accompanied sacrifices, including the foregrounding of civil rights through legal remedies to discrimination over human rights strategies that fought for equality on a number of fronts including legal ones in the United States, which (Penny M. Von Eschen argues) led, in part, to the collapse of leftist and Black diasporic coalition's utopian imaginary, produced as an antidote to the atrocities of World War II. Following the Truman Doctrine of 1947, "the criticism of American foreign policy gave way to an acceptance of America's claim to be the legitimate leader of the free world. In a fundamental reshaping of black American political and rhetorical strategies, anticolonialism did not disappear but, for liberals, was increasingly justified by an anti-Communist agenda. The repression of the McCarthy era devastated the anticolonialism of the left as well, destroying the vestiges of the 1940s politics."[11] As a result, Higashida argued, "African American liberals delinked decolonization movements abroad from domestic civil rights struggles."[12]

Von Eschen uses the term "destroying" to describe the impact of McCarthy era repression on U.S.-based international Black freedom movements, but earlier she makes a less totalizing claim, suggesting, "anticolonialism did not disappear." Appearance and disappearance, the hallmarks of performance, point to the extra-legal and communal modes of resistance that Black feminist leftists produced from the 1940s through the 1960s.[13] While "Embodied memory, because it is live, exceeds the archive's ability to capture it," according to Diana Taylor, "performances also replicate themselves through their own structures and codes," including daily practices of freedom passed down intergenerationally.[14] Higashida notes the importance of Hansberry working with Alice Childress, Dorothy Burnham, and Eslanda Goode Robeson during the early days of *Freedom*. Even though the archive offers scant evidence of the nature of their relationships, Hansberry was invested in equal proportion to Black internationalism through feminist webs of affiliation. Webs of affiliation connect performances in the present to those enacted in the past but not through a direct line. Black freedom movements occur in time but also shape our relationship to time. Temporal multiplicity—that is, time working in counterpoint rather than linearly—shapes artists and activists' relationship to categories of the human and the citizen.

Hansberry's investment in diasporic Black freedom movements foregrounded self-determination without reinscribing patriarchal structures of nationalism, which echoes the work of Childress, Burnham, and Robeson. If one looks to Hansberry's writing from the early 1950s until her death, anti-colonialism never disappears. Although Hansberry's work certainly bears the signs of the Cold War and Black internationalism, understanding all performances as acts of memory situates meaning making and the constitution of the public sphere within historical contexts that move in multiple directions simultaneously.

Les Blancs connects Black freedom struggles in the late twentieth century to a diasporic form of international humanism that was imagined in the aftermath of World War II but that artists and activists routed underground through the pragmatic political wrangling of midcentury in the United States.[15] At the same time, Hansberry's play engages with and anticipates the social and political shifts that occurred following the major victories of the civil rights movement (the Civil Rights Act and the Voting Rights Act). The revolutionary energy of making new worlds that inspired civil rights activism and art did not disappear following the passage of the Voting Rights Act. It was rechanneled into the militancy of the Black Power movement, which accounted for the ongoing social, cultural, and political work that exceeded juridical frameworks. *Les Blancs* marks a turning point and a continuation of artist-activists that capture the shifts in the Black freedom movements of the mid-twentieth century in their dramatic work, including Baldwin, Childress, and Aimé Césaire. Hansberry's play demands that we reconsider the relationship between civil rights and human rights. The question enables an understanding of Black subjects' inability to find full incorporation in the national body and provides an opportunity to unmask the working of global capitalism and neoliberalism (in part the fulfillment of democracy through the totalizing and unyielding agency of the individual), which found a foothold in the wake of World War II. Hansberry was deeply invested in civil rights and saw the categories of civil rights and human rights as interwoven.

The multiple temporalities that Hansberry negotiates in her play are not only those of the mid- and late twentieth century, but also the Renaissance. She writes back to Shakespeare as a way to rethink the relationship of postcolonial movements to a colonial past that still structures the present. Similar to the multiple constituencies that informed Hansberry's life and work, her characters are diasporic Black subjects whose identities require speaking from multiple vantage points. In particular, Hansberry returns to *Hamlet* because Shakespeare's play presents a rupture in the conceptualization of the thinking subject as it calls into question the organization of the national body. C.L.R. James contends, "in Hamlet [Shakespeare] had isolated and pinned down the psychological streak which characterized the communal change from the medieval world to the world of free individualization."[16] *Hamlet* is one of Shakespeare's most well known tragedies and comes to inspire theories of political action and inaction, but most importantly the play establishes that while Hamlet faces a new historical juncture, he must still actively engage with the past. *Les Blancs* shifts the negotiations from the context of the Renaissance to the Black freedom movements of the mid-twentieth century and the debates among different organizations, including the NAACP, the SCLC, the SNCC, and CORE, as to how to proceed. In addition, Hansberry engages Shakespeare because, as Ania Loomba and Martin Orkin contend, "he became, during the colonial period, the quintessence of Englishness and a measure of humanity itself. Thus the meanings of Shakespeare's plays were both derived from and used to establish colonial authority."[17] *Les Blancs* calls forth a set of pasts (ones that come to define the citizen and one that comes to define the human) to imagine futures for Black citizen-subjects that are unimaginable in prior contexts. Therefore it is important to consider how the work not only rethinks the present but also the past.

Hansberry's dance with the ghosts of the past secured her guiding philosophical imperative to activate what makes us human by commanding the force of history. Nevertheless, her play takes the form of tragedy and models its protagonist on Hamlet in order to rethink the prototypical tragic figure. In his examination of C.L.R. James's *The Black Jacobins,* David Scott insists that although much of the book follows the formal conventions of romance with a focus on a progressive narrative that moves toward redemption, James made revisions in the 1963 edition that enable a reading of the text as a contemplation of the political implications of tragedy. The revisions serve to reframe the text's structure, making it speak to what Scott describes as the tragic times of the postcolonial period. According to Scott, "tragedy questions, for example, the view of human history as moving teleologically and transparently toward a determinate end, or as governed by a sovereign and omnisciently rational agent." He concludes, "In short, tragedy sets before us the image of a man or woman obliged to act in a world in which values are unstable and ambiguous."[18]

Scott sees the references to tragedy in the revised edition of *The Black Jacobins* as an opportunity to read James's text against its grain in order to open it up to what he describes as the tragic times of the twenty-first century: "Our present, unlike Toussaint's and unlike James's, does not ring with the strong cadences of revolutionary anticipation. To the contrary, our present is characterized much more by a profound skepticism about the teleology of nationalist and socialist liberation in which those cadences rang. And therefore if we wish neither to simply lament the passing of that heroic past nor to merely valorize the self-congratulatory present, we may wish to press *The Black Jacobins* in directions it itself signals but, understandably, does not develop."[19] The ambiguity fundamental to tragedy echoes with the uncertainty of the twenty-first century and the feeling Hansberry registers at the end of her life. Many of the critiques of nationalist independence movements Higashida explained, "in their perpetuation of male-dominated, heteronormative ideologies; their inability to establish transparent, democratic governments; and their economic dependence on transnational corporations, former colonial masters, and neoliberal policy," appeared for Hansberry from her position as a lesbian Black feminist.[20] In part, Tshembe's characterization as a tragic figure that must give up his comforts and domestic patriarchal privilege to fight for the unknown with a mysterious Black woman as his guiding force disrupts male-dominated, heteronormative ideologies. The instability of political outcomes for Black freedom movements that emerges in the years following the classical phase of the civil rights movement also resonates in Hansberry's play.

Even though Hansberry models the central figure of her play on Hamlet (the tragic hero that Scott endorses), the play's conclusion does require the circumscription of *the movement.* Rather, the play's ambiguous ending provides an alternative structure of meaning making for modernity to institute itself, a diasporic form of international humanism that redefines national belonging. The ending focuses attention on citizenship as a process, situating it as a movement, not a position. Hansberry's play not only stages Tshembe choosing between his brothers but also deciding which parts of his father's legacy that he will honor. The mapping of a political drama on to a familial one may seem to resonate most forcefully in the portrayal of a monarchy, but an examination of the personal lives of many civil rights activists (Hansberry, Martin Luther King, Jr., Ella Baker, Nina Simone) will demonstrate the central relationship between communal allegiances and political ones. Hamlet becomes a political subject in the play and must negotiate personal and social histories in order to command his political present. In Hansberry's life she had to make uncommon choices in order to align her political vision with her personal investments. Hansberry and Nemiroff quietly divorced in 1964 but continued to work together. In a letter dated March 3, 1964, he gave her more than seven typed pages of notes on the full draft of Les Blancs. The exchange typifies a long-standing collaboration that aided the dissemination of Hansberry's work. Hansberry's relationship with Nemiroff evolved as her political commitments shifted. Her personal allegiances were central and not ancillary to her political ones. In such a configuration, national belonging becomes an act, not a state or possession.

Given Hansberry's understanding of *the movement* as a process, perhaps it is fitting that Les Blancs was one of her unfinished works. Questioning the script that resulted in the first production of the play, which was staged on Broadway in 1970, *New York Times* critic Clive Barnes explained: "The play was not completed on Miss Hansberry's death in 1965, although she had been working on it for four years, completed several drafts and was still polishing it when she died. The present 'final text' has been adapted by Robert Nemiroff, and as the play was still being adapted and put into final shape less than a week ago, it is not at all certain that this is the play Miss Hansberry had in mind. It is conjecture, but unquestionably this is an unusually mixed play, and perhaps Miss Hansberry, given time, could have surrounded Tshembe with people worthier of him."[21] Other critics also found fault with the language, final outcome, and plot development of the play.[22]

The dissonance produced by Les Blancs anticipated the wrangling over the unfinished business of the civil rights movement, which continues to shape Black political debate in the twenty-first century.[23] The play, however, did receive some positive reviews, such as Ray Robinson's in the *New York Amsterdam News,* which stated of the opening night: "The vast majority of people sensed that this particular evening would be one of serious thought and introspection; they could not have been more correct." *The Nation* theater critic Harold Clurman wrote: "I confess to have been more impressed by Lorraine Hansberry's *Les Blancs* (Longacre Theatre) than I expected to be; more, indeed, than most of the professional theatre-tasters. At a time when rave reviews are reserved for plays like *Sleuth* and *Conduct Unbecoming,* I am tempted to speak of *Les Blancs* in superlatives. I suspect, too, that resistance to the play on the ground of its simplistic argument is a rationalization for social embarrassment. *Les Blancs* is not propaganda, as has been inferred; it is a forceful and intelligent statement of the tragic impasse of white and black relations all over the world, as well as of the complexity of motivation and effect where European nations colonize undeveloped lands inhabited by blacks."[24] Clurman suggested the articulation of Hansberry's political project in *Les Blancs,* a project that *A Raisin in the Sun* first introduced to a mass international commercial audience in the more digestible register of integration, striking a discordant note in the political present following the civil rights era.

Although critics disagreed about the merits of *Les Blancs,* they consistently agreed that the acting distinguished the play. Many reviews raved about James Earl Jones's performance as Tshembe and Lili Darvas's portrayal of Madame Neilsen. Darvas was nominated for a Tony award for her performance. Considered one of the best American actors, Jones won a Tony in 1969 for his performance in *The Great White Hope.* His magnetic star power certainly helped to bolster audience and critical attention in Hansberry's play. Jones's stature, both physical and professional, also surely lent Hansberry's central character a gravitas that helped communicate his shift from ambivalence to action. Rounding out the trio of brothers, Earle Hyman played Abioseh and Harold Scott performed the role of Eric. The collaboration did not result in critical acclaim but did produce a template that would inform Scott's direction of the Huntington Theatre's revival of the play in 1989 and the National Theatre's production in 2016.[25]

HANSBERRY'S CROSSROADS

Hansberry's work expresses the political desire for decolonial and not just postcolonial consciousness. For Hansberry, the interracial coalition of Black and white radicals required attention to the material history of slavery and imperialism not only in the United States but also throughout the world. *Les Blancs* asserts the importance of independence movements and resists the patriarchal privilege implicit in much of the rhetoric of the civil rights movement and, later, the Black Power movements, and it also foregrounds the fluidity and inconsistency of social change. The final scene of *A Raisin in the Sun,* for example, which in an earlier version of the play featured the Younger family sitting in the living room of their new home with shotguns, qualifies as (at the least) ambivalent or (as Hansberry would put it) "*between* despair and joy." Similarly, *Les Blancs* ends moments after the insurgents bomb the missionary hospital and kill the matriarch of the settler community. She writes, "man is unique in the universe, the only creature who has in fact the power to transform the universe."[26] Tshembe's action calls forth a historical connection that ties him to the insurgency of his father and what is yet to come. At the same time, his choice anticipates a painful splintering of the social fabric that threatens his humanity as it enables a redirection of the course of history. The play communicates this redirection, instructing that "the Woman appears" in "a pool of light" as Tshembe cries.[27]

Tshembe's final decision in the play, to kill his brother, affirms a vision of self- and collective determination that required severing a familial tie and a disruption of the presumed social order to prioritize family.[28] In order to clear some space for her international humanism, Hansberry had to disrupt the logics of the heteronormative family unit as the primary social unit. She categorized *the* movement as a struggle for human and civil rights, gender equality, and peace.[29] The movement sought to demonstrate that, according to Hansberry, "all human questions overlap. ... Men continue to misinterpret the second-rate status of women as implying a privileged status for themselves; heterosexuals think the same way about homosexuals; gentiles about Jews; whites about blacks; haves about have-nots. And then, always, come the reckoning."[30] The quote appears in an unpublished letter that Hansberry wrote in response to a split "at a homophile conference at which Gay men called for open public advocacy of a 'Bill of Rights for Homosexuals' and Lesbian women opposed them."[31] Hansberry's letter explains the women's reluctance to endorse a "Bill of Rights for Homosexuals," and it articulates the problem in members of liberation movements not being able to act in reciprocity with their allies. It also calls for a capacious understanding of connecting across difference that realizes mutuality as fundamental to Black freedom struggles. As Hansberry remained an outsider, she bore witness to what the movement could be.

Hansberry invests in citizenship because she sees social contracts as having the potential to safeguard human rights. To achieve a meaningful form of citizenship, she realized, according to Higashida, "a conflictual Hegelian dialectic is not the only possible relationship between individuals. There can be reciprocity and mutual recognition between equal consciousnesses, which de Beauvoir associates with travel and contact zones."[32] Hansberry argues:

Now—this, I think, may be part at least part of the source of confusion for the dividing off at the conference. The men seemed to have confused the women by speaking in the time-honored manner of the socially insurgent of "demands" and "rights." There is, of course, hardly another way to speak of exactly that; for that is what the homosexual HAS to do in America and everywhere else: assert to the world that no crime is committed in his sexual habits . . . not to understand it as a question of "rights" is to suggest that what we are seeking then is indeed a privileged status—and there should be no privileged groups. The question is always understood when it is "taxation without representation" because that is now a reasonably decided issue in the United States since 1776. However, the PRINCIPLE, of unjust laws as an abstraction is what escapes people when the unjust law is current. Our ancestors fought against the above and demanded the repeal of its complementary laws because they were in violation of their human rights.[33]

Hansberry understood civil rights as governing social interactions that created the contexts for a fuller flourishing of human rights. The exercise of unjust laws served as cover for the graver injustice of denying an individual's humanity. The inability of activists to meet across difference denied opportunities for recognition, which served as the first stepping-stone toward a different form of citizenship predicated on reciprocity. Therefore even though Hansberry's memories of her father cemented her understanding of the limitations of juridical means of redress, she understood the protection and equal access to civil rights as a necessary strategy to protect human rights. Hansberry's rhetorical "our" refers to U.S. citizens, which implicitly shifts the position of her audience, the members of a homophile conference, from margin to center.

The movement in Hansberry's letter from the "we" seeking a purportedly privileged status to the group claiming "our ancestors" that "fought against" taxation without representation redefines the ideal revolutionary. In midcentury America, all independence movements were not equal. Whereas the U.S. independence movement of the eighteenth century symbolized a just and necessary exercise of self-determination, the independence movements in Africa and the Caribbean threatened the loose hold of the United States democracy during the Cold War. Hansberry's letter questions how "the PRINCIPLE, of unjust laws . . . escapes people when the unjust law is current." She also imagines figures that counter such contradictions. In *Les Blancs,* Eric, the youngest brother, is queer sexually, socially, and politically, as he is the most alienated and radical of the brothers. Eric is the first brother to join the independence movement and able to see the virtue of action well before Tshembe because his revolutionary democratic action serves to secure his humanity in ways that do not apply to his heterosexual, Western-educated brothers.

HANSBERRY AND THE AMERICAN THEATER

Hansberry's drama anticipates the tragic times that Scott describes in *Conscripts of Modernity*, as *Les Blancs* wrestles with the Pandora's box of ethical dilemmas World War II unleashed. Two giant voices in American theater, Arthur Miller (American theater's ethical playwright) and Hansberry (American theater's visionary playwright), struggle to come to terms with the political landscape that Miller described in the title of his 1964 play *After the Fall*. The title refers to the loss of Eden-like conditions in the Western world after the use of atomic warfare. *After the Fall* presents the futility of individual sacrifice in the name of communal redemption, one of the central devices in Miller's earlier domestic drama. In Miller's *All My Sons* (1947), the central character, Joe Keller, owns a manufacturing company that sells defective engine parts to the Army, which results in the death of soldiers. He chooses to sell the cracked cylinder heads because he knows that if he does not meet the Army's demand for parts, his business will fold and he will have nothing left to leave his sons. One of Joe's sons, Larry, does not return from his military deployment. In order for Joe's decision to warrant the costs of Larry's probable death, Joe's other son Chris must accept the company as his inheritance. Chris must redeem his father by confirming the worth of the company in accepting his inheritance. Once Chris learns, however, of his father's criminal business practices, he refuses to have any part of the company, and Joe (defeated) kills himself.

Although *All My Sons* leaves Chris's final outcome ambiguous, the play establishes that Joe will deem his actions worth the cost if Chris benefits. *Les Blancs* inserts itself in the well-established American theater convention of thwarted paternal succession, absenting the paternal figure from the play. And like *All My Sons*, *Les Blancs* weaves the most important political struggle of the time—the battle for independence—into a domestic drama. Hansberry's play extends the battle for home, taken up in earlier work, to the battle for homeland. In so doing, she links her concerns about spatial justice to her critique of gender and sexual hierarchies. The second act of the play features a standoff between brothers Tshembe and Abioseh. The brothers disagree about the role of settlers in their country. Tshembe believes that the Africans should have governmental control, whereas Abioseh sides with the colonizing Europeans. In an effort to undermine the Africans' struggle for independence, Abioseh betrays a family friend, Peter, and reveals that Peter participates in the insurgency. As a result, the colonial military leader Major George Rice executes Peter.

Owing to his betrayal and his investment in the colonial government, Tshembe and Abioseh have their final standoff. According to the stage directions: "Sensing his brother's presence, Abioseh looks up, regards Tshembe for a moment and then, with fateful premonition, begins to back away as Tshembe advances. Abioseh turns. Warriors appear over the rise and at the edges of the stage, rifles in hand. Among them is Eric—who blocks the way."[34] The triangulated confrontation speaks to the spatial dynamics that Hansberry employs to communicate the complexity of her vision. Abioseh represents the assimilated African subject. He has profited from his education and association with the missionary while in Africa and has moved on to study Catholic theology in order to become a priest. Tshembe too enjoys the freedom of being an expatriate. In the beginning of the play, he brags to his half-brother Eric of the ease that comes along with his new life and his marriage to a European woman. Throughout the play, however, Tshembe's encounters with the revolutionary spirit and conversations with those whom he left behind spark a desire in him to aid the insurgency. Meanwhile, Eric, the youngest brother, accepts an invitation to join the resistance. Eric differs from his older brothers in many ways, being gay and biracial. Eric's father, Major George Rice, raped his mother, and she died in childbirth. Therefore Eric symbolizes the loss of their mother and the shame of colonial domination. Politically the brothers represent different points along a spectrum instead of oppositional points of view. "The first of his brothers to join the uprising, Eric challenges the homophobic ideologies of Black nationalism," Higashida claimed.[35] In triangulating the final scene, Hansberry draws attention to what Scott would call the "collision" of forces that Tshembe must negotiate.[36]

Forced to confront his brother, "As Abioseh turns back to him," and Tshembe, after a moment of quiet consideration and "aware of all the universal implications of the act," kills his brother and watches him fall to the ground.[37] Although *Les Blancs* complicates the lines of affiliation, placing Eric on the stage in the final confrontation between Abioseh and Tshembe, the play also clarifies that difficult decisions do not and must not amount to indecision. The play insists that the slaying of one brother by another brother has personal and social consequences. Choosing to act enables Tshembe to claim freedom in action but does not guarantee a permanent state. The perpetuation of freedom adheres in understanding and taking action as part of a movement.

Hansberry's drama makes clear that the conflict she depicts in Africa has ties to a larger movement that has a long history. Understanding the conflict in her play as a part of the movement opens up space to consider how Hansberry presents the division of a family as not devastating but open to possibilities that bisect generations, creating lines of affiliation that do not necessarily flow from one generation to the next. Her drama suggests that the sacrifices that each individual character makes may be understood as participating in shifting the course of history, not with the assumption of immediate payoff but necessary nonetheless to supply the movement with the energy that ultimately redirects history.

In *Les Blancs,* Peter, a leader of the insurgency, tells Tshembe the story of Modingo to encourage the native son to join the resistance, describing the perils of inaction. Modingo, a hyena, lived between the elephants and the hyenas. As a wise hyena, Modingo had a keen understanding of the land dispute between his brethren and the elephants. "The elephants said they needed more space because of their size, and the hyenas because they had been *first* in that part of the jungle and were accustomed to running free." The hyenas came to Modingo, whose name means "one who thinks carefully before he acts," and he pondered the situation. Modingo waited and thought, "the elephants gathered their herds and moved at once—and drove them from the jungle altogether. That is why the hyena laughs until this day and why it is such terrible laughter." In recounting the story of Modingo, Peter warned of the peril of inaction, and how it facilitates domination. He also provided another note in the soundtrack of the play, which begins with "the unearthly 'laughter of a hyena' " and replays in Act 2.[38] The tortured sound adds a sonic layer to the narrative of colonization and decolonization that communicates the affective register of the conflict and points in different directions than what language may allow. After the post-colonial movements of the mid-twentieth century, Anthony Bogues confirms that we must develop a political language that adequately gives voice to what Glenda Carpio calls "laughing fit to kill"—a register affectively different from the blues people, which typifies routinely Black political subjectivity in the twentieth century.[39] The designation blues people, taken from Amiri Baraka's influential work, names a long history of Black cultural production. Theorists including Eddie Glaude use the term "blues people" to establish the political subjectivity of Black folks in America.[40]

Rather, "laughing fit to kill" registers an oscillation between the violence of self-deprecation in the name of appropriating racist stereotypes and the anger that undergirds trenchant critique. The laughter-imbued rage communicates the "defeat *and* triumph in the face of absurdity" that Hansberry confronted in response to what historians have depicted as the waning years of the movement she helped shape. The soundings register a political desire to attend to the unspeakable things that defy legislation, as Michele Elam explained, "the tension between aspiration and limitation, between idealism and expedient materialism, truth and delusion," and also demand attention to "the unpredictable vagaries of consciousness," "the subtleties of personality," and "the opacities of culture," according to Scott.[41] The laughter communicates an affective dynamic to political subjectivity distinctive from the blues.

As with the conflict among three brothers that *Les Blancs* presents, sound has many layers that communicate varied emotional responses. The same sound has the potential to evoke despair and joy or something in between. It also has the ability to express the manic laugh of the defeated hyena and the mournful cry of the warrior after suffering casualties in battle. The play uses the various sonic references to map the affective movements of the struggle onto the play and offer a correlation between the political and emotional landscapes. Hansberry's drama and political writing confronted but did not give in to the seduction of despair; for Hansberry, succumbing to despair amounts to facilitating one's own oppression. Conversely, the act of choosing perpetuates the movement and affirms the subject's humanity and citizenship.

In a letter written in response to Miller's play *After the Fall,* which opened on Broadway in January 1964, Hansberry lambasted Miller for his "despair" about "the destructiveness of our age" and "all this Camusian guilt." She critiques: "[Miller] is trying like hell for the respectability of fashionable despair because nothing else, in the West, really is right now. Fashionable, I mean."[42] *After the Fall* creates a connection among Miller's crumbling personal life (most sharply indicated by the suicide of his ex-wife, Marilyn Monroe), his being called to testify before the House Un-American Activities Committee, and the looming legacy of World War II.[43] *After the Fall* marks a distinctive shift in Miller's drama. Hansberry writes, "I think it is fundamentally, a shameful work. A distinguished artist is kopping [*sic*] out when his culture most needs him. Miller has been punished and punished hard for seeing 'too much' and now he wants in and I think that he has written a play which he thought would get the 'thesis playwright' stigma off his back."[44] Hansberry's demarcation suggests that Miller's early work, although complicated, had a didactic quality. Conversely, she critiques *After the Fall* for reveling in absurdity and relinquishing personal responsibility by asserting universal complicity of all Americans in the violation of human rights at home and abroad.

Hansberry also calls to task the theater of the absurd in general through the title of her play, which signifies Genet's *The Blacks.*[45] If time had held up, in time, Genet and Hansberry might have been friends. His play, written for white people, questions the outcome of Black independence movements, suggesting that they would result in the same tyranny as current "democratic" structures in the West. "*The Blacks,* with its exploration of power's tendency to corrupt within the context of African decolonization, spoke to the anomie and anxieties of Cold War life under the threats of totalitarianism and mass annihilation."[46] While Hansberry deeply understood power's ability to corrupt, she found the notion of white liberals using that complication as an excuse for apathy infuriating and Genet's retreat to abstraction politically anemic.[47]

Although many well-known Black artists, some of whom were activists, participated in the U.S. production of *The Blacks* in 1961, some would later regret the responses of white audiences to the play. The cast featured James Earl Jones, Roscoe Lee Brown, Louis Gossett, Cicely Tyson, Godfrey Cambridge, Maya Angelou, and Abbie Lincoln. Perhaps the casting of Jones in *Les Blancs* allowed him to pay his penitence. "Angelou's autobiography, which concludes its chapter about performing in *The Blacks* by describing Angelou's encounter with a white woman who expresses support and comprehension of the play but recoils when Angelou pointedly asks, 'Would you take me home with you? Would you become my friend?' " Higashida recalled.[48] The woman's response demonstrates liberals' abstraction of race rather than material engagement with it. The intimacy of friendship that Hansberry depicts in her work and cultivated in her life required working through the histories that made audiences comfortable with seeing Genet's play but not living in the same communities with Black people.

Hansberry's critique of the theater of despair establishes her resistance to the slow death of racism, in the midst of her own political and personal crisis. In July 1964, four months after Nemiroff wrote his notes on the complete draft of *Les Blancs,* Hansberry wrote in her journal, "It's an effort to walk straight. Going to Leahy Clinic." The next day she lamented, "Health: NOT good. Continue to lose weight. Down to 107." "And the truth is that I am so tired of hurting at this point that I wouldn't mind something rather drastic. I don't mean an operation. I do mean death. I feel as if I am being sucked away."[49] The confluence of personal and social challenges produce in Hansberry a political vision between despair and joy, and between mirth and rage; a vision that draws from a rigorous political discipline.

REVOLUTIONARY ACTION

Following Peter's recounting of the Modingo fable, *Les Blancs* stages the debate over diplomacy versus action, presenting Tshembe as an advocate for negotiation and Peter as a proponent of action. The debate has particular purchase in the years directly following the classical phase of the civil rights movement for activists considering the merits of nonviolent protest versus direct action and self-defense. Tshembe reassures Peter that the leader of the resistance "Kumalo is coming home." In a sobering reply, Peter counters, "There has been enough talk. The Council speaks for the people not Kumalo." Peter's vehemence shocks Tshembe and inspires the well-intentioned native son to offer to go to Zatembe—to speak with Kumalo, a character modeled on Jomo Kenyatta. "I will tell him the mood of our people. I will tell him the settlers have *one* season to grant our demands . . . *One* season." Peter, already weary of talking and waiting, charges, "We have waited a thousand seasons . . ." His comment, though intentionally hyperbolic, links the fight for independence in the mid-twentieth century to freedom struggles in the eighteenth and nineteenth centuries. Ultimately unmoved, Peter agrees but warns, "Tshembe Matoseh, the Wanderer—who has come home with the white man's tongue . . . I hope you do not have his heart." By the end of the scene, Tshembe's belief in diplomacy and hope for no additional bloodshed drives him to advocate for the native Africans. But before he can travel to Zatembe to speak to Kumalo, the leader is jailed. Rocked to the core and broken, when Tshembe learns of Kumalo's arrest (similar to the hyena), the stage directions read: "at last it comes—laughter, slowly at first, then rising uncontrollably. The drums build to a climax and—abruptly—silence: the laughter dies in his throat as the Woman appears. He straightens slowly to face her."[50]

Confronted with the haunting legacy of the revolutionary spirit his father expressed and the inadequacy of "the white man's tongue," Tshembe (like Modingo) must face the limits of diplomacy. The laughter that bursts from his lips gives a sonic expression to the loss of an ideal and the panic that accompanies that loss. Tshembe is fully invested in the hopes of reconciliation, of serving as the force that could bridge the competing interests of his country and of his family. He finally agrees to speak on behalf of his people and learns that, although he decided to speak, his words have lost all power. Leaving emptiness in the wake of diplomacy's promise of equality, the play strips Tshembe of words and reduces him to sound. A soul-rocking chuckle builds into hysterics until Tshembe realizes what he must do. The play choreographs Tshembe turning toward the Woman instead of away from her. The laughter signals a shift in political subjectivity reinforced in the interaction between Tshembe and the Woman. Through the laughter, Hansberry foregrounds the sardonic tone that emerges in the work of many artists after the classical phase of the civil rights movement.

The reconciliation made available through sound, to mark a difference but not necessarily a complete break, recalls the healing properties of civil rights music. "Before Hansberry died in 1965, Nina [Simone] came to her hospital bedside to perform 'In the Evening by the Moonlight' for her friend," music critic Joe Hagan recalled. Simone's version of the song, "a stormy narrative about black creativity in the face of work's exhausting claim to the body," must have resonated profoundly with Hansberry, with *Les Blancs* still on her mind.[51] Similar to Baldwin, Simone and Hansberry shared visions of what the world could be. When they both lived in New York, Lorraine would go to the Village Gate to hear Nina play. Poet Nikki Giovanni noted of their friendship, "What is important is that [Nina] loved her and she was loved in return."[52] The intertwining of sound, solidarity, and movement toward becoming free emanated from Hansberry's hospital bed and in *Les Blancs,* fusing intimacy and action into the struggle for Black life.

Hansberry's unwavering commitment to collectivity needs to be qualified in light of a discussion she depicts in *Les Blancs.* At the same time that she insisted upon a connection between the students fighting for freedom in the streets of Birmingham and the citizens uprising in Kenya, she critiqued the notion of a unilateral Black position. Taking direct aim at Genet's *The Blacks,* Tshembe counters the prodding of a white U.S. reporter, Mr. Morris, declaring, "Mr. Morris, have it your way! No matter what delusions of individuality infect *my* mind, to *you* I am not an individual but a tide, a flood, a monolith: 'The *Bla-a-acks!*'"[53] Hansberry understood the problems of presenting race as a unifying ideology. Her coalition does, however, mean to acknowledge that collective integration will not address the United States' moral dilemma.

In the year following her meeting with Kennedy, Hansberry finished *The Sign in Sidney Brustein's Window* and continued to work on *Les Blancs* and a play about Toussaint L'Ouverture. On June 7, 1964, she wrote in her journal, "Free from physical discomfort. No depression. I fear addiction to the drug. Fear of having to earn a living. I don't know how. Had trouble keeping a job in the early days. Hospital tomorrow at 10:30 shall leave Croton about 9:00. Not drinking. Started smoking again." Later that day she reflected, "Suddenly a great night! Bob came to drive me in tomorrow—and to talk about Les Blancs. Persistence, thy name is Nemiroff! He likes the changes but wants more. We talked, worked, hollered, fought, scene by scene . . . 4 hours and no pain! I know what I must do now, But can I?" Her physical pain gave meaning to how she conceptualized political struggle as did her collaboration with Bob. On June 17 she wrote, "Decision. When I get back from Cape must complete Les Blancs—confusion everywhere demanding it. And must confront the African corruption á la Tshembe—and, I fear, Kenyatta." In the margin she wrote "Et Tu Brute?" signaling her understanding of African independence movements' complicated and tragic histories.[54] Hansberry knew Black leaders did not mean saviors and that becoming free required perpetual action and accountability.

She felt the same dejection expressed in *Les Blancs* when Tshembe learns of Kumalo's arrest following her meeting with Kennedy, so she returned to her work. Although critics have argued about what the final scene of the play reveals about Hansberry's political evolution and whether it serves as her call to arms, in her life she responded to the shortcomings in diplomacy through an act of imagination. Her aesthetic vision compensated for the limitations of political negotiations. Hansberry felt that the theater served as a rarefied form of communication. She says, "Well, I think it's because I'm particularly attracted to a medium where not only do you get to do what we do in life every day—you know, talk to people—but to be very selective about the nature of the conversation."[55] Hansberry's exchange with Kennedy reflects a well-known narrative of the civil rights movement: a white liberal asking a Black political activist for patience. We are also familiar with the ways the civil rights movement failed to adequately address gender inequality and hierarchies of class and sexuality. These shortcomings add fuel to what would become the fires, metaphorically and literally (as a result of riots), of the Black Power movement and third-wave feminism. Hansberry's drama recalls and forecasts history, making an important contribution to political imagination of the civil rights movement period. In the same way that Miller's work of the midcentury affirmed and pointed to the limitations of the American Dream, Hansberry crafts a Black imaginary that may serve as the measuring stick against which society judges its democracies.

As does her protagonist, Hansberry paid a great price for her activism. Baldwin recalls leaving the meeting with Kennedy and seeing Hansberry walk down the street. "We passed Lorraine, who did not see us. She was walking toward Fifth Avenue—her face twisted, her hands clasped before her belly, eyes darker than any eyes I had ever seen before—walking in an absolutely private place."[56] As much as Hansberry's work critiques individuality and focuses on collectivity, she knew all too well the personal nature of suffering. Although an individual could not and will not lead the movement to victory, individuals had to sacrifice in the name of the movement. Hansberry's drama ends with Tshembe alone on stage. However, following his final expression of anger, the stage directions say, "in a pool of light facing him,—the woman appears." The female dancer in Hansberry's play should not be read as only the embodiment of nationalism but comes instead to represent the power of unspeakable pasts to spark political consciousness. Her dancing functions similarly to the cries heard in the play expressing an imaginative possibility that bypasses the limitations of the colonizer's language to communicate the position and political vision of the colonized. In crucial turning points of Tshembe's character development, the dancer appears; she confronts him on stage with history. In the final scene of Act I, "She circles in movement symbolic of the life of the people, binding him closer . . . She signifies the slaughter, the enslavement . . . She drops and writhes in agony . . . She rises: a warrior summoning him urgently, insistently, unrelentingly."[57] With each movement, Tshembe responds with protest, but the Woman will not relent. Even given her persistence, the play suggests Tshembe must act in order to align with the revolutionary collectivity she represents, placing him in relation to not only his father but his brother Eric too.

Hansberry provides an answer to the problem of individuality that plagues the historiography of the civil rights movement, most notably in the person of Martin Luther King, Jr., through an aesthetic turn. As mentioned earlier, Hansberry offers a trans-historical conception of the movement that links insurgent slaves fighting for freedom with civil rights activists. In order to move something, you have to make it kinetic, which disrupts stasis. Whether the flow of history or the political tide, Hansberry's movement implicitly relies on physical movement, which takes an idealized form in dramatic performance.

Displacing that association from Tshembe onto the unknown woman, Hansberry makes the mythical ghostly figure both bodily and disembodied, both all-encompassing and singular, both a sign of male leadership (as a force associated with Tshembe's father) and superficially a woman, in order to call attention to the movement as a moral crisis whose true costs would be addressed after the battle. The final scene of the play shows ambivalence toward the native Africans taking up arms in defense of independence. What it does address with certainty is communicating the need for mechanisms that will create human connections in the aftermath of the turmoil. In the final scene, the woman not only serves as a signal of the insurgency to come, she also functions as a comfort to Tshembe, arriving in response to his "animal-like cry of grief." As Hansberry suffered with her own mortality, she left as part of her rich legacy a means of connection through performance. *Les Blancs* offers an expression of the heart-rending losses in the name of human rights and serves as a testimony to the sacrifice that drives the movement.

The soundings produced in *Les Blancs* imagine an alternative representational field that disrupts the portending malaise of the postcolonial nation-state. The cries serve to create a disruption that seeks to refocus the freedom movements on the larger struggle for freedom and away from the immediate "triumph" of independent nation-states. The cries therefore have a temporal effect that works to leverage the time between revolution and national independence in the service of an insurgent imagination that accounts for and exceeds pragmatic concerns. Therefore, one might read Tshembe's cry as demonstrative of the work yet to be done in the political movement; work that will require new sounds, as well as alternative modes of hearing. Yet to hear differently may require opening oneself up to the human concerns that distinguish the citizen from the insurgent.

Epilogue: Alternative Endings

"People do not understand who I am yet, they will. 'Baby Life is Merry' indeed!!!"
—Lorraine Hansberry

This story does not end in death. The encounters at the heart of Hansberry's work extend to the archive, inviting the reader into alternative worlds and future possibilities. In the version of Hansberry's never televised screenplay *The Drinking Gourd* submitted to Dore Schary at NBC, she depicted an alternative to the ending of the published version. In the published version, at the end of the screenplay Hannibal, the central enslaved figure in the play, runs away with his lover Sarah and his nephew Joshua. In the version submitted to NBC, she offered another set of fugitives and, therefore, rethinks fugitivity. She depicts Rissa, Hannibal's mother, stealing a gun and taking it with Joshua to Sarah in the clearing. Hansberry directs, "We stay with them until they come to Hannibal's clearing where Sarah stands, poised for traveling, and trembling mightily. Rissa locks the other woman's hand about one of those of the child and thrusts the gun in the other. There is a swift embrace and the woman and the child turn and disappear in the woods.

Rissa watches after them and the singing of the 'Drinking Gourd' goes on as we pan away from her to the quarters."[1] Hansberry's ending tableau of an armed woman with child recalls her own mother's posture of protection at 6140 South Rhodes Avenue. It also calls to mind the fierce determination of Harriet Tubman for self-defense and determination. These expressions of Black womanhood contextualize activism historically and particularly during the civil rights movement. Nannie Louise Perry taught school, served as a ward leader for the Republican Party, and protected her family with a gun. Her movements for freedom combined institutional reform and fugitivity. Hansberry understood that becoming free required both forces. Her archive bears witness to this mutuality and writes her radical feminist self into being as an encounter in the archive.

Although playwrights, including Bruce Norris, have speculated about the Youngers' future following *A Raisin in the Sun*, this epilogue takes up the alternative endings to Hansberry's self and world creation provided by those that appear in drafts of *A Raisin in the Sun* and *The Drinking Gourd* and that responded to her speech "To Be Young, Gifted, and Black."[2] As we saw, an early version of *A Raisin in the Sun* ended with the Younger family huddled in their new home, armed and awaiting the vigilante violence of their neighbors. Together the plays establish Hansberry's attention to the material demands of becoming free through the protection of life. Attending to material demands meant understanding how social, economic, and cultural forces situate Black women in time and space, requiring them historically to practice modes of self-protection and determination that may not stereotypically align with womanhood. This positioning of Black women both within and in excess of womanhood informed Hansberry's understanding of becoming free as a child, her work for *Freedom*, and her early days observing life in the Village. It informed her letters to *The Ladder*, her characterization of Beneatha Younger, and what we find in the archive. In *The Drinking Gourd*, Rissa, the figure that functions as the intermediary between the plantation owners and the enslaved, arms Sarah after the brutal mutilation of her son. Hannibal loses his eyes as a punishment for learning to read, but throughout the screenplay he actively and outwardly refuses the injustices of slavery. His public refusal serves as a foil to his mother's stealth ability to go unnoticed as she gathers information to arm her resistance.

The final scene shows women working intergenerationally to support and challenge prototypical expressions of Black masculinity. These moments of alliance with and challenge to Black masculinity reinforce the Black women's transgressive performances of gender. Depicting Sarah leaving with Joshua suggests a shifting and queering of the family unit. It replicates the mother-son relationship of Rissa and Hannibal, but in this case, the mother has no biological ties to the child and expresses the "stealth of the stolen" through underground movements.[3] Hansberry's ending offers a continuance of becoming free that requires going off the grid. This movement may mean leaving the nation-state that could not contain Black freedom (as her father attempted to do and her dear friend Jimmy did) or in establishing, whether through her associations with the left or emergent queer communities, underground networks. These webs of affiliation expanded Hansberry's reach and demonstrated her understanding of the limits to Black nationalism as a geographically bound framework. She deeply invested in the ideas of self-determination, but her work also expresses an understanding of community that connects across geographies and generations to produce forms of kinship and care that flourish as diasporic connections. Just as anti-Black racism functioned in and through the state, its extralegal mechanisms (lynch mobs and church bombings) required fugitive responses.

The Drinking Gourd elaborates a line of thought in Hansberry's work that she began with the alternative ending to *Raisin in the Sun* and, arguably, culminates with the ending of *Les Blancs*. Distinctively, the ending to *The Drinking Gourd* establishes Hansberry's understanding of the formative role race plays in shaping gender as the expression of a set of repeated acts. Just as the memory of her trip to the south with her mother serves as the preface to the play, Hansberry maps her experience onto the figure of Sarah to establish a prehistory of insurgence for Black women. This history, Hansberry suggests, will keep them safe in the days of freedom work yet to come. Her learning ground as an activist, peopled by Robeson, Du Bois, and Burnham, also featured Childress, Goode Robeson, and the Sojourners for Truth and Justice. In the archive, we find the imprint of women on Hansberry's understanding of the historical acts that make freedom practices in the present possible.

In writing herself into being, Hansberry provided alternative endings that inscribe Black feminist radicalism and her fugitive vision. Near the end of her life, Hansberry gave a speech for the United Negro College Fund titled ". . . To Be Young, Gifted, and Black . . ." The speech not only cemented Hansberry's perception of freedom as a process of becoming that unfolded over time, it also encouraged ongoing engagement with her dear friends Nina and Bobby. The speech, occasioned by a writing contest, gave Hansberry the opportunity to read the work of burgeoning artists. In speaking directly to the three award winners, Miss Purvis, Miss Yeldell, and Mr. Lewis, she said, "You are, after all, the product of a presently insurgent and historically vivacious and heroic culture, a culture of an indomitable will for freedom and aspiration to dignity." Hansberry references the history of political possibility during Reconstruction and notes the cultural impact of Black people to establish what still awaits to be. Her speech suggests both a joyful assertion of a current state, oh "to be," as well as a future horizon. She said, "Though it be a thrilling and marvelous thing to be merely young and gifted in such times, it is doubly so—doubly dynamic—to be young, gifted and black. Look at the work that awaits you!"[4] Hansberry understood blackness as an expression of a dynamic historical force that shaped her era and that provided a material foundation for becoming free. Even in the midst of the challenges that activists faced in 1964, Hansberry emphasized "in such times" "look at the work that awaits you."

Hansberry's address emphasizes the importance of the racial designation, Black, well in advance of its popularization by Stokely Carmichael. Carmichael became the chairman of SNCC in May 1966. In June, James Meredith, the first Black student to attend the University of Mississippi, began a solitary walk, the "Walk Against Fear," from Memphis, Tennessee, to Jackson, Mississippi. Just twenty miles into Mississippi, Meredith was shot. Carmichael called on SNCC activists to continue walking in Meredith's place. Once the group reached Greenwood, Mississippi, Carmichael gave a speech in which he asserted, "We been saying 'freedom' for six years. What we are going to start saying now is 'Black Power.' " Hansberry shared Carmichael's investment in the designation "Black" as an expression of a diasporic identity and had long thought about the circulation of power, but she understood freedom as the goal of intervening in power's circulation. She understood power as an expression that enabled becoming free but that would never substitute for it.

Hansberry's parting words urged the students to use their art as a source of continued transformation. She urged them, "Write! Work hard at it, CARE about it. Eschew the unstructured and the undisciplined and the pointless; no matter what anyone tells you—they are cheap evasions of art. And write about our people, tell their story. Leave the convoluted sex preoccupations to the convoluted; you have something glorious to draw on begging for attention. Use it."[5]

Hansberry's insistence on the process of transformation, calling the students to draw on the story of Black life and "Use it" functions as an extension of the work of Reconstruction she mentions earlier in the speech and continues through the circulation of her ideas and encounters in her archive. Still smarting from the racism and sexism of the homophile movement, Hansberry's writing suggests that she understood blackness to implicitly include what we would now describe as queerness. She resented, however, the disjoining of blackness and gender from the material conditions that produced them. As she argued in her letters to *The Ladder*, these same material conditions challenged expressions of same-sex desire. Although her comment, "Leave the convoluted sex preoccupations to the convoluted," seems oddly out of place, it represents her still unreconciled striving for coherence in a world that misapprehended her. For Hansberry, the bohemian expressions of sexual liberation divorced from the material conditions of gender as a racial category undermined becoming free.

Hansberry's speech served as an invitation to the young, gifted, and Black *and* a sight of memory for her dearests. James Baldwin's "Sweet Lorraine" offers a poignant tribute to the figure's life and legacy. And Hansberry's imprint emerges forcefully in Nina Simone's song "To Be Young, Gifted, and Black," recorded in 1969 and released on the album *Black Gold* (1970). In the intro to the song she remembers her friend, who, she insists, "comes alive more every day."[6] Simone calls Hansberry into the space. The song, which CORE adopted as the Black National Anthem to replace James Weldon Johnson and J. Rosamond Johnson's Negro National Anthem, "Lift Ev'ry Voice and Sing," calls attention to the growing emphasis on internationalism in U.S. Black freedom struggles. Simone with CORE emphasized the Black feminist internationalism always present in Hansberry's writing. In Hansberry's version of Black internationalism, like with the work of STJ, women's work laid the foundation for revolutionary change and, after, building the world anew. Simone's singing moved her and activists closer to accomplishing Hansberry's chief concern, "that was not a question of victory but one of how to rebuild Black communities on the other side of that inevitability," according to Shana Redmond.[7]

Nemiroff's adaptation, *To Be Young, Gifted, and Black*, creates a play based on Hansberry's published and unpublished writing. It draws her work into a nonsequential montage that highlights Hansberry's primary ideas. The organization of the play demonstrates how her ideas cohere through different modes of expression, from journal entries to creative writing. The prologue to the play ends with the speaker called Playwright saying, "it is still not unthinkable to me that the human race might just do what the apes never will:—impose the reason of life on life. (Turns . . . to reveal . . . a poster with the words 'To Be Young, Gifted, and Black.')"[8] The movement from one speech act to another one shows how Hansberry's multiple and interrelated selves reemerge through her different texts and contexts. Her steadfast investment in life, the living of it, every day as a protest, forestalled death and despair and uplifted the beauty of things Black. The imposition of impossibility within possibility remains the work that awaits you.

Notes

INTRODUCTION: NOTES OF A NATIVE DAUGHTER

Epigraph: Lorraine Hansberry's Journal, March 11, 1964, Restricted Box 1963–1964, Folder 4, *Lorraine Hansberry Papers,* Schomburg Center for Research in Black Culture, New York Public Library, New York. Hansberry's journal entry says that her father died in 1945, but he actually died in 1946. *A Raisin in the Sun* premiered on Broadway on March 11, 1959, but its first preview was on March 10.

1. Correspondence from "Mother" to "Mamie," March 4, 1946–March 11, 1946, Box 2, Folder 1, *Lorraine Hansberry Papers,* Schomburg Center for Research in Black Culture, New York Public Library, New York. A telegram dated March 11, 1946, reads: "DADDY PASSED WILL BE HOME AS SOON AS POSSIBLE WITH BODY BE BRAVE."
2. Mamie Hansberry Mitchell quoted in Anne Cheney, *Lorraine Hansberry* (New York: Twayne, 1994), 2, 3.
3. Imani Perry, *Looking for Lorraine: The Radiant and Radical Life of Lorraine Hansberry* (Boston: Beacon, 2018), 13.
4. Carl had a brain aneurysm, which caused his death, according to Perry, *Looking for Lorraine,* 22.
5. "Talk of the Town," *New Yorker,* May 9, 1959, 34.
6. Philip Bump, "When Did Black Americans Start Voting so Heavily Democratic?" *Washington Post,* July 7, 2015 (www.washingtonpost.com/news/the-fix/wp/2015/07/07/when-did-black-americans-start-voting-so-heavily-democratic/?noredirect=on&utm_term=.170de4dadode, accessed February 3, 2019).

7. Mary L. Dudziak, *The Cold War Civil Rights: Race and the Image of American Democracy* (Princeton: Princeton University Press, 2000), 24–26; Martha Biondi, *To Stand and Fight: The Struggle for Civil Rights in Postwar New York City* (Cambridge: Harvard University Press, 2006), 142.

8. Walter Benjamin, *Illuminations,* ed. Hannah Arendt, trans. Harry Zohn (New York: Harcourt Brace Jovanovich, 1968), 257; Hannah Arendt, "Introduction" to Walter Benjamin, *Illuminations,* ed. Hannah Arendt (New York: Schocken, 1968), 17–18.

9. Lillian Ross, "How Lorraine Hansberry Wrote 'A Raisin in the Sun,' " *New Yorker,* May 2, 1959 (www.newyorker.com/magazine/1959/05/09/playwright, accessed November 20, 2019).

10. Jacquelyn Dowd Hall, "The Long Civil Rights Movement and the Political Uses of the Past," *The Journal of American History* 91, no. 4 (March 2005): 1235; Dayo F. Gore, Jeanne Theoharis, and Komozi Woodard, eds., *Want to Start a Revolution? Radical Women in the Black Freedom Struggle* (New York: New York University Press, 2009); Dayo F. Gore, *Radicalism at the Crossroads: African American Women Activists in the Cold War* (New York: New York University Press, 2011); and Jeanne F. Theoharis and Komozi Woodard, eds., *Freedom North: Black Freedom Struggles Outside the South, 1940–1980* (New York: Palgrave Macmillan, 2003). Sundiata Keita Cha-Jua and Clarence Lang, "The 'Long Movement' as Vampire: Temporal and Spatial Fallacies in Recent Black Freedom Studies," *The Journal of African American History* 92, no. 2 (Spring 2007): 265–288, offers a critique of the Long Civil Rights Movement.

11. Hansberry moved to New York City in 1950, according to her FBI file, part 1, page 19; United States [U.S.] Dept. of Justice, *Lorraine Vivian Hansberry Nemiroff,* Assorted documents dated July 21, 1952, to January 22, 1965, Internal case file No. 100-107297 (New York: U.S. Federal Bureau of Investigation Freedom of Information/Privacy Acts Section, 1952), 19.

12. Gore, Theoharis, and Woodard, *Want to Start a Revolution?* 7, 11. Biondi, *To Stand and Fight,* has a description of the different organizations shaped by Black radicalism (5).

13. Lori Jo Marso, *Politics with De Beauvoir: Freedom in the Encounter* (Durham: Duke University Press, 2017), 3.

14. The relational quality at the heart of Hansberry's understanding of human existence resonates with chapter 25 in Hannah Arendt, *The Human Condition* (1958), which explores "the web of human relationships" (Chicago: University of Chicago Press, 1998).

15. For a scholarly examination of Black women's self-invention through an examination of their art, see Farah Griffin, *If You Can't Be Free, Be a Mystery* and *Harlem Nocturne.*

16. Lisa Lowe, "Autobiography Out of Empire," *Small Axe,* Number 28, 13.1 (March 2009): 102.

17. My book joins a rich group of texts that explore the life stories of Black women radicals, including Carole Boyce Davies, *Left of Karl Marx,* Dayo Gore, *Radicalism at the Crossroads,* Sherie M. Randolph, *Florynce "Flo" Kennedy,* and Barbara Ransby, *Ella Baker and the Black Freedom Movement* and *Eslanda.*

18. Hansberry also said that her father died in 1945 in Lillian Ross, "How Lorraine Hansberry Wrote 'A Raisin in the Sun,' " *New Yorker,* May 2, 1959 (www.newyorker.com/magazine/1959/05/09/playwright, accessed November 20, 2019).

19. Lorraine Hansberry, *To Be Young, Gifted, and Black: Lorraine Hansberry in Her Own Words* (New York: Vintage, 1995), 228.
20. Ibid., 4.
21. In addition to the renewed attention to Hansberry, the mounting interest in women's roles in the classical phase of the civil rights movement, including Ransby's *Ella Baker and the Black Freedom Movement* and Danielle L. McGuire's investigation of Rosa Parks in *At the Dark End of the Street* (New York: Vintage, 2011), provide contexts to consider not only how Hansberry contributed to what she called "the movement," but also how her freedom dreams required acts of imagination. Hansberry's work functions as a vehicle to consider how the arts intersect with political theory and action.
22. Simone de Beauvoir, *The Second Sex*, trans. Constance Borde and Sheila Malovany-Chevallier (New York: Vintage, 2011; originally published 1949), 17.
23. John Fitzgerald Kennedy, "Radio and Television Address to the American People on the Soviet Arms Build-up in Cuba" (Speech, Address During the Cuban Missile Crisis, White House, Washington, D.C., October 22, 1962), (www.jfklibrary.org/learn/about-jfk/historic-speeches/address-during-the-cuban-missile-crisis, accessed January 3, 2019).
24. According to Garry Wills: "To the American public, [Fidel] Castro's acceptance of Russian missiles looked unprovoked, mysteriously aggressive, and threatening. There was no way for Americans to know—and, at that point, no Kennedy could bring himself to inform them—that Cuban protestations of a purely defensive purpose for the missiles were genuine. We did not know what Castro knew—that thousands of [CIA] agents were plotting his death, the destruction of his government's economy, the sabotaging of his mines and mills, the crippling of his sugar and copper industries. We had invaded Cuba once; officials high in Congress and the executive department thought we should have followed up with overwhelming support for that invasion; by our timetable of a year to bring Castro down, the pressure to supply that kind of support in a new 'rebellion' was growing. All these realities were cloaked from the American people, though evident to the Russians and the Cubans." Garry Wills, "Did Kennedy Cause the Crisis?" *The Atlantic*, February 1, 2018 (www.theatlantic.com/magazine/archive/2013/08/did-kennedy-cause-the-crisis/309488, accessed January 3, 2019).
25. Hansberry's FBI file reports the date of the speech as October 24; part 1, page 15. In the Caedmon recording, the speech is dated October 25, and titled, "My Government Is Wrong." In the *Freedomways*, the speech is dated October 27, titled "A Challenge to Artists." It is possible that Hansberry gave the speech more than once. The FBI file and the Caedmon recording both have the speech taking place at the Manhattan Center; *Freedomways* places the event at Carnegie Hall.
26. Lorraine Hansberry, "A Challenge to Artists," *Freedomways* 3, no. 1 (Winter 1963): 31–35. Also, Caedmon, "My Government Is Wrong" (Speech to abolish the House Un-American Activities Committee, Manhattan Center on October 25, 1962), 6:13, *Lorraine Hansberry Speaks Out: Art and the Black Revolution* (New York: Harper Audio/Caedmon Records, 2009).
27. Ibid.
28. Ibid.
29. Frantz Fanon, *Black Skin, White Masks* (New York: Grove, 1967), 112.

30. De Beauvoir, *The Second Sex*, 7.

31. De Beauvoir, *The Second Sex*, 17. I am grateful for a collaborative conversation with Paige McGinley and Amber Musser about teaching *The Second Sex* that helped clarify my thinking about the text and how it relates to Hansberry's work. Soyica Colbert, Amber Musser, Paige McGinley, "Teaching the Second Sex: A Conversation," *Feminist Formations* 32, no. 1 (spring 2020): 98–116.

32. Lorraine Hansberry, "Simone de Beauvoir and *The Second Sex:* An American Commentary," in *Words of Fire,* ed. Beverly Guy-Sheftall, 133.

33. Joshua Chambers-Letson, *After the Party: A Manifesto for Queer of Color Life* (New York: New York University Press, 2018), xii, xx, 9. Also, as Steven R. Carter argues, "In [Hansberry's] 'Tribute' to the black intellectual giant W.E.B. Du Bois, she observed 'that certainly Du Bois's legacy teaches us to look forward and work for a socialist organization of society as the next great and dearly won universal condition of mankind.' She thought that the socialist organization of society held the greatest possibility of providing the basic necessities for a decent life for all and a potentially more democratic approach to managing social relationships so that no individual or group had too much power. Also, whether in their own fully achieved societies or still striving for them, socialists, perhaps, would nurture creativity and teach people to appreciate and even applaud individual and cultural differences. Hansberry did not want a socialism that would impose a homogeneous culture and a party line." Steven R. Carter, *Hansberry's Drama: Commitment Amid Complexity* (Urbana: University of Illinois Press, 1991), 12.

34. Chambers-Letson, *After the Party,* 25.

35. Carter, *Hansberry's Drama,* 10.

36. Hansberry, "A Challenge to Artists." Slightly different wording in Caedmon, "My Government Is Wrong."

37. Lisa Lowe, "Autobiography Out of Empire," *Small Axe,* no. 28, 13.1 (March 2009): 102.

38. Hansberry, "A Challenge to Artists."

39. Ibid.

40. Ibid.

41. Ibid.

42. Ibid.; also, Caedmon, "My Government Is Wrong."

43. Hansberry went to great lengths to correct the record when she thought she was misrepresented or misquoted by writing letters to the editor. See, for example, Ernest Kaiser and Robert Nemiroff, "A Lorraine Hansberry Bibliography," *Freedomways: A Quarterly Review of the Freedom Movement* 19, no. 4 (1979), 286–287; Lorraine Hansberry, "Miss Hansberry on 'Backlash,' " *Village Voice,* July 23, 1964, 10; Lorraine Hansberry, "Genet, Mailer, and the New Paternalism," *Village Voice,* June 1, 1961, 10, 14–15.

44. W.E.B. Du Bois, *The Souls of Black Folk* (Oxford: Oxford University Press, 2007), 3.

45. In *Abstractionist Aesthetics,* Phillip Brian Harper references the history of African American art being conceived of as a political project. He argues that racialized norms "presuppose the social-critical function of African American culture" and "generally assume that the function is best served by a type of realist aesthetic that casts racial blackness in overridingly 'positive' terms" (2). Hansberry did not invest in "verisimilitude so highly prized within the realist framework" (2–3). Instead her work sought to

call attention to how history framed the appearance of certain bodies and actions in order to produce collaboration, mutuality, and freedom practices (New York: New York University Press, 2015).

46. See Jean-Paul Sartre, *Sartre on Theatre* (Pantheon, 1976); Simone de Beauvoir, *Simone de Beauvoir: "The Useless Mouths" and Other Literary Writings*, ed. Margaret A. Simons and Marybeth Timmermann (Urbana: University of Illinois Press, 2011); Camus wrote the following plays: *Caligula, The Just Assassins, The Misunderstanding, The Possessed, Requiem for a Nun, The State of Siege.*

47. José Esteban Muñoz, "Feeling Brown: Ethnicity and Affect in Ricardo Bracho's *The Sweetest Hangover (and Other STDs)*," *Theatre Journal* 52, no. 1 (March 2000): 71.

48. See Lauren Berlant, *Cruel Optimism* (Durham: Duke University Press, 2011), and Robert J. Patterson, *Destructive Desires: Rhythm and Blues Culture and the Politics of Racial Equality* (New Brunswick: Rutgers University Press, 2019).

49. Lorraine Hansberry, "Letter to the Editor," under the pseudonym L. H. N., *The Ladder*, vol. 1 (August 1957): 27.

50. As Tavia Nyong'o asks, "What would it mean to consider the genesis of what becomes queer theory, its dark precursor, if you will, as not having taken place in intellectual discussions at particular academic institutions or in the pages of particular journals, but in the railroad flats of bohemian Greenwich Village in the 1960s?" Tavia Nyong'o, *Afro-Fabulations: The Queer Drama of Black Life* (New York: New York University Press, 2019), 158.

51. Darlene Clark Hine, "Rape and the Inner Lives of Black Women in the Middle West," *Signs* 14, no. 4 (Summer 1989): 912.

52. Nina Simone and Stephen Cleary, *I Put a Spell on You: The Autobiography of Nina Simone* (Cambridge, Mass.: Da Capo, 1993), 87.

CHAPTER 1. PRACTICES OF FREEDOM

Epigraph: Lorraine Hansberry, "Simone de Beauvoir and the Second Sex—An American Commentary," Box 59, Folder 1, page 15, *Lorraine Hansberry Papers*, Schomburg Center for Research in Black Culture, New York Public Library, New York. An edited version of the essay appears in *Words of Fire: An Anthology of African-American Feminist Thought*, ed. Beverly Guy-Sheftall (New York: New Press, 1995), 128–142.

1. Murali Balaji, *Professor and the Pupil: The Politics and Friendship of W.E.B. Du Bois and Paul Robeson* (New York: Nation, 2007), 115–116.

2. Martin Duberman, *Paul Robeson: A Biography* (New York: New Press, 1989), 307.

3. Balaji, *Professor and the Pupil*, xxiv.

4. Alan Rogers, "Passports and Politics: The Courts and the Cold War," *The Historian* 47, no. 4 (August 1985): 501.

5. Biondi, *To Stand and Fight*, Gore, *Radicalism and the Crossroads*, and Washington, *The Other Blacklist.*

6. Barbara J. Beeching, "Paul Robeson and the Black Press: The 1950 Passport Controversy," *The Journal of African American History* 87 (Summer 2002): 339.

7. Deborah Willis, "The Image of Robeson," in *Paul Robeson: Artist and Citizen*, ed. Jeffrey C. Stewart (New Brunswick: Rutgers University Press, 1998), 62.

8. Balaji, *Professor and the Pupil,* 323.

9. Analysis of Robeson as a target of McCarthyism appears in Martha Biondi, *To Stand and Fight: The Struggle for Civil Rights in Postwar New York City* (Cambridge: Harvard University Press, 2006), 153.

10. In "Sisters Outside," Carole Boyce Davies makes a similar point about how the deportation of Claudia Jones had an impact on St. Clair Drake's perspective about radicalism. She asserts, "[Kevin] Gaines points out that in rendering Jones a 'tragic' figure, she would have been a 'cautionary example for [St. Clair] Drake and those of his generation' because of the brutal treatment which she received. But this is precisely the point that my book makes, that is, that a specific targeting of black radicalism had in many ways 'deported the radical black subject' from consideration, not just the subject Claudia Jones herself but what she represented in terms of ideas and practice. So, basically, this brings us to the contemporary period of recovery" (220). Hansberry too knew Jones and would have taken note of the state's brutal treatment of her. Unlike Drake, however, Hansberry continued to cling to not only the ideals of radicalism but also the identity of radical, which begs the question of what Hansberry thought of Jones's fate as portent for her own? *Small Axe,* no. 28, 13.1 (March 2009).

11. It is not clear what month Hansberry moved to New York. In a letter to Edythe Cohen, Hansberry indicated that she had moved in November 1950. Lorraine Hansberry to Edythe Cohen, n.d., Box 1, Folder 5, *Lorraine Hansberry Papers,* Schomburg Center for Research in Black Culture, New York (hereafter *Hansberry Papers*). In an interview with the *New Yorker,* Hansberry said she moved to New York in the summer of 1950. Lillian Ross, "How Lorraine Hansberry Wrote 'A Raisin in the Sun,'" *New Yorker,* May 2, 1959 (www.newyorker.com/magazine/1959/05/09/playwright, accessed November 20, 2019). In a cover letter she sent to the *New York Times* in 1953, she wrote that she had moved to New York in March 1950. In that letter, she claimed to have graduated from the University of Wisconsin and listed her date of birth as May 19, 1928. Hansberry was born on May 19, 1930, and she left the University of Wisconsin without graduating. Lorraine Hansberry to the personnel manager at the *New York Times,* July 9, 1953, Box 66, Folder 4, *Hansberry Papers.* An entry in Hansberry's FBI file on December 18, 1953, says that the University of Wisconsin, Madison, placed her on final scholastic probation, February 10, 1950.

12. Although Lorraine Hansberry's published writing, excluding speeches, does not qualify as life writing, making truth claims about the subject matter of her experiences, relationships, and events as the basis for the narrative, her archive, as a specific curation of her published and unpublished works, shares with eighteenth- and nineteenth-century Black life writing "that the black narrator was, despite all prejudice and propaganda, a truth-teller, a reliable transcriber of the experience and character of black folk"; William L. Andrews, *To Tell a Free Story: The First Century of Afro-American Autobiography, 1760–1865* (Champaign: University of Illinois Press, 1986), 1. Approaching her archive as a source that speaks to her intellectual life produces resonance with historic forms of life writing. Andrews argues: "Reaching 'the hearts of men' was the rhetorical aim of practically all black autobiography in the first century of its existence, whether produced by an ex-slave or not. Afro-American literature of the late eighteenth and early nineteenth centuries is dominated by treatises, pamphlets, addresses, and appeals,

all of which employ expostulatory means to confront the problem of the black situation in white America" (5). Reading Hansberry's archive evidences how her writing, as an expression of herself, confronted "the problem of the black situation in white America."

13. Lorraine Hansberry, *To Be Young, Gifted, and Black* (New York: Signet 2011), 10.

14. Joshua Chambers-Letson, *After the Party: A Manifesto for Queer of Color Life* (New York: New York University Press, 2018), 6.

15. Margaret B. Wilkerson, "The Sighted Eyes and Feeling Heart of Lorraine Hansberry," *Black American Literature Forum* 17.1 (Spring 1983): 8–13, 9.

16. William W. Demastes, ed., *Realism and the American Dramatic Tradition* (Tuscaloosa: University of Alabama Press, 1996), xi.

17. Reference to Hansberry working as a Tag-maker is in a document titled "Lorraine Hansberry," Box 1, Folder 1, *Lorraine Hansberry Papers,* Schomburg Center for Research in Black Culture, New York Public Library, New York.

18. Imani Perry, *Looking for Lorraine: The Radiant and Radical Life of Lorraine Hansberry* (Boston: Beacon, 2018), 46.

19. Lorraine Hansberry's FBI File, entry dated November 27, 1953; Perry, *Looking for Lorraine*, 53; Mary Helen Washington, *The Other Blacklist: The African American Literary and Cultural Left of the 1950s* (New York: Columbia University Press, 2014), 143.

20. Denise Lynn, "Socialist Feminism and Triple Oppression: Claudia Jones and African American Women in American Communism," *Journal for the Study of Radicalism* 8, no. 2 (Fall 2014): 8. Also see Carole Boyce Davies, *Left of Karl Marx: The Political Life of Black Communist Claudia Jones* (Durham: Duke University Press, 2007), 3.

21. Washington, *The Other Blacklist*, 143.

22. Peniel E. Joseph, *Waiting 'til the Midnight Hour: A Narrative History of Black Power in America* (New York: Henry Holt, 2006), 26–27.

23. My description of Hansberry's writing as a freedom practice is also informed by what Michel Foucault theorized in a 1984 interview in which he considered freedom as "practice of the self" as "an exercise" of self-improvement "which one tries to work out, to transform one's self and to attain a certain mode of being"; Michel Foucault, "Michel Foucault The Ethical Care for the Self as a Practice of Freedom: An Interview with Michel Foucault," in *The Final Foucault,* edited by James Bernauer (Cambridge: MIT Press, 1998), 2. Foucault explained that working on one's self should be understood as "practices of freedom" rather than liberation: practice calls attention to the ongoing and necessary negotiations of power that sustain an act of liberation (2–3). For Foucault, self-improvement necessarily entails repeated practices of freedom. Hansberry, following Jones, saw these practices of self-transformation as linked to a network or a movement.

24. For a discussion of gender hierarchies in the Black labor movement of the 1930s, '40s, and '50s, see Robin D. G. Kelley, *Race Rebels* (New York: Free Press, 1994), chapters 5 and 6.

25. Hansberry, "Simone de Beauvoir and the Second Sex—An American Commentary," 16. Also see letter to Molly written in 1957, Restricted File, Page 11–14, *Hansberry Papers.* She wrote it while working as a recreation leader for the Federation for the Handicapped. She writes about gender as a performance in the letter and her own investments, or lack thereof, in labels.

26. Hansberry, "Simone de Beauvoir and the Second Sex—An American Commentary," 4.

27. Shatema Threadcraft, *Intimate Justice: The Black Female Body and the Body Politic* (Oxford: Oxford University Press, 2016), 27.

28. Lorraine Hansberry, "Flag from a Kitchenette Window," *Masses & Mainstream* 3, no. 9 (September 1950): 39.

29. Hansberry, "Flag from a Kitchenette Window," 40. The war song refers to the Korean War (June 25, 1950–July 27, 1953).

30. Lorraine Hansberry, *The Movement: Documentary of a Struggle for Equality* (New York: Simon and Schuster, 1964).

31. Quoted in Washington, *The Other Blacklist*, 141.

32. Lorraine Hansberry, Letter to Edythe Cohen, Box 1, Folder 5, *Lorraine Hansberry Papers,* Schomburg Center for Research in Black Culture, New York Public Library, New York.

33. Michael Anderson, "Lorraine Hansberry's Freedom Family," *American Communist History* 7, no. 2 (December 17, 2008): 266.

34. Lorraine Hansberry, Hansberry's Reflection on Employment at *Freedom,* Box 2, Folder 13, *Lorraine Hansberry Papers,* Schomburg Center for Research in Black Culture, New York Public Library, New York.

35. Ibid.

36. Erik S. McDuffie, *Sojourning for Freedom: Black Women, American Communism, and the Making of Black Left Feminist* (Durham: Duke University Press, 2011), 173.

37. Brian Richard, "The Initiating Committee of the Sojourn for Truth and Justice," September 25, 1951, Box 12, Folder 17, *Louise Thompson Patterson Papers,* Stuart A. Rose Manuscript, Archives and Rare Book Library, Emory University, Atlanta.

38. See Kevin Gaines, "Locating the Transnational in Postwar African American History," *Small Axe,* no. 28, 13.1 (March 2009): 192–202, 196, and Dayo F. Gore, *Radicalism at the Crossroads: African American Women Activists in the Cold War* (New York: New York University Press, 2011), 85–89.

39. Gore, *Radicalism at the Crossroads,* 3.

40. Lorraine Hansberry, "Women Demand Justice Done," *Freedom* (October 1961): 6.

41. J. Clay Smith, Jr., *Emancipation: The Making of the Black Lawyer, 1844–1944* (Philadelphia: University of Pennsylvania Press, 1993), 187 note 322.

42. Hansberry, "Women Demand Justice Done," 6.

43. Ibid.

44. Ibid.

45. Lorraine Hansberry, "They Dried Their Tears," *Freedom* (October 1961): 6; Lorraine Hansberry, "Women Voice Demands in Capital Sojourn," *Freedom* (October 1951): 6; Hansberry "Women Demand Justice Done," 6.

46. Hansberry, "They Dried Their Tears," 6.

47. McDuffie, *Sojourning for Freedom,* 165.

48. Ingram said that "me and my children were getting along all right until he started at me. He could not make me go his way and he was mad. And this is just what it was about[—]me not having him." Quoted in Herbert Shapiro, *White Violence and Black Response: From Reconstruction to Montgomery* (Amherst: University of Massachusetts Press, 1988), 360.

49. Charles Martin, "Race, Gender, and Southern Justice: The Rosa Lee Ingram Case," *The American Journal of Legal History* 29, no. 3 (1985): 251–252.

50. See Robin D. G. Kelley, *Race Rebels,* chapters 5 and 6, for a discussion of gender hierarchies in the Black labor movement of the 1930s, '40s, and '50s.

51. McDuffie 2011, Kindle locations 3356–3359; Castledine 2012, Kindle locations 2210–2215 and 2232–2238.

52. Lorraine Hansberry and Alice Childress, "Negro History Festival," February 29, 1952, Box 45, Folder 25, *Alice Childress Papers,* Schomburg Center for Research in Black Culture, New York Public Library, New York.

53. Carole Boyce Davies, "Sisters Outside: Tracing the Caribbean/Black Radical Intellectual Tradition," *Small Axe,* no. 28, 13.1 (March 2009): 218. Davies argues, "In this article's particular application of outsiderness, black women have become sisters outside the black radical intellectual tradition; Caribbean women, sisters outside the Caribbean radical tradition and US African American civil rights discourse and sisters outside Pan-Africanist discourse. In other words, while there has been, for example, tremendous headway in black women writers claiming a space within the canon of African American or Caribbean letters, the same has not happened substantially in intellectual and political traditions" (218). While several Black feminist historians have worked to call attention to the contribution of Black women radicals, including Angela Davis, Kevin Gaines, Patricia Saunders, Barbara Ransby, Dayo Gore, Imani Perry, Sherie M. Randolph, and Keisha Blain, work still remains to be done to fully articulate the history of the tradition to account for women's intellectual contributions.

54. Lorraine Hansberry, "Lynchsong," *Masses & Mainstream,* vol. 4, no. 7 (July 1951): 19.

55. "Mississippi Lynches a Slayer: Overpowers Sheriff and Takes Negro Convicted Friday to Bridge on Victim's Farm," *New York Times,* October 18, 1942, 49.

56. Hansberry, "Lynchsong," 20.

57. The woman who called herself Rosalee McGee was not Willie McGee's wife or the mother of his children. His ex-wife Eliza Jane Payton McGee was the mother of Willie's four children. In July 1951, Hansberry would not have known of Rosalee's misrepresentation of her identity. See Alexander Heard, *The Eyes of Willie McGee: A Tragedy of Race, Sex, and Secrets in Jim Crow South* (New York: HarperCollins, 2010), 16–17.

58. Heard, 5–6; Bridgettte McGee-Robinson, "My Grandfather's Execution," *All Things Considered,* produced by Joe Richman and Samara Freemark of Radio Diaries, with help from Anayansi Diaz-Cortes, Deborah George, and Ben Shapiro, *NPR,* May 7, 2010.

59. Hansberry, "Lynchsong," 20.

60. Ibid.

61. William L. Patterson, ed. *We Charge Genocide* (New York: Civil Rights Congress, 1951), n.p.

62. Patterson, *We Charge Genocide,* xi. "Convention on the Prevention and Punishment of the Crime of Genocide," adopted by the General Assembly of the United Nations on 9 December 1948 (https://treaties.un.org/doc/Publication/UNTS/Volume%2078/volume-78-I-1021-English.pdf).

63. Brian Richardson, "Introduction: The Struggle for the Real—Interpretive Conflict, Dramatic Method, and the Paradox of Realism," in *Realism and the American Dramatic Tradition,* ed. William W. Demastes (Tuscaloosa: University of Alabama Press, 1996), 2.

64. Lorraine Hansberry, "Frederick Douglass School Opens Its Doors in Harlem," *Freedom* 2 (March 1952), 2, 7. Advertisement, *Freedom* 3 (September 1953), 8.

65. Shirley Graham Du Bois quoted in Gerald Horne, *Race Woman: The Lives of Shirley Graham Du Bois* (New York: New York University Press, 2008), 18. Also see Judith E. Smith, *Visions of Belonging: Family Stories, Popular Culture, and Postwar Democracy, 1940–1960* (New York: Columbia University Press, 2004), 295.

66. Lorraine Hansberry, "Africa . . . For Europeans Only?" *New Challenge*, vol. 4, no. 7 (1955): 19.

67. Anthony Bogues, "And What About the Human? Freedom, Human Emancipation, and the Radical Imagination," *Boundary 2*, vol. 39, no. 3 (2012): 38.

68. Lorraine Hansberry, "Kenya's Kikuyu: A Peaceful People Wage Heroic Struggle Against British," *Freedom* (December 1952): 3.

69. Ibid.

70. Elsie Robbins, "This Little Piggy Got Dumped on the Sidewalk," *Freedom*, vol. 2, no. 4 (April 1952): 7.

71. "It was also in Madison, on January 7, 1950, that Hansberry attended a Communist recruitment party. Apparently she did not join the party until later in the year, after she abandoned her college studies and moved to New York, where she almost immediately was a presence on picket lines, tenants' protests, and as a street-corner orator, where, an acquaintance remembered, 'she spoke with the fierceness of a young Harriet Tubman' " (Anderson, "Lorraine Hansberry's Freedom Family," 264).

72. Lorraine Hansberry, "Noted Lawyer Goes to Jail; Says Negroes' Fight for Rights Menaced," *Freedom*, vol. 2, no. 5 (May 1952): 3.

73. Mary L. Dudziak, *Cold War Civil Rights: Race and the Image of American Democracy* (Princeton: Princeton University Press, Kindle Edition, 2011), 28, chapter 2.

74. Lorraine Hansberry, "The Negro Writer and His Roots: Toward a New Romanticism," Box 56, Folder 4, *Lorraine Hansberry Papers*, Schomburg Center for Research in Black Culture, New York Public Library, New York, presented at the American Society of African Culture (AMSAC) Conference of Negro Writers, February 28–March 1, 1959.

75. Lorraine Hansberry, "A Negro Woman Speaks for Peace," *The Worker*, June 22, 1952, 8.

76. Lorraine Hansberry, " 'Illegal' Conference Shows Peace Is Key to Freedom," *Freedom*, vol. 2, no. 4 (April 1952): 3.

77. Lorraine Hansberry, "Speech at APC, May 28th 1952," Box 66, Folder 3, *Lorraine Hansberry Papers*, Schomburg Center for Research in Black Culture, New York Public Library, New York.

78. Hansberry, " 'Illegal' Conference Shows Peace Is Key to Freedom," 3.

79. Hansberry, "Speech at APC, May 28th 1952." The document titled "Speech at APC" includes a speech given at a rally in New York on April 17, 1952, as well as a draft of a story that she wrote for *Freedom* about the conference.

80. Lorraine Hansberry, Letter to the staff of *Freedom* on stationery of the Palacio Florida Hotel in Montevideo, Uruguay, Box 66, Folder 3, *Lorraine Hansberry Papers*, Schomburg Center for Research in Black Culture, Schomburg Center for Research in Black Culture, New York Public Library, New York.

81. Hansberry, "Speech at APC, May 28th 1952." Hansberry participated in the Inter-Continental Peace Congress Conference at a time when many activists began

to shy away from being identified as Black radicals. Subsequently, as Mary Helen Washington, Kevin Gaines, and Carole Boyce Davies argue, "the political and ideological strictures of cold war anticommunism lingered long after the mid-1950s, not only restricting the freedom of expression and mobility of black dissenters but subsequently shaping the perspective of scholars of US civil rights and antiracist struggles." Thus "the US academy tended to dismiss the black left and emphasize mainstream civil rights organizations" (Gaines quoted in Davies, 221). Although Hansberry's work emerges alongside the classical phase of the civil rights movement, it activated the philosophy and practices of Black radicalism as a mass movement for freedom that required the sharing of resources, the redistribution of power, and the dismantling of capitalism through a resistance to accumulation. See the introduction to Mary Helen Washington's *The Other Blacklist* and Carole Boyce Davies, "Sisters Outside," 221.

82. Lorraine Hansberry, "The Real Reasons Behind the Murder," *New Challenge*, vol. 4, no. 8 (November 1955): 16.

83. Lorraine Hansberry, "The Truth About the South," *New Challenge*, vol. 5, no. 1 (February 1956): 20–21. "In May 1954, when the Supreme Court issued its historic decision on desegregation in education, young Americans everywhere—North and South, Negro and white—rejoiced. But in South Carolina, Dixiecrat Gov. Byrnes warned: 'blood would flow in the streets' before democracy came to the South. He urged open defiance of the Supreme Court ruling—and thus of the U.S. Constitution itself. Today the blood is flowing. The hideous murder of Emmett Till was—as NEW CHALLENGE reported in special 10-page coverage last month—a direct result of the racist incitement which has followed. We warned then that it could be either the beginning of the end of lynching in these United States—if the Federal Gov't intervened—or the 'go-ahead' for a reign of terror of unprecedented scope and brutality. Since that time the Government has refused to do a thing. And the result has been exactly what responsible youth and adult leaders everywhere had predicted—A 'growing racist terror,' says the National Association for the Advancement of Colored People, today rides unchecked in Dixie. And thus far its prime, though not exclusive, victim has been youth." Lorraine Hansberry, "Terror in Dixie," *New Challenge*, vol. 4, no. 9 (December 1955): 20–21.

84. See Lorraine Hansberry, "1954 Season at Camp Unity: A Report," Box 66, Folder 5, *Lorraine Hansberry Papers*, Schomburg Center for Research in Black Culture, Schomburg Center for Research in Black Culture, New York Public Library, New York.

85. Bruce Weber, "Philip Rose, 'Raisin' and 'Purlie' Producer, Dies at 89," *New York Times*, June 2, 2011 (www.nytimes.com/2011/06/02/theater/philip-rose-broadway-producer-dies-at-89.html, accessed December 25, 2017), and Theatertalk, "Creating A Raisin In the Sun with Ossie Davis, Ruby Dee & Phil Rose (2002)," YouTube, September 3, 2013 (www.youtube.com/watch?v=fPQVrkKOJ68, accessed December 25, 2017).

86. Lorraine Hansberry, "Some Basic Conclusions," Letter to Robert Nemiroff, December 26, 1952, Box 2, Folder 0, *Lorraine Hansberry Papers*, Schomburg Center for Research in Black Culture, New York Public Library, New York.

87. Lorraine Hansberry, "You Are Never to Fly Again!" Letter to Robert Nemiroff, March 10, no year, Box 2, Folder 0, *Lorraine Hansberry Papers*, Schomburg Center for Research in Black Culture, New York Public Library, New York.

88. Lorraine Hansberry, "Chicago—Christmas 1955," 1955, Box 1, Folder 1, *Lorraine Hansberry Papers,* Schomburg Center for Research in Black Culture, New York Public Library, New York.

89. Lorraine Hansberry, "Letter to the Editor," under the pseudonym L. N., *The Ladder,* vol. 1 (August 1957): 27.

90. Amy C. Steinbugler, *Beyond Loving: Intimate Racework in Lesbian, Gay, and Straight Interracial Relationships* (Oxford: Oxford University Press, 2012), 12.

91. John D'Emilio, *Sexual Politics, Sexual Communities* (Chicago: University of Chicago Press, 1998), 49.

92. Lorraine Hansberry, Letter about "Her," July 8, 1954, Restricted Box, Folder 1, *Lorraine Hansberry Papers,* Schomburg Center for Research in Black Culture, New York Public Library, New York.

93. Lorraine Hansberry, Letter about her "chief characteristic," August 1954, Restricted Box, Folder 1, *Lorraine Hansberry Papers,* Schomburg Center for Research in Black Culture, New York Public Library, New York.

94. Lorraine Hansberry, "Notes on Women's Liberation," 1955, Box 56, Folder 6, *Lorraine Hansberry Papers,* Schomburg Center for Research in Black Culture, New York Public Library, New York. Audre Lorde warns against creating a hierarchy of oppression in "Learning from the '60s," in *Sister Outsider* (Berkeley: Cross Press, 1984), 139.

95. "When she looked for actors to translate her language and ideas into action, she turned to the tightly knit group from her days with the Committee for the Negros in the Arts, the actors Sidney Poitier, Lonnie Elder III, Ruby Dee, and Ossie Davis." Lawrence P. Jackson, *The Indignant Generation: A Narrative History of African American Writers and Critics, 1934–1960* (Princeton: Princeton University Press, 2011), 487.

96. Lisbeth Lipari, "Lorraine Hansberry," in *Black Writers of the Chicago Renaissance,* ed. Steven C. Tracy (Urbana: University of Illinois Press, 2011), 205.

97. James Baldwin, "Sweet Lorraine," *The Price of the Ticket: Collected Nonfiction, 1948–1985* (New York: St. Martin's, 1985), 444.

98. In 1976, Barbara Grier, a former editor of *The Ladder,* identified Hansberry as the author of these two letters. See Lisbeth Lipari, "The Rhetoric of Intersectionality: Lorraine Hansberry's 1957 Letters to the *Ladder,*" in *Queering Public Address: Sexualities in American Historical Discourse,* edited by Charles E. Morris, III (Columbia: University of South Carolina Press, 2007), 220.

99. Lorraine Hansberry, "Letter to the Editor," signed "L.H.N.," *The Ladder,* vol. 1, no. 8 (May 1957): 27.

100. See Washington, *The Other Blacklist,* 257, and John D'Emilio, *Sexual Politics, Sexual Communities,* 76–81.

101. Lorraine Hansberry, "Hansberry's Notes on Homosexual Self-determination," 1957, Restricted Box, Folder 8, Schomburg Center for Research in Black Culture, New York Public Library, New York.

102. Hansberry, "Letter to the Editor," signed L.N., 27, 28–29.

103. D'Emilio, *Sexual Politics, Sexual Communities,* 100. According to D'Emilio: "In 1955, when a few gay women in San Francisco commenced autonomous organizing for

their own emancipation, their efforts reflected the particularities of lesbian existence. The extreme isolation and invisibility of gay women projected concerns about social life to the forefront of their goals. A smaller subculture [than gay men] made recruitment difficult, while the precarious economic circumstances of women and their limited options heightened the risks of participating in a movement," 100.

104. Hortense Spillers, "Mama's Baby, Papa's Maybe: An American Grammar Book," *Diacritics,* vol. 17, no. 2 (1987): 80.

105. Lipari, "Rhetoric of Intersectionality," 220.

106. See Elise Harris, "The Double Life of Lorraine Hansberry," *Out* (September 1999): 96–101, 174–175.

107. In the *Lorraine Hansberry Papers,* Box 60, folder 17 contains a short story by Emily Jones. Cheryl Higashida, *Black Internationalist Feminism: Women Writers of the Black Left, 1945–1995* (Urbana: University of Illinois Press, 2011), 197, notes that Hansberry used the pseudonym Emily Jones.

108. Demastes, *Realism and the American Dramatic Tradition,* xi.

109. Lorraine Hansberry, "The Budget," *The Ladder,* vol. 2, no. 12 (September 1958): 20.

110. Hansberry, "The Budget," 21.

111. Lorraine Hansberry, "Chanson du Konallis," written under the pseudonym Emily Jones, *The Ladder,* vol. 2, no. 12 (September 1958): 20.

112. Hansberry, "Chanson du Konallis," 25.

113. Lorraine Hansberry, "The Anticipation of Eve," written under the pseudonym Emily Jones, *One Magazine,* vol. 6, no. 12 (December 1958): 29.

114. Hansberry "The Anticipation of Eve," 29, emphasis added.

115. See Jackson, *The Indignant Generation,* 475.

116. Lorraine Hansberry, "The Negro Writer and His Roots: Toward a New Romanticism."

117. Ibid.

118. Ibid.

CHAPTER 2. THE SHAPING FORCE OF *A RAISIN IN THE SUN*

Epigraphs: Audre Lorde, "Poetry Is Not a Luxury," *Sister Outsider* (Berkeley: Crossing Press, 2007), 39; Lorraine Hansberry, "The Negro Writer and His Roots: Toward a New Romanticism," *The Black Scholar,* March–April 1981, 12.

1. According to Simone in *What Happened, Miss Simone?* a documentary film directed by Liz Garbus (Brooklyn: Moxie Firecracker Films, 2016).

2. For a detailed recounting of critics' misunderstanding of *A Raisin in the Sun* and Hansberry's comments about the play, see Steven R. Carter, *Hansberry's Drama: Commitment Amid Complexity* (Urbana: University of Illinois Press, 1991), 20–21.

3. See Lillian Ross, "How Lorraine Hansberry Wrote 'A Raisin in the Sun,' *New Yorker,* May 2, 1959 (www.newyorker.com/magazine/1959/05/09/playwright, accessed November 20, 2019). In a preface to the interview, Hansberry is described as "the twenty-eight-year-old author of the hit play 'A Raisin' in the Sun. Miss Hansberry is a relaxed, soft-voiced young lady with an intelligent and pretty face, a particularly vertical hairdo, and large brown eyes, so dark and so deep that you get lost in them."

4. Wil Haygood, "45 Years Ago, a 'Raisin' to Cheer," *Washington Post,* March 28, 2004 (www.washingtonpost.com/archive/lifestyle/style/2004/03/28/45-years-ago-a-

raisin-to-cheer/cafa33bd-853b-4c19-bab3-e011a580284f/?utm_term=.9a55a3fd50d8, accessed February 28, 2019).

5. Ibid.

6. "National Archives at Chicago: Civil Rights Cases," *The U.S. National Archives and Records Administration,* August 30, 2017 (www.archives.gov/chicago/finding-aids/civil-rights-movement.html, accessed March 1, 2019).

7. Affidavit Signed by Carl A. Hansberry and Perry Hansberry, Box 2, Folder 17, *Lorraine Hansberry Papers,* Schomburg Center for Research in Black Culture, New York Public Library, New York.

8. Wedding Book of Lorraine Hansberry and Robert Nemiroff, Box 5, Folder 2, *Lorraine Hansberry Papers,* Schomburg Center for Research in Black Culture, New York Public Library, New York.

9. Michael Anderson, "Lorraine Hansberry's Freedom Family," in *Red Activists and Black Freedom: James and Esther Jackson and the Long Civil Rights Revolution,* ed. David Levering Lewis, Michael H. Nash, Daniel J. Leab (New York: Routledge, 2012), 96.

10. Lorraine Hansberry, Letter dated July 8, 1954, Box 1, Folder 1, *Lorraine Hansberry Papers,* Schomburg Center for Research in Black Culture, New York Public Library, New York.

11. Lorraine Hansberry, Letter dated October 19, 1956, Box 1, Folder 1, *Lorraine Hansberry Papers,* Schomburg Center for Research in Black Culture, New York Public Library, New York.

12. Recall Hansberry's letters to *The Ladder* were published in the summer of 1957.

13. Imani Perry, *Looking for Lorraine: The Radiant and Radical Life of Lorraine Hansberry* (Boston: Beacon, 2018), 92–93.

14. Lauren Berlant, *Cruel Optimism* (Durham: Duke University Press, 2011), 23–50.

15. Edward Soja, *Seeking Spatial Justice* (Minneapolis: University of Minnesota Press, 2010), 20.

16. Studs Terkel, "Make New Sounds: Studs Terkel Interviews Lorraine Hansberry," *American Theatre,* vol. 1, no. 7 (1984): 6.

17. Tommie Shelby, "Justice, Deviance, and the Dark Ghetto," *Philosophy & Public Affairs,* vol. 35, no. 2 (2007): 144.

18. Arnold R. Hirsch, *Making the Second Ghetto: Race and Housing in Chicago, 1940–1960* (Cambridge: Cambridge University Press, 1983), 9–10.

19. Diane Fisher, "Miss Hansberry & Bobby K.: Birthweight Low, Jobs Few, Death Comes Early," *Village Voice* June 6, 1963, 9.

20. Lorraine Hansberry, *A Raisin in the Sun and The Sign in Sidney Brustein's Window* (New York: Vintage, 1995), 148.

21. Ta-Nehisi Coates, "The Case for Reparations," *The Atlantic,* May 21, 2014 (www.theatlantic.com/features/archive/2014/05/the-case-for-reparations/361631, accessed June 16, 2017).

22. See Lorraine Hansberry's Unpublished Short Stories, Box 60, Folder 16, *Lorraine Hansberry Papers,* Schomburg Center for Research in Black Culture, New York Public Library, New York. Also see Perry, *Looking for Lorraine,* 14–15.

23. Soja, *Seeking Spatial Justice,* 45.

24. Hansberry, *A Raisin in the Sun and The Sign in Sidney Brustein's Window,* 73.

25. See Margaret B. Wilkerson, "'A Raisin in the Sun': Anniversary of an American Classic," *Theatre Journal* 38.4 (Dec. 1986): 450–451.

26. Hansberry, *A Raisin in the Sun and The Sign in Sidney Brustein's Window,* 133, 134.

27. Ibid., 135.

28. Audre Lorde, *Sister Outsider: Essays and Speeches* (New York: Crossing Press, 2007), 111.

29. Terkel, "Make New Sounds," 6. The interview took place May 12, 1959 but was not published until 1984.

30. Sidney Fields, "Housewife's Play Is a Hit," *New York Daily Mirror,* March 16, 1959, 4.

31. *Ebony,* "Negro Playwrights," May 10, 2016, Box 7, Folder 10, *Lorraine Hansberry Papers,* Schomburg Center for Research in Black Culture, New York Public Library, New York.

32. Lorraine Hansberry, *A Raisin in the Sun and The Sign in Sidney Brustein's Window,* 121.

33. See *Ebony* magazine story which explains that the producers of *A Raisin in the Sun* tried to finance the play with Black people's donations. Also see Aliyyah I. Abdur-Rahman, *Against the Closet: Black Political Longing and the Erotics of Race* (Durham: Duke University Press, 2012), 100.

34. *Ebony* "Negro Playwrights."

35. From Lawrence P. Jackson, *The Indignant Generation: A Narrative History of African American Writers and Critics, 1934–1960* (Princeton: Princeton University Press, 2011), 485:

> Lorraine Hansberry had the excellent personal fortune of being introduced to the American public at almost precisely the same moment as the Nation of Islam national spokesman Malcolm X. The television broadcaster Mike Wallace interviewed Hansberry for his news program on May 8, 1959, the result of her winning the New York Drama Critics Circle Award. Wallace was then hard at work on the exposé of the Nation of Islam called *The Hate That Hate Produced,* a five-part series televised in July. The famous broadcast would be the first time that most Americans, black or white, had ever heard of organized black nationalism, proponents of black segregation and separatism, and black supremacy. Nor had people typically been exposed to the articulate, charismatic, and visibly convinced ex-convict Malcolm X. These topics were of considerable interest to Wallace when he interviewed Hansberry, apparently so much so that he ignored questions from two other areas.
>
> The first area he neglected was Hansberry's long association with Paul Robeson, *Freedom* newspaper, the Committee for the Negro in the Arts, and the Communist Party. The other point in the news, never brought up by Wallace, was the startling fact that an NAACP president in Monroe, North Carolina, named Robert F. Williams had also said in May 1959, 'We must be willing to kill . . . if it's necessary to stop lynching with lynching, then we must be willing to resort to that method.' The May 7, 1959, *New York Times* headline ran 'N.A.A.C.P. Leader Urges Violence.' In some respects, Williams, a committed integrationist who wanted to organize African American self-defense efforts, a strategy that he called 'armed self-reliance,' seemed a more threatening black leader than Malcolm X, a black separatist and devotee to a cult like religion. It was better not to invoke a man like Williams at all."

36. Lorraine Hansberry, "The Beauty of Things Black—Towards Total Liberation," an interview with Mike Wallace on May 8, 1959, 21:34, *Lorraine Hansberry Speaks Out: Art and the Black Revolution* (New York: Harper Audio/Caedmon Recordings, 2009).

37. Lorraine Hansberry's review of Richard Wright's *The Outsider, Freedom,* vol. 14 (April 1953): 7.
38. Mary Helen Washington, *The Other Blacklist: The African American Literary and Cultural Left of the 1950s* (New York: Columbia University Press, 2014), 241, 239.
39. Lorraine Hansberry, "The Negro Writer and His Roots: Toward a New Romanticism," *The Black Scholar* (March–April 1981), 6.
40. Washington, *The Other Blacklist,* 243.
41. See Mary L. Dudziak, *Cold War Civil Rights: Race and the Image of American Democracy* (Princeton: Princeton University Press, 2000), 65–78.
42. Washington, *The Other Blacklist,* 240.
43. Hansberry, "The Negro Writer and His Roots," 5.
44. Washington, *The Other Blacklist,* 261.
45. Nan Robertson "Dramatist Against Odds," *New York Times,* May 8, 1959, 3.
46. Lorde, *Sister Outsider,* 115, 112.
47. See Robin Bernstein, "Inventing a Fishbowl: White Supremacy and the Critical Reception of Lorraine Hansberry's *A Raisin in the Sun,*" *Modern Drama* 42, no. 1 (Spring 1999): 18.
48. Robertson, "Dramatist Against Odds," 3.
49. Ernest Kaiser and Robert Nemiroff, "A Lorraine Hansberry Bibliography," *Freedomways: A Quarterly Review of the Freedom Movement* 19, no. 4 (1979): 286–287.
50. Lloyd W. Brown, "Lorraine Hansberry as Ironist: A Reappraisal of *A Raisin in the Sun,*" *Journal of Black Studies* 4, no. 3 (March 1974): 237.
51. Peniel E. Joseph, *Waiting 'til the Midnight Hour: A Narrative of Black Power in America* (New York: Henry Holt, 2006), 311 note 58.
52. Stefano Harney and Fred Moten, *The Undercommons: Fugitive Planning & Black Study* (New York: Minor Compositions, 2013), 93.
53. Michelle Gordon, " 'Somewhat Like War': The Aesthetics of Segregation, Black Liberation, and *A Raisin in the Sun,*" *African American Review* 42, no. 1 (2008): 122.
54. Douglas S. Massey, "Residential Segregation and Neighborhood Conditions in U.S. Metropolitan Areas," in *America Becoming: Racial Trends and Their Consequences,* vol. 1, ed. Neil Smelser, William Julius Wilson, and Faith Mitchell (Washington, D.C.: National Academies Press, 2001), 398, 396 (https://doi.org/10.17226/9599).
55. Ibid.
56. Ibid., 425.
57. Ibid., 399.
58. Gordon, " 'Somewhat Like War,' " 122.
59. Quoted in Lorraine Hansberry, *To Be Young, Gifted, and Black: Lorraine Hansberry in Her Own Words* (New York: Signet, 2011), 117.
60. Lorraine Hansberry, "Your Play Is Performed," *Lorraine Hansberry Audio Collection: A Raisin in the Sun, To Be Young Gifted and Black, and Lorraine Hansberry Speaks Out,* read by Ruby Dee and James Earl Jones (New York: Caedmon Records, 2009).
61. Ibid.
62. Joseph-Achille Mbembé and Libby Meintjes, "Necropolitics," *Public Culture,* vol. 15, no. 1 (Winter 2003): 39, 40.
63. "Homecoming," Box 60, Folder 9, *Lorraine Hansberry Papers,* Schomburg Center for Research in Black Culture, New York Public Library, New York.

64. Stefano Harney and Fred Moten, *The Undercommons: Fugitive Planning & Black Study* (New York: Minor Compositions, 2013), 96.

65. Walter Kerr, "*A Raisin in the Sun:* No Clear Path and No Retreat," *New York Herald Tribune,* March 22, 1959, 1.

66. Brooks Atkinson, "The Theatre: 'A Raisin in the Sun'; Negro Drama Given at Ethel Barrymore," *New York Times,* March 12, 1959, 27.

67. Lawrence P. Jackson, *The Indignant Generation: A Narrative History of African American Writers and Critics, 1934–1960* (Princeton: Princeton University Press, 2011), 488.

68. Hansberry moved to Harlem in 1951 to attend the New School for Social Research; Erin Cabrey, "Historic Plaque Marks the NYC Home of Playwright Lorraine Hansberry," Untapped Cities, October 19, 2017 (https://untappedcities.com/2017/10/19/historic-plaque-marks-the-nyc-home-of-playwright-lorraine-hansberry, accessed May 26, 2019). See also Audrey W., "Author Spotlight: Lorraine Hansberry," Arcadia Publishing (www.arcadiapublishing.com/Navigation/Community/Arcadia-and-THP-Blog/May-2019/Author-Spotlight-Lorraine-Hansberry, accessed May 26, 2019).

69. Lorraine Hansberry, "I Saw Your Play," *Lorraine Hansberry Audio Collection: A Raisin in the Sun, To Be Young Gifted and Black, and Lorraine Hansberry Speaks Out,* read by Ruby Dee and James Earl Jones (New York: Caedmon Records, 2009).

70. Hansberry, "The Negro Writer and His Roots," 8–9.

71. Ibid., 9.

72. Hansberry, "I Saw Your Play."

73. E. Franklin Frazier, *Black Bourgeoisie* (New York: Free Press Paperbacks, 1957), 50–51.

74. Terkel, "Make New Sounds," 7.

75. Frazier, *Black Bourgeoisie,* 237.

76. Hansberry, "I Saw Your Play."

77. Harold Cruse, *The Crisis of the Negro Intellectual* (New York: New York Review Books, 1967), 273.

78. Hansberry, "Your Play Is Performed."

79. Ibid.

80. Malcolm X, "A Summing Up: Louis Lomax Interviews Malcolm X," interview by Louis Lomax, Teaching American History, 1963 (http://teachingamericanhistory.org/library/document/a-summing-up-louis-lomax-interviews-malcolm-x, accessed May 20, 2019).

81. Ossie Davis, "Interview with Ossie Davis," interview by Madison Davis Lacy, Jr., Washington University Digital Gateway Texts, July 6, 1989 (http://digital.wustl.edu/e/eii/eiiweb/dav5427.0777.037ossiedavis.html, accessed June 16, 2017).

82. Adrienne D. Davis, "The Private Law of Race and Sex: An Antebellum Perspective," *Stanford Law Review* 51, no. 2 (January 1999): 227.

83. See the introduction to Alan B. Anderson and George W. Pickering's *Confronting the Color Line: Broken Promise of the Civil Rights Movement in Chicago,* particularly page 3. (Athens: University of Georgia Press, 1987).

84. Davis, "The Private Law of Race and Sex," 266.

85. Ibid., 246, 243.

86. Allen R. Kamp quoting *Burke v. Kleiman,* 277 Ill. App. 519, 523 (1934), in "The History Behind *Hansberry v. Lee,*" *U.C. Davis Law Review* 20 (1986–1987): 484, 490.

87. Davis, "The Private Law of Race and Sex," 237.
88. Coates, "The Case for Reparations."

CHAPTER 3. ORIGINS

1. Dayo F. Gore, Jeanne Theoharis, and Komozi Woodard, eds., *Want to Start a Revolution? Radical Women in the Black Freedom Struggle* (New York: New York University Press, 2009), 7.
2. Letter to Molly written in 1957, Restricted File, Page 11–14, *Hansberry Papers*.
3. Lorraine Hansberry, "Myself in Notes," Restricted Box, Folder 15, *Lorraine Hansberry Papers*, Schomburg Center for Research in Black Culture, New York Public Library, New York.
4. In part 1 of Hansberry's FBI file, an agent wrote: "It is noted that the subject and spouse reside at two different addresses, the wife living at 112 Waverly Place, NYC, and the husband residing at 337 Bleecker Street, NYC. It is believed that the purpose of these two addresses is for business reasons inasmuch as during the above-mentioned pretext subject's spouse stated that his wife was unavailable and had 'retreated' to her private residence at 112 Waverly Place, where she was unavailable for interview. The spouse mentioned that this was the customary practice of his wife whenever she was engaged in writing." Part 17 of the file notes, "On 3/14/60, advised writer that subject resides with her husband at 337 Bleecker St., NYC. Subject was interviewed by Herald Tribune writer, Don Rose and interview published in MARCH 13 . . . of Tribune. Article reflects subjects and husband own and reside in 3 story walk-up On Waverly Place in the Village." United States [U.S.] Dept. of Justice, *Lorraine Vivian Hansberry Nemiroff*, Assorted documents dated July 21, 1952, to January 22, 1965, Internal case file No. 100-107297 (New York: U.S. Federal Bureau of Investigation Freedom of Information/Privacy Acts Section, 1952), 19.
5. Lorraine Hansberry, "Myself in Notes."
6. Ibid.
7. Robert Nemiroff quotes Hansberry in Lorraine Hansberry, *Drinking Gourd*, in *Les Blancs: The Collected Last Plays* (New York: Vintage, 1994), 143.
8. Imani Perry, *Looking for Lorraine: The Radiant and Radical Life of Lorraine Hansberry* (Boston: Beacon, 2018), 11.
9. Lorraine Hansberry, "Simone de Beauvoir and the Second Sex—An American Commentary," Box 59, Folder 1, Page 6, *Lorraine Hansberry Papers*, Schomburg Center for Research in Black Culture, New York Public Library, New York.
10. See the introduction to Saidiya V. Hartman's *Scenes of Subjection: Terror, Slavery, and Self-Making in Nineteenth Century America*, in which she discusses the concept of fungibility as a characteristic of the enslaved (Oxford: Oxford University Press, 1997). Hortense Spillers makes a distinction between body and flesh in her classic essay "Mama's Baby, Papa's Maybe: An American Grammar Book," *Diacritics*, vol. 17, no. 2 (1987): 65–81.
11. Lorraine Hansberry, "Integration into A Burning House," from the WBAI NYC radio symposium on "The Negro Writer in America" on January 1, 1961, two excerpts from a Civil War Centennial program that included James Baldwin, Langston Hughes, Nat

Hentoff, Alfred Kazin, and Emile Capouya, 4:49, *Lorraine Hansberry Speaks Out: Art and the Black Revolution* (New York: Harper Audio/Caedmon Recordings, 2009).

12. Margaret Wilkerson quotes Hansberry in Lorraine Hansberry, *Drinking Gourd*, in *Les Blancs: The Collected Last Plays* (New York: Vintage, 1994), 5.

13. See Manning Marable, *Race, Reform, and Rebellion: The Second Reconstruction and Beyond in Black America, 1945–2006* (Jackson: University of Mississippi Press, 2007).

14. Jewell Nemiroff quoting Hansberry in Lorraine Hansberry, *Drinking Gourd*, in *Les Blancs: The Collected Last Plays* (New York: Vintage, 1994), xx.

15. Lisa Lowe, "Autobiography Out of Empire," *Small Axe*, no. 28, 13.1 (March 2009): 98–111, 98.

16. See the Introduction to *Race and Performance After Repetition* edited by Soyica Diggs Colbert, Douglas Jones, and Shane Vogel (Durham: Duke University Press, 2020).

17. Lorraine Hansberry, *Drinking Gourd*, in *Les Blancs: The Collected Last Plays* (New York: Vintage, 1994), 185

18. Hansberry, *Drinking Gourd*, 175.

19. Aida Levy-Hussen, *How to Read African American Literature: Post Civil Rights Fiction and the Task of Interpretation* (New York: New York University Press, 2016), 70.

20. Levy-Hussen writes, quoting José Muñoz and Elizabeth Freeman, "For [Muñoz and Freeman] . . . queer time is a utopian imagining of the otherwise that emerges in part from the traumas and hostilities of the now. Thus it is most often experienced as a fleeting, private, or phantasmatic glimpse of possibility, bounded by the trauma of its own negation. 'The present,' Muñoz writes, 'is impoverished and toxic for queers and other people who do not feel the privilege of normative belonging.' Yet it is precisely this toxicity of exclusion that forms the precondition for his utopian vision" (43–44). The historical arrangement relies on an origins narrative that does not fully account for Black people's participation in and resistance to the institution of slavery, or how blackness and sexuality emerge outside normative formulations of gender and Western formulations of humanity (70). Muñoz's formulation of utopian possibility, similar to Simone de Beauvoir's, depicted a yet to be political horizon. Hansberry's work, however, drew from the material history of the enslaved and native populations as foundation for contemporary political and aesthetic possibilities. Through realism Hansberry produced shared moments of fleeting possibility that harnessed political practices of the past to organize them into practices that structure the present and future movements. Hansberry's depiction of fugitivity in *The Drinking Gourd* anticipates the theorization of it in Fred Moten's *In the Break: The Aesthetics of the Black Radical Tradition* (Minneapolis: University of Minnesota Press, 2003) and C. Riley Snorton's *Black on Both Sides: A Racial History of Trans Identity* (Minneapolis: University of Minnesota Press, 2017).

21. Hansberry, *Drinking Gourd*, 176.

22. Ibid., 201.

23. Martin Luther King, Jr., "Sermon at Temple Israel of Hollywood" (speech, Shabbat Synagogue Service, Temple Israel of Hollywood, Los Angeles, February 26, 1965; www.americanrhetoric.com/speeches/mlktempleisraelhollywood.htm, accessed May 24, 2019).

24. Hansberry, *Drinking Gourd*, 210.

25. Ibid., 214, 215.

26. Ibid., 186.

27. Ibid., 188.

28. Ibid., 199 (emphasis added), 206.

29. An entry for April 21, 1959, in Hansberry's FBI file says that she sold the play for $300,000 and that David Susskind and Philip Rose would co-produce it.

30. Lorraine Hansberry, "Me Tink Me Hear Sounds in de Night," *Theatre Arts* (October 1960): 8, 10.

31. James Baldwin, "Sweet Lorraine," *The Price of the Ticket: Collected Nonfiction, 1948–1985* (New York: St. Martin's, 1985), 445.

32. Lorraine Hansberry, "Me Tink Me Hear Sounds in de Night," 10.

33. Ibid.

34. Lorraine Hansberry, "Stanley Gleason and the Lights that Need Not Die," *New York Times,* January 17, 1960, 11.

35. Robin D. G. Kelley, *Race Rebels: Culture, Politics, and The Black Working Class* (New York: Free Press, 1996), chapter 7, examines how the zoot suit serves as a cultural adornment of opposition to racism and respectability.

36. Lorraine Hansberry, "Stanley Gleason and the Lights that Need Not Die," 11.

37. Ibid.

38. Countee Cullen, "Thesis: The Poetry of Edna St. Vincent Millay: An Appreciation," 1925, Box 13, Folder 6, *Countee Cullen Papers, 1900–1947,* Amistad Research Center, Tulane University, New Orleans (http://amistadresearchcenter.tulane.edu/archon/?p=collections/findingaid&id=41&q=&rootcontentid=24425, accessed December 17, 2017).

39. Lorraine Hansberry, "Ode to Edna St. Vincent Millay," January 30, 1960, Box 61, Folder 10, *Lorraine Hansberry Papers,* Schomburg Center for Research in Black Culture, New York Public Library, New York.

40. Lorraine Hansberry, "Queer Beer," Restricted Box, Folder 1, *Lorraine Hansberry Papers,* Schomburg Center for Research in Black Culture, New York Public Library, New York.

41. Ibid.

42. Ibid.

43. See Paul Kleinpoppen, "Some Notes on Oliver La Farge," *Studies in American Indian Literatures* 10, no. 2 (Spring 1986): 70.

44. Lorraine Hansberry, "Queer Beer."

45. Ibid.

46. Ibid.

47. Ibid.

48. Daphne Lamothe, *Inventing the New Negro: Narrative, Culture, and Ethnography* (Philadelphia: University of Pennsylvania Press, 2008), 9.

49. Lorraine Hansberry, "Untitled and Unpublished Short Story About 'Austin,' " Box 60, Folder 16, *Lorraine Hansberry Papers,* Schomburg Center for Research in Black Culture, New York Public Library, New York.

50. Richard Schechner, *Between Theater and Anthropology* (Philadelphia: University of Pennsylvania Press, 1985).

51. Kleinpoppen, "Some Notes on Oliver La Farge," 70.

52. Lorraine Hansberry, third draft of "Laughing Boy," January–February 1963, Box 1, Folder 3, *Lorraine Hansberry Papers,* Schomburg Center for Research in Black Culture, New York Public Library, New York.

53. Schechner, *Between Theater and Anthropology,* 6.

54. Lorraine Hansberry, "Draft of *Toussaint* for 'Playwright at Work,' " May 21, 1961, Box 42, Folder 6, *Lorraine Hansberry Papers,* Schomburg Center for Research in Black Culture, New York Public Library, New York.

55. Postcard from Lonnie Bunch to Lorraine Hansberry and Robert Nemiroff, Box 42, Folder 5, *Lorraine Hansberry Papers,* Schomburg Center for Research in Black Culture, New York Public Library, New York.

56. Correspondence from Clarence Cameron White to Lorraine Hansberry, March 16, 1959, Box 42, Folder 5, *Lorraine Hansberry Papers,* Schomburg Center for Research in Black Culture, New York Public Library, New York.

57. Correspondence from Lorraine Hansberry to Clarence Cameron White, March 20, 1959, Box 42, Folder 5, *Lorraine Hansberry Papers,* Schomburg Center for Research in Black Culture, New York Public Library, New York.

58. Lorraine Hansberry Papers, "Toussaint," Folder 42, Box 4, *Lorraine Hansberry Papers,* Schomburg Center for Research in Black Culture, New York Public Library, New York.

59. Ibid.

60. Ibid.

61. Margaret B. Wilkerson quoting Lorraine Hansberry in the "Introduction" to *Les Blancs: The Collected Last Plays* (New York: Vintage, 1994), 8.

62. Lorraine Hansberry Papers, "Toussaint."

63. Ibid.

64. Darlene Clark Hine, "Rape and Inner Lives of Southern Black Women: Thoughts on the Culture of Dissemblance," *Signs* 14, no. 4 (1989): 912–920.

65. Quoted in Jeremy Matthew Glick, *The Black Radical Tragic: Performance, Aesthetics, and the Unfinished Haitian Revolution* (New York: New York University Press, 2016), 184.

CHAPTER 4. THE MOVEMENT

1. Cheryl Lynn Greenberg, *A Circle of Trust: Remembering SNCC* (New Brunswick: Rutgers University Press, 1998), 1.

2. Bonita Lawrence and Enakshi Dua, "Decolonizing Antiracism," *Social Justice,* vol. 32, no. 4 (2005): 130. See also Ikuko Asaka, *Tropical Freedom: Climate, Settler Colonialism, and Black Exclusion in the Age of Emancipation* (Durham: Duke University Press, 2017), 15–18.

3. For an examination of how masculinity and individuality informed leadership during the civil rights movement, see Eric Edwards, *Charisma and the Fictions of Black Leadership* (Minneapolis: University of Minnesota Press, 2012); and Robert J. Patterson, *Exodus Politics: Civil Rights and Leadership in African American Literature and Culture* (Charlottesville: University of Virginia Press, 2013).

4. Greenberg, *A Circle of Trust,* 4.

5. Layhmond Robinson, "Robert Kennedy Consults Negroes Here About North," *New York Times,* May 25, 1963, 1 (www.nytimes.com/1963/05/25/archives/robert-kennedy-consults-negroes-here-about-north-james-baldwin.html, accessed May 25, 2019).

6. Taylor Branch, *Parting the Waters: America in the King Years, 1954–1963* (New York: Simon & Schuster, 1989), 809, 810.

7. In the Bay of Pigs invasion, April 1961, the U.S. government sent armed forces to overthrow the Cuba government.

8. Joanne Grant, "The Little Man Who Wasn't There: Negro Intellectuals Just Can't Reach Robert Kennedy," *National Guardian*, June 13, 1963, 5. Also see Lena Horne and Richard Schickel, *Lena* (New York: Doubleday, 1965), 280, and Branch, *Parting the Waters,* 810–811.

9. The exchange also called attention to a shift in protocol from the Double V campaign of World War II in which W.E.B. Du Bois called for Black people to assist the war effort as a mechanism to bolster freedom in the United States.

10. James Baldwin, *The Fire Next Time* (New York: Vintage, 1993), 102.

11. James Baldwin, "Lorraine Hansberry at the Summit," *Freedomways Reader: Prophets in Their Own Country* (Boulder: Westview, 2000), 80.

12. Terrence Johnson, *Tragic Soul-Life: W.E.B. Du Bois and the Moral Crisis Facing American Democracy* (Oxford: Oxford University Press, 2012), 17.

13. Jackie Robinson, "Jim Baldwin and Bob Kennedy," *New York Amersterdam News,* June 8, 1963, 11.

14. Lorraine Hansberry, *To Be Young, Gifted, and Black: Lorraine Hansberry in Her Own Words* (New York: Vintage, 1995), 220. A similar version of Hansberry's statement appears in Lorraine Hansberry, "We Are One People," Remarks to a civil rights rally, Croton-on-Hudson on June 16, 1963, 4:16, *Lorraine Hansberry Speaks Out: Art and the Black Revolution* (New York: Harper Audio/Caedmon Recordings, 2009). Lena Horne agreed with Hansberry's assertion about the "exceptional Negro," writing in her autobiography: "I had begun to convince myself that all of us 'firsts'—first glamour girl, first baseball player, first this-that-and-the-other—had reached the end of our usefulness. We were not symbols of the approaching rapprochement between the races. We were sops, tokens, buy-offs for the white race's conscience. Now millions of Negro people were reaching out, as a mass, to take what had been so long denied them. I did not want to be used to remind them of the old days. I wanted to join this movement not as a tired symbol but simply as me, as a private Negro person. I wondered if I still had that right." Lena Horne and Richard Schickel, *Lena* (New York: Doubleday, 1965), 276.

15. Faith S. Holsaert et al., eds., *Hands on the Freedom Plow: Personal Accounts by Women in SNCC* (Urbana: University of Illinois Press), 1.

16. Steven Kasher, *The Civil Rights Movement: A Photographic History, 1954–1968* (New York: Abbeville, 1996), 10.

17. Nicole Fleetwood, *Troubling Vision: Performance, Visuality, and Blackness* (Chicago: University of Chicago Press, 2011), 3.

18. Rebeccah Welch, "Spokesman of the Oppressed? Lorraine Hansberry at Work: The Challenge of Radical Politics in the Postwar Era," in *The New Black History: Revisiting the Second Reconstruction,* ed. Manning Marable and Elizabeth Kai Hinton (New York: Palgrave, 2011), 74.

19. Stuart Hall, "Notes on Deconstructing 'The Popular,'" *Cultural Theory and Popular Culture: A Reader,* ed. John Storey (Essex, England: Pearson Education, 2009), 514.

20. Diane Nash, quoted in *A Circle of Trust: Remembering SNCC,* ed. Cheryl Lynn Greenberg (New Brunswick: Rutgers University Press, 1998), 22, 23–24.

21. Clayborne Carson, *In Struggle: SNCC and the Black Awakening of the 1960s* (Cambridge: Harvard University Press, 1981), 12.

22. Welch, "Spokesman of the Oppressed?" 73.

23. On perceptions of Hansberry's looks see ibid., 77.

24. Lillian Ross, "How Lorraine Hansberry Wrote 'A Raisin in the Sun,' " *New Yorker,* May 2, 1959 (www.newyorker.com/magazine/1959/05/09/playwright, accessed May 25, 2019).

25. Leigh Raiford, " 'Come Let Us Build a New World Together': SNCC and Photography of the Civil Rights Movement," *American Quarterly* 59, no. 4 (December 2007): 1132.

26. Nicole Fleetwood, *Troubling Vision: Performance, Visuality, And Blackness* (Chicago: The University of Chicago Press, 2010), 8.

27. Danny Lyon, quoted in *A Circle of Trust: Remembering SNCC,* ed. Cheryl Lynn Greenberg (New Brunswick: Rutgers University Press, 1998), 38.

28. Raiford, " 'Come Let Us Build a New World Together,' " 1133.

29. Charles E. Connerly, *"The Most Segregated City in America": City Planning and Civil Rights in Birmingham, 1920–1980* (Charlottesville: University of Virginia Press, 2005), 2 (www.jstor.org/stable/j.ctt6wrnnn, accessed May 25, 2019), 2, 84; Spike Lee's *Four Little Girls* (Burbank, Calif.: HBO Documentary Film and 40 Acres & a Mule Filmworks, 2010), DVD.

30. Raiford, " 'Come Let Us Build a New World Together,' " 1154.

31. For evidence of the symposium speakers see "In Her Own Words," Lorraine Hansberry Literary Trust (www.lhlt.org/quotes?quote=id_588&tid=25, accessed December 27, 2017).

32. Lorraine Hansberry, "Yankee Doodle," Box 3, Folder 16, *Lorraine Hansberry Papers,* Schomburg Center for Research in Black Culture, New York Public Library, New York.

33. Lorraine Hansberry, "Integration into A Burning House," from the WBAI NYC radio symposium "The Negro Writer in America" on January 1, 1961, two excerpts from a Civil War Centennial program that included James Baldwin, Langston Hughes, Nat Hentoff, Alfred Kazin, and Emile Capouya, 4:49, *Lorraine Hansberry Speaks Out: Art and the Black Revolution.* (New York: Harper Audio/Caedmon Recordings, 2009).

34. Ibid.

35. W.E.B. Du Bois, *Black Reconstruction in America, 1860–1880* (New York: Free Press, 1998), 15.

36. Cedric Robinson, *Black Marxism: The Making of the Black Radical Tradition* (Chapel Hill: University of North Carolina Press, 2000), 200.

37. Hansberry, "Integration into a Burning House."

38. Lorraine Hansberry, *The Movement: Documentary of a Struggle for Equality* (New York: Simon and Schuster, 1964), 13.

39. Mary L. Dudziak, *Cold War Civil Rights: Race and the Image of American Democracy* (Princeton: Princeton University Press, 2000), 153.

40. Hansberry, "Integration into a Burning House."

41. Ibid.

42. See Fidel Castro, *Fidel Castro Reader* (North Melbourne, Victoria, Australia: Ocean Press, 2008), 137–139.

43. Steven Cohen, "When Castro Came to Harlem," *New Republic,* March 21, 2016 (https://newrepublic.com/article/131793/castro-came-harlem, accessed December 28, 2017).

44. Hansberry, "Integration into a Burning House."

45. See Correspondence from Daisy Bates to Lorraine Hansberry and Robert Nemiroff, Box 2, Folder 16, *Lorraine Hansberry Papers,* Schomburg Center for Research in Black Culture, New York Public Library, New York.

46. Ibid.

47. Lorraine Hansberry, "Dialogue with an Uncolored Egghead Containing Wholesome Intentions and Some Sass," *The Urbanite: Images of the American Negro,* May 24, 1961, 10.

48. Lawrence P. Jackson, *The Indignant Generation: A Narrative History of African American Writers and Critics, 1934–1960* (Princeton: Princeton University Press, 2011), 488.

49. Hansberry, "Dialogue with an Uncolored Egghead," 11.

50. Ibid., 36.

51. Lorraine Hansberry, Hansberry's Journal, September 16th, 1963, Box Restricted, Folder 4, *Lorraine Hansberry Papers,* Schomburg Center for Research in Black Culture, New York Public Library, New York.

52. Hansberry, *The Movement,* 98.

53. Ibid., 104, 105.

54. Ibid., 122.

55. Clayborne Carson, *In Struggle,* 51.

56. Ibid., 28.

57. Fleetwood, *Troubling Vision,* 45.

58. Hansberry, *The Movement,* 52.

59. See Raiford, " 'Come Let Us Build a New World Together,' " 1130.

60. Clayborne Carson, *In Struggle,* 63.

61. Hansberry, *The Movement,* 118.

62. See Welch, "Spokesman of the Oppressed?"

63. Hansberry, *The Movement,* 122.

64. See Clayborne Carson, *In Struggle,* 20.

CHAPTER 5. FROM LIBERALS TO RADICALS

Epigraph: Lorraine Hansberry, "The Black Revolution and the White Backlash," from the Town Hall forum with Imamu Baraka, Ossie Davis, Ruby Dee, John O. Killens, Paule Marshall, Charles Silberman, David Susskind, and James Weschler on June 15, 1964, 10:46, *Lorraine Hansberry Speaks Out: Art and the Black Revolution* (New York: Harper Audio/Caedmon Recordings, 2009).

1. Norman Mailer, "Theatre: The Blacks," *Village Voice,* May 11, 1961, 14 (https://news.google.com/newspapers?nid=KEtq3P1Vf8oC&dat=19610511&printsec=frontpage&hl=en, accessed May 26, 2019).

2. Cyrus Ernesto Zirakzadeh, "Political Prophecy in Contemporary American Literature: The Left-Conservative Vision of Norman Mailer," *The Review of Politics* 69, no. 4 (Fall 2007): 625–626.

3. Ibid., 632.

4. Norman Mailer, "The White Negro (Fall 1957)," *Dissent Magazine,* June 20, 2007 (www.dissentmagazine.org/online_articles/the-white-negro-fall-1957, accessed April 19, 2019).

5. Ibid.
6. Lorraine Hansberry interview with Studs Terkel, "Lorraine Hansberry discusses her play 'A Raisin in the Sun'" (https://studsterkel.wfmt.com/programs/lorraine-hansberry-discusses-her-play-raisin-sun, accessed August 8, 2019).
7. Mailer, "Theatre: The Blacks," 14.
8. Lorraine Hansberry, "Genet, Mailer, and the New Paternalism," *Village Voice*, June 1, 1961, 14.
9. Ibid.
10. Ibid.
11. James Baldwin, *The Fire Next Time* (New York: Dial, 1963), 88.
12. Lorraine Hansberry's Journal, April 21, 1962, entry, Restricted Box, Folder marked "Autobiographical Notes," *Lorraine Hansberry Papers,* Schomburg Center for Research in Black Culture, New York Public Library, New York.
13. Wallace Terry, "Novelist Baldwin Links Civil Rights and Peace," *Washington Post,* April 1, 1961, 44; Vincent J. Intondi, *African Americans Against the Bomb: Nuclear Weapons, Colonialism, and the Black Freedom Movement* (Stanford: Stanford University Press, 2015), 63.
14. Intondi, *African Americans Against the Bomb,* 51, 52.
15. Lorraine Hansberry, *A Raisin in the Sun and The Sign in Sidney Brustein's Window* (New York: Vintage, 1995), 295.
16. Simone de Beauvoir, *The Ethics of Ambiguity* (New York: Open Road Integrated Media, 2015), 8–9.
17. Jean-Paul Sartre, *Existentialism and Humanism,* trans. and Introduction by Philip Mairet (London: Methuen, 1982), 39.
18. See Soyica Diggs Colbert, "Black Rage: On Cultivating Black National Belonging," *Theatre Survey* 58, no. 3 (September 2016): 336–357.
19. Lorraine Hansberry, "Books: The Outsider," *Freedom,* vol. 3, no. 4 (April 1953): 7.
20. Lorraine Hansberry's Journal, December 7, 1962, entry, Box Restricted, Folder 4, April 21, 1962, entry, Box Restricted, Folder marked "Autobiographical Notes," *Lorraine Hansberry Papers,* Schomburg Center for Research in Black Culture, New York Public Library, New York.
21. Letter from LeRoi Jones to Lorraine Hansberry, June 13, 1961, Box 63, Folder 15, *Lorraine Hansberry Papers,* Schomburg Center for Research in Black Culture, New York Public Library, New York.
22. Letter from LeRoi Jones to Lorraine Hansberry, June 23, 1961, Box 63, Folder 15, *Lorraine Hansberry Papers,* Schomburg Center for Research in Black Culture, New York Public Library, New York.
23. Ibid.
24. De Beauvoir, *The Ethics of Ambiguity,* 14, 84.
25. Ibid., 32–33.
26. Ibid., 27.
27. Hansberry, *A Raisin in the Sun,* 136.
28. Hansberry, *The Sign in Sidney Brustein's Window,* 215, 218.
29. Ibid., 229.
30. Ibid., 269.

31. Ibid., 271–272.

32. Ibid., 273–274, 234.

33. James Baldwin, "Sweet Lorraine," in *The Price of the Ticket: Collected Nonfiction, 1948–1985* (New York: St. Martin's, 1985), 445; Hansberry, *The Sign in Sidney Brustein's Window,* 291.

34. Hansberry, *The Sign in Sidney Brustein's Window,* 292, 293–294.

35. Ibid., 298–299, 316.

36. Lorraine Hansberry's Journal, Box Restricted, Folder 4, *Lorraine Hansberry Papers,* Schomburg Center for Research in Black Culture, New York Public Library, New York, entries for Dec. 9, 1963; Dec. 13, 1963, Jan. 9, 1964; June 7, 1964; July 17, 1964.

37. Lorraine Hansberry's Journal, Dec. 28, 1963, entry, Box restricted, Folder 4, *Lorraine Hansberry Papers,* Schomburg Center for Research in Black Culture, New York Public Library, New York.

38. Imani Perry, *Looking for Lorraine: The Radiant and Radical Life of Lorraine Hansberry* (Boston: Beacon, 2018), 128, 119.

39. Hansberry interview with Studs Terkel.

40. Quoted in Perry, *Looking for Lorraine,* 120.

41. Hansberry interview with Studs Terkel.

42. Hansberry, *The Sign in Sidney Brustein's Window,* 263.

43. Albert Camus, *The Myth of Sisyphus and Other Essays* (New York: Vintage, 1991), 3, 6, 64.

44. See Sally Banes, *Greenwich Village, 1963: Avant-Garde Performance and the Effervescent Body* (Durham: Duke University Press, 1993), 9, 32.

45. John Strausbaugh, *The Village: 400 Years of Beats and Bohemians, Radicals and Rogues, a History of Greenwich Village* (New York: HarperCollins, 2013); Banes, *Greenwich Village, 1963,* 4, 36. Strausbaugh argues, "Marxism was on its way out. Younger artists still heard some Trotskyist rhetoric from the older ones, but it was increasingly just that. Downtown's arty bohemians still dressed and tried to drink like workingmen—a lasting legacy of the old American idea that only girly men would want to be artists—but for the most part they gave up trying to make art for them, or for the middle class, or for anyone else" (245).

46. Hansberry, *The Sign in Sidney Brustein's Window,* 300, 301–302.

47. Ibid., 309.

48. Mark Hodin, "Lorraine Hansberry's Absurdity: The Sign in Sidney Brustein's Window," *Contemporary Literature* 50, no. 4 (Winter 2009): 742–774, 757.

49. Ibid., 763.

50. Margaret B. Wilkerson, "Excavating Our History: The Importance of Biographies of Women of Color," *Black American Literature Forum* published by *African American Review* 24, no. 1 (Spring 1990): 80.

51. Hodin, "Lorraine Hansberry's Absurdity," 763–764.

52. Biondi, *To Stand and Fight,* 162.

53. In an early assessment of *A Raisin in the Sun,* LeRoi dismissed the play as concerns of the middle class. After Hansberry's death, he reassessed the play and retracted his criticism. See Steven Carter, *Hansberry's Drama: Commitment and Complexity* (Urbana: University of Illinois Press, 1990), 25.

54. David Leeming, *James Baldwin: A Biography* (New York: Simon and Schuster, 1994), 161. In recounting the story in *The Village*, Strausbaugh says that Baldwin was with cinematographer Richard Bagley and two white women (283). The other details of the story are consistent with Leeming's recounting.

55. Jerry Watts, *Amiri Baraka: The Politics and Art of a Black Intellectual* (New York: New York University Press, 2001), 142.

56. Strausbaugh, *The Village*, 281.

57. Hansberry, *The Sign in Sidney Brustein's Window*, 330–331.

58. William Flanagan, "The Art of the Theatre IV: Edward Albee: An Interview," in *Conversations with Edward Albee*, ed. Philip C. Kolin (Jackson: University of Mississippi Press, 1988), 52.

59. Lorraine Hansberry, "The Negro Writer and His Roots: Toward a New Romanticism," *The Black Scholar* 12, no. 2 (March–April 1981): 6.

60. In *Greenwich Village, 1963*, Banes asserts, "the arts seemed to hold a privileged place in the democratic vision, not merely as a reflection of a vibrant, rejuvenated American society, but as an active register of contemporary consciousness—as its product, and also its catalyst" (3).

61. Lorraine Hansberry's Journal, December 17, 1963, entry, Box restricted, Folder 4, *Lorraine Hansberry Papers*, Schomburg Center for Research in Black Culture, New York Public Library, New York.

62. Hansberry, *The Sign in Sidney Brustein's Window*, 338.

63. Ibid., 338, 339.

64. Lorraine Hansberry's Journal, January 1, 1964, entry, Box restricted, Folder 4, *Lorraine Hansberry Papers*, Schomburg Center for Research in Black Culture, New York Public Library, New York.

65. Hansberry *A Raisin in the Sun and The Sign in Sidney Brustein's Window*, 339–340.

66. Robert Nemiroff, "The 101 'Final' Performances of Sidney Brustein," in *A Raisin in the Sun/The Sign in Sidney Brustein's Window* (New York: Vintage, 1995), 269, 283–284.

67. Richard Gilman, "Borrowed Bitchery," *Newsweek*, October 26, 1964, 101–102.

68. Howard Taubman, "Theater: 'Sidney Brustein's Window': Lorraine Hansberry's Play at Longacre," *New York Times* (1923–Current file), October 16, 1964, 32, ProQuest Historical Newspapers: New York Times, accessed August 9, 2018.

69. Richard P. Cooke, "The Theater: Miss Hansberry's Success," *Wall Street Journal* (1923–Current file), October 19, 1964, 20, ProQuest Historical Newspapers: The Wall Street Journal, accessed August 9, 2018.

70. Nemiroff, "The 101 'Final' Performances of Sidney Brustein," 172–173.

71. Ibid., 181, 182.

72. Ibid., 185.

73. See Anna McMullan, "When Beckett Wrote Waiting for Godot He Really Didn't Know A Lot About Theatre," Interview by Daisy Bowie-Sell, *The Telegraph*, January 5, 2013 (www.telegraph.co.uk/culture/theatre/theatre-features/9780077/When-Beckett-wrote-Waiting-for-Godot-he-really-didnt-know-a-lot-about-theatre.html, accessed September 24, 2018).

74. Brooks Atkinson, "Theatre: Beckett's 'Waiting for Godot': Mystery Wrapped in Enigma at Golden The Cast," *New York Times* (1923–Current file), April 20, 1956, 21, ProQuest Historical Newspapers: The New York Times, accessed August 8, 2018.

75. Brooks Atkinson, " 'Godot' Is No Hoax: Eccentric Drama Has Something To Say Joycean Style," *New York Times* (1923–Current file), April 29, 1956, 129, ProQuest Historical Newspapers: The New York Times, accessed August 9, 2018.

76. Brooks Atkinson, "Theatre: 'Godot' Is Back: Beckett Play Staged With Negro Cast," *New York Times*, January 22, 1957, 25, ProQuest Historical Newspapers: The New York Times, accessed August 9, 2018.

77. Lorraine Hansberry, "What Use Are Flowers?" in *Les Blancs: The Last Collected Plays*, edited with a Critical Background by Robert Nemiroff, with a Foreword by Jewell Handy Gresham Nemiroff, and an Introduction by Margaret B. Wilkerson (New York: Vintage, 1994), 224.

78. Brooks Atkinson, "Theatre: 'Godot' for Fair: Coast Troupe Here on Way to Brussels," *New York Times* (1923–Current file), August 6, 1958, 22, ProQuest Historical Newspapers: The New York Times, accessed August 9, 2018.

79. W. F. Minor, "They Are Waiting for Godot in Mississippi, Too," *New York Times*, January 31, 1963, 3, ProQuest Historical Newspapers: The New York Times, accessed August 9, 2018.

80. Bertolt Brecht, *Mother Courage and Her Children* (New York: Grove Press, 1955), 110.

81. Lorraine Hansberry, "Gedachtnis," Box 60, Folder 8, *Lorraine Hansberry Papers*, Schomburg Center for Research in Black Culture, New York Public Library, New York.

82. Hansberry, *What Use Are Flowers?* 232.

83. Ibid., 237.

84. Fred Moten, *In the Break* (Minneapolis: University of Minnesota Press, 2003), 9.

85. Hansberry quoted in Nemiroff's Critical Background, *What Use Are Flowers?* 223.

86. Lorraine Hansberry, "Accident of the Cosmos," Box 60, Folder 1, *Lorraine Hansberry Papers*, Schomburg Center for Research in Black Culture, New York Public Library, New York.

87. Lorraine Hansberry, "The Arrival of Mr. Todog," Box 50, Folder 5, manuscript page 1, *Lorraine Hansberry Papers*, Schomburg Center for Research in Black Culture, New York Public Library, New York.

88. Ibid., manuscript page 1–2.

89. Ibid., manuscript pages 2, 3.

90. Ibid., manuscript page 8.

91. Ibid., manuscript pages 8, 9, 10.

CHAPTER 6. WITH HER MIND STAYED ON FREEDOM

Epigraphs: Lorraine Hansberry's Journal, November 27, 1961, entry, Box 1, Folder 3, *Lorraine Hansberry Papers*, Schomburg Center for Research in Black Culture, New York Public Library, New York; James Baldwin, interview in *The Negro Protest: James Baldwin, Malcolm X, and Martin Luther King, Jr., Talk with Kenneth B. Clark* (Boston: Beacon, 1963), 13–14.

1. Lorraine Hansberry, *To Be Young, Gifted, and Black: Lorraine Hansberry in Her Own Words* (New York: Vintage, 1995), 257.

2. Margaret B. Wilkerson, "The Dark Vision of Lorraine Hansberry: Excerpts from a Literary Biography," *The Massachusetts Review* 28, no. 4 (1987): 642.

3. Lorraine Hansberry, *Les Blancs: The Last Collected Plays,* edited with a Critical Background by Robert Nemiroff, with a Foreword by Jewell Handy Gresham Nemiroff, and an Introduction by Margaret B. Wilkerson (New York: Vintage, 1994), 79.

4. Barbara Ransby, *Ella Baker and the Black Freedom Movement: A Radical Democratic Vision* (Chapel Hill: University of North Carolina Press, 2003), 211, 212.

5. Martin Luther King Jr., "Martin Luther King Jr.—Acceptance Speech," Speech, the Nobel Peace Prize 1964 Award Ceremony, University of Oslo, Oslo, Norway, December 10, 1964 (www.nobelprize.org/nobel_prizes/peace/laureates/1964/king-acceptance_en.html, accessed February 9, 2016).

6. See Soyica Colbert, "A Pedagogical Approach to Understanding Rioting as Revolutionary Action in Alice Childress's *Wine in the Wilderness,*" *Theatre Topics,* vol. 19, no. 1 (2009): 79.

7. Lorraine Hansberry, "The Black Revolution and the White Backlash," in *Black Protest: History, Documents, and Analysis, 1619 to the Present,* edited by Joanne Grant (New York: Fawcett Premier, 1968), 22.

8. Hansberry, *Les Blancs,* 60.

9. Lorraine Hansberry, "Myself in Notes," 1950, Restricted Box, Folder 15, *Lorraine Hansberry Papers,* Schomburg Center for Research in Black Culture, New York Public Library, New York.

10. Cheryl Higashida, *Black Internationalist Feminism: Women Writers of the Black Left, 1945–1995* (Urbana: University of Illinois Press, 2011), 60.

11. Penny M. Von Eschen, *Race Against Empire: Black Americans and Anti-Colonialism, 1937–1957* (Ithaca: Cornell University Press, 1997), 6.

12. Higashida, *Black Internationalist Feminism,* 41.

13. Ibid., 41.

14. Diana Taylor, *The Archive and the Repertoire* (Durham: Duke University Press, 2003), 20–21.

15. See Mary Helen Washington, *The Other Blacklist: The African American Literary and Cultural Left of the 1950s* (New York: Columbia University Press, 2015).

16. C.L.R. James, "Notes on Hamlet," *The C.L.R. James Reader,* edited by Anna Grimshaw (1953), 244.

17. Ania Loomba and Martin Orkin, *Post-Colonial Shakespeares* (London: Routledge, 1998), 1.

18. David Scott, *Conscripts of Modernity: The Tragedy of Colonial Enlightenment* (Durham: Duke University Press, 2004), 12, 13.

19. Ibid., 97.

20. Higashida, *Black Internationalist Feminism,* 8.

21. Clive Barnes, "Theater: '*Les Blancs*': Hansberry Work, Left Unfinished, Opens," *New York Times,* November 16, 1970, 47.

22. Sandra Schmidt, " 'Les Blancs,' a Political Play," *Los Angeles Times,* November 21, 1970, 6; Haskel Frankel, "Staging 'Les Blancs' Ill Serves Miss Hansberry," *National Observer,* November 30, 1970, 21; M.G. " 'Les Blanc,' " *Women's Wear Daily,* November 16, 1970, 2; George Oppenheimer, "Flaws Present But '*Les Blancs*' Still Looms High," *Reporter Dispatch,* White Plains, N.Y., Nov. 16, 1970, 26.

23. See Erica R. Edwards, *Charisma and the Fictions of Black Leadership* (Minneapolis: University of Minnesota Press, 2012); Robert J. Patterson, *Exodus Politics: Civil Rights*

and *Leadership in African American Literature and Culture* (Charlottesville: University of Virginia Press, 2013); Eddie Glaude, *Exodus! Religion, Race, and Nation in Early Nineteenth-Century Black America* (Chicago: University of Chicago Press, 2000); and Jacquelyn Dowd Hall, "The Long Civil Rights Movement," *Journal of American History* 91, no. 4 (2005): 1233–1263.

24. Ray Robinson, "Hansberry's Anxiously Awaited Play Opens," *New York Amsterdam News,* November 21, 1970, 22. See Harold Clurman, "Theatre," *The Nation,* November 30, 1970, and Harold Clurman, "Theatre," *The Nation,* December 7, 1970; Shirley Harrison, "The Spotlight," *Tri-Boro Post,* New York, N.Y., November 26, 1970, 15.

25. Harold Scott directed a revival of the play at the Huntington Theatre, Boston, January 13–February 5, 1989. The New York City Lincoln Center Library of the Performing Arts Theatre on Film and Tape Archive has a recording of the Huntington Theatre production.

26. Hansberry, *To Be Young, Gifted, and Black,* 40.

27. Hansberry, *Les Blancs,* 128.

28. Steven R. Carter, Harry J. Elam Jr., Cheryl Higashida, Joy L. Abell, and Philip Uko Effiong create a critical context to examine the play, whereas Nemiroff and Hansberry's biographer Margaret B. Wilkerson offers insights into Hansberry's life. Higashida's essay notes that although Hansberry expressed strong concerns about the despair implicit in the existentialist writing of many of her contemporaries (most notably Jean Genet's *The Blacks: A Clown Show,* translated by Bernard Frechtman, 1960), the existentialist feminist Simone de Beauvoir informed the gender politics in *Les Blancs* and helped Hansberry imagine a nonpatriarchal form of Black internationalism.

29. Margaret B. Wilkerson's essay "The Sighted Eyes and Feeling Heart of Lorraine Hansberry" informs my understanding of the nature of Hansberry's activist aesthetic. Wilkerson argues, "Hansberry's 'sighted eyes' forced her to confront fully the depravity, cruelty, and utter foolishness of men's actions, but her 'feeling heart' would not allow her to lose faith in humanity's potential for overcoming its own barbarity. This strong and uncompromising belief in the future of humankind informed her plays and sometimes infuriated her critics," *Black American Literature Forum,* vol. 17, no. 1 (1983): 10.

30. Lorraine Hansberry quoted in Steven R. Carter, *Hansberry's Drama: Commitment Amid Complexity* (Chicago: University of Illinois Press, 1991), 6.

31. Lorraine Hansberry, Letter from Hansberry in Response to the "Bill of Rights for Homosexuals," 1957, Restricted Box, Folder 8, *Lorraine Hansberry Papers,* Schomburg Center for Research in Black Culture, New York Public Library, New York. Also quoted in Carter, *Hansberry's Drama,* 6.

32. Higashida, *Black Internationalist Feminism,* 69.

33. Lorraine Hansberry, Letter from Hansberry in Response to a "Bill of Rights for Homosexuals," 1957. Emphasis on original.

34. Hansberry, *Les Blancs,* 128.

35. Higashida, *Black Internationalist Feminism,* 77.

36. Scott, *Conscripts of Modernity,* 161.

37. Hansberry, *Les Blancs,* 128.

38. Ibid., 95, 41.

39. Glenda Carpio, *Laughing Fit to Kill,* which takes its title from Charles Chesnutt's short fiction (New York: Oxford University Press, 2008), 8.

40. See the introduction to Eddie Glaude's *In a Shade of Blue: Pragmatism and the Politics of Black America* (Chicago: University of Chicago Press, 2007).

41. Michele Elam, *The Souls of Mixed Folk: Race, Politics, and Aesthetics in the New Millennium* (Stanford: Stanford University Press, 2011), 183; Scott, *Conscripts of Modernity,* 139.

42. Lorraine Hansberry, "On Arthur Miller, Marilyn Monroe, and Guilt," Letter to a friend in 1963; excerpt published in *Women in Theatre: Compassion and Hope,* edited by Karen Malpede (New York: Drama Book Publishers, 1983), 174.

43. I owe this insight to Donald Pease's brilliant reading of *After the Fall* (New York: Dramatists Play Service, 1964), on which I heard him lecture in an American Drama course that we co-taught in the spring 2009.

44. Hansberry, "On Arthur Miller, Marilyn Monroe, and Guilt," 175.

45. For more on Hansberry's resistance to the theater of the absurd, see Carter, *Hansberry's Drama,* 2.

46. Higashida, *Black Internationalist Feminism,* 61.

47. On Genet's use of abstraction in *Les Nègres,* see Jeremy Matthew Glick, *The Black Radical Tragic: Performance, Aesthetics, and the Unfinished Haitian Revolution* (New York: New York University Press, 2016), 172.

48. Higashida, *Black Internationalist Feminism,* 61–62.

49. Lorraine Hansberry's Journal, July 28 and July 29, 1964, entries, Restricted Box, Folder 4, *Lorraine Hansberry Papers,* Schomburg Center for Research in Black Culture, New York Public Library, New York.

50. Hansberry, *Les Blancs,* 96, 97, 106.

51. Joshua Chambers-Letson, *After the Party: A Manifesto for Queer of Color Life* (New York: New York University Press, 2018), 62, 63.

52. Joe Hagan, "I Wish I Knew How It Would Feel to Be Free," *Believer,* August 2010 (https://believermag.com/i-wish-i-knew-how-it-would-feel-to-be-free, accessed August 9, 2019).

53. Hansberry, *Les Blancs,* 91.

54. Lorraine Hansberry's Journal, June 17, 1964, entry, Restricted Box, Folder 4, *Lorraine Hansberry Papers,* Schomburg Center for Research in Black Culture, New York Public Library, New York.

55. Hansberry, *To Be Young, Gifted, and Black,* 150.

56. James Baldwin, "Lorraine Hansberry at the Summit," *Freedomways: A Quarterly Review of the Freedom Movement* 19, no. 4 (1979): 272.

57. Hansberry, *Les Blancs,* 128, 81.

EPILOGUE: ALTERNATIVE ENDINGS

Epigraph: Lorraine Hansberry's Journal, January 1, 1964, entry, Box Restricted, Folder 4, *Lorraine Hansberry Papers,* Schomburg Center for Research in Black Culture, New York Public Library, New York.

1. Lorraine Hansberry, "The Drinking Gourd Script," copy of the mimeographed version for Dore Schary, Producer-Director, Box 43, Folder 5, *Lorraine Hansberry Papers,* Schomburg Center for Research in Black Culture, New York Public Library, New York.

2. Since the play's Broadway premiere in 1959, the artistic, political, social, and cultural contexts have changed, but its impact remains. Several playwrights have written plays inspired by *A Raisin in the Sun:* Bruce Norris, Robert O'Hara, Gloria Bond Clunie, Branden Jacobs-Jenkins, George C. Wolfe, and Kwame Kwei-Armah. Differing drastically in style, the plays serve as one marker among many of the ongoing engagement with Hansberry's work.

3. Fred Moten, "The Case of Blackness," *Criticism,* vol. 50, no. 2 (Spring 2008): 179.

4. Lorraine Hansberry, "To Be Young, Gifted, and Black," Box 59, Folder 3, *Lorraine Hansberry Papers,* Schomburg Center for Research in Black Culture, New York Public Library, New York.

5. Ibid.

6. Nina Simone, "To Be Young, Gifted, and Black (Live)," *Forever Young, Gifted & Black: Songs of Freedom and Spirit,* RCA, Sony BMG Music Entertainment.

7. Shana L. Redmond, *Anthem: Social Movements and the Sound of Solidarity in the African Diaspora* (New York: New York University Press, 2014), 194.

8. Lorraine Hansberry, *To Be Young, Gifted, and Black,* adapted by Robert Nemiroff (New York: Samuel French, 1999), 24.

Index

abolitionists, 7, 155, 157
absurdism, 89, 168, 169, 184, 185, 198, 200, 205, 206, 216, 217
African independence movement, 27, 43–45, 49, 51, 70, 78, 116, 140, 147–149, 151–153, 155, 164, 168, 175, 201–203, 209, 213, 218; Hansberry's view of, 220–221, 222
Albany (Ga.) protests, 157–158
Albee, Edward, 189; *Who's Afraid of Virginia Woolf?* 184, 185
Algerian war, 140, 148, 149, 152, 153, 202
alienation, 152, 153, 176
Allen, Billie Jo Thornton, 157
American exceptionalism, 137, 143, 148, 162
American Society of African Culture (AMSAC), 65–66; conference (1979), 78–79, 80, 87, 88
Anderson, Michael, 35
Angelou, Maya, 218
Arkansas, Little Rock Nine, 150, 159

assimilation, 67, 90, 151, 162; opposition to, 80–81, 92, 151; self-determination vs., 58
Atkinson, Brooks, 76, 191–193

Bagley, Richard, 255n54
Baker, Ella, 79, 133, 160, 203–204, 210
Baldwin, James, 58, 91, 97–98, 145, 146, 171, 181–185, 200, 208, 220; civil rights activism, 134, 135, 158; on equality, 166–168; Greenwich Village life, 183–184, 255n54; Hansberry friendship, 23, 56–57, 108, 179–180, 228; peace rally speech, 167; racism and, 183–185; on *Sign in Sidney Brustein's Window,* 190–191; works: *Another Country,* 153, 160, 179, 184; *Blues for Mr. Charlie,* 179; *The Fire Next Time,* 87, 148, 197; *Giovanni's Room,* 56; "Sweet Lorraine," 228
Bandung Conference (1955), 80
Banes, Sally, 181, 255n60